SAILORS, STATESMEN AND THE IMPLEMENTATION OF NAVAL STRATEGY

SAILORS, STATESMEN AND THE IMPLEMENTATION OF NAVAL STRATEGY

Edited by
Richard Harding and Agustín Guimerá

THE BOYDELL PRESS

© Contributors 2024

All Rights Reserved. Except as permitted under current legislation
no part of this work may be photocopied, stored in a retrieval system,
published, performed in public, adapted, broadcast,
transmitted, recorded or reproduced in any form or by any means,
without the prior permission of the copyright owner

First published 2024
The Boydell Press, Woodbridge

ISBN 978 1 83765 120 7

The Boydell Press is an imprint of Boydell & Brewer Ltd
PO Box 9, Woodbridge, Suffolk IP12 3DF, UK
and of Boydell & Brewer Inc.
668 Mt Hope Avenue, Rochester, NY 14620–2731, USA
website: www.boydellandbrewer.com

A CIP catalogue record for this book is available
from the British Library

The publisher has no responsibility for the continued existence or accuracy
of URLs for external or third-party internet websites referred to in this book,
and does not guarantee that any content on such websites is, or will remain,
accurate or appropriate

This collection aims to explore how states accessed essential professional naval expertise in the making and implementation of strategy. Political and naval leaders must share expertise and understand each other. These essays point to the ways different states, at different times, have managed that relationship and the limitations it placed upon effective strategic policy.

CONTENTS

List of Contributors ix

Introduction: Naval Leadership: Expertise and Strategy 1
RICHARD HARDING

1. The Evolution of French Naval Leadership: Defining the
Admiralty of France from the Sixteenth to the Eighteenth Century 18
ALAN JAMES

2. The Makers of Spanish Naval Strategy in the Eighteenth Century:
Strategy, Tactics, and Shipbuilding Policy 31
IVAN VALDEZ-BUBNOV

3. Naval Strategic Leadership in Britain, 1739–1748: Political
Leaders and Professional Knowledge 52
RICHARD HARDING

4. The Statesman and the Naval Leader: The Count of Floridablanca
and Navy Minister Antonio Valdés, 1783–1792 70
AGUSTÍN GUIMERÁ

5. Defining French Eighteenth-Century Naval Strategy 92
OLIVIER CHALINE

6. Casto Méndez Núñez: The Admiral who could have been Regent,
1861–1868 104
AGUSTÍN RAMÓN RODRÍGUEZ GONZÁLEZ

7. Teaching by Example: Julian Corbett's *The Campaign of
Trafalgar* of 1910 120
ANDREW LAMBERT

8. Spanish Naval Leadership during the Second Republic:
José Giral Pereira 141
ADOLFO MORALES TRUEBA

9.	The Quest to Understand Naval Leadership: Educating Admirals for High Command in the U.S. Navy from the Eighteenth Century into the Twenty-first Century JOHN B. HATTENDORF	159
10.	Reflections RICHARD HARDING	179

Bibliography	185
Index	202

CONTRIBUTORS

Professor Olivier Chaline, Sorbonne Université, Paris FED 4124. Professor Chaline is a French modernist historian. He has held professorships at the University of Rennes II (1999–2001), and the University of Paris IV (Paris-Sorbonne). He is Director of the Centre for Maritime Archaeology and Historical Research and Head of the international research programme investigating Admiral de Grasse's fleet. He has authored many books and articles including *La Mer et la France: quand les Bourbons voulaient dominer les oceans* (2016), *Les armées du Roi: le grand chantier xviie–xviiie siècle* (2016) and with Jean-Marie Kowalski (eds.), *L'amiral de Grasse et l'Indépendance américaine: Commander en opérations* (Paris: SUP, 2023).

Dr Agustín Guimerá of the Instituto de Historia, Consejo Superior de Investigaciones Científcas, Madrid, is the author of numerous studies of comparative naval leadership: *Liderazgo estratégico en España, 1475–2018* (Madrid, Instituto Universitario General Gutiérrez Mellado, 2019); *El liderazgo estratégico: una aproximación interdisciplinar* (Madrid, Ministerio de Defensa, 2018); Guimerá, A., and Chaline, O. (eds.). *La real armada: la marine des Bourbons d'Espagne au xviiie siècle* (Paris: PUPS).

Professor Richard Harding is an emeritus professor at the University of Westminster. He is author of *Modern Naval History: Debates and Perspectives* (2015); *The Emergence of Britain's Global Naval Supremacy: The War of 1739–1748* (2010). He has edited and co-edited numerous books, including *Naval Leadership in the Atlantic World: The Age of Reform and Revolution, 1700–1850* (2017) with Dr Agustín Guimerá; *Naval Leadership and Management, 1650–1950* (2012) with Dr Helen Doe. His most recent works are co-edited with Professor Olivier Chaline, *L'Angleterre vue de la mer au temps de la voile, XVIe–XIXe siècles, histoire, économie et société: époques modernes et contemporaines* (Paris: Cairn, 2020); 'Ideology and Operational Impact in Eighteenth Century Britain', in *Ideologies of Western Naval Power, c. 1500 – 1815.* Edited by J.D. Davies, Alan James, and Gijs Rommelse (Abingdon: Routledge, 2020), pp. 262–279.

Professor John B. Hattendorf, US Naval War College, Newport, Rhode Island. Professor Hattendorf is the Ernest J. King Professor Emeritus of Maritime History, a chair he occupied at the U.S. Naval War College from 1984 to 2016. He is a distinguished author who has written or edited over fifty books on many aspects of naval history.

Dr Alan James King's College, London. Dr James is a senior lecturer at King's College. His works include *Navy and Government in Early Modern France, 1572–1661* (2004); Les arsenaux français avant Colbert", *Neptunia* 263 (September 2011); La Bataille du Cap Béveziers (1690): une glorieuse victoire pour le roi stratège. *La Bataille: du fait d'armes au combat idéologique, XIe–XIXe siècle*. Edited by A. Boltanski, Y. Lagadec, and F. Mercier (Rennes: Universitaires de Rennes, 2015); he is also co-editor of *Ideologies of Western Naval Power, 1500–1815* (Abingdon, Routledge, 2019).

Professor Andrew Lambert, King's College, London. Professor Lambert is the Laughton Professor of Naval History in the Department of War Studies. Some of his more recent works include *Crusoe's Island: A Rich and Curious History of Pirates, Castaways and Madness* (2016); *21st Century Corbett: Maritime Strategy and Naval Policy for the Modern Era* (2017); *Seapower States: Maritime Culture, Continental Empires and the Conflict that made the Modern World* (2018).

Dr Agustín R. Rodríguez González, Real Academia de la Historia, Madrid. Dr Rodríguez has worked on many aspects of the Spanish navy from the eighteenth to the twentieth centuries. His works on the Spanish navy include, *Trafalgar y el conficto naval anglo-español del siglo XVIII* (2005); *La reconstrucción de la escuadra: planes navales españoles, 1898*–1920 (2009); *Corsarios españoles* (2020).

Lt. Col. Dr Adolfo Morales Trueba, Ministerio de Defensa, Universidad Nacional de Educación Distancia. Lt. Col. Dr Trueba is an expert on the Spanish navy of the Second Republic (1931–1939) and a writer on contemporary naval affairs. His work includes 'Las dimensiones de la política naval de la Segunda República española en su contexto internacional', *Aportes Revista de Historia Contemporánea* (2017); 'El escenario naval tras la Primera Guerra Mundial', *Revista de Estudios en Seguridad Internacional* (2017).

Professor Ivan Valdez-Bubnov, Instituto de Investigaciones Históricas, Universidad Nacional Autónoma de México. Professor Valdez-Bubnov is the author of numerous works on the Spanish navy and naval power in early modern world. These include *Poder naval y modernización del estado: política de construcción naval española (siglos XVI–XVIII).* (2011); 'Spanish Naval Strategy and the United States, 1763–1819', *Mariner's Mirror* (2015).

Introduction

Naval Leadership: Expertise and Strategy

RICHARD HARDING

Since the first few months of 2020 the world economy has been faced by crises that it had not seen for over seventy years. The sudden progress of the virus COVID-19 throughout most of the world forced an unprecedented economic shut-down, bringing predictions of an economic jolt whose repercussions are likely to be felt for many years to come. So new was the virus that most national governments quickly turned to the scientific community to help them understand the epidemiology. They looked to this community to inform decisions relating to the immediate political questions about ending 'lockdowns' and organising life in the post-virus world. They barely dared to make a move without the endorsement of some part of the scientific community. However, it was not long before citizens became restless in many parts of the world, particularly the western world. This was reflected in political backlashes and even violence. It was a stark reminder of an old tension that exists within societies between political authority and the authority of experts.[1]

Barely had the global concern over COVID subsided when another major crisis jolted world politics. In January 2022 increasingly aggressive displays of Russian military power on the borders of Ukraine sent tremors through the world's diplomatic channels. While Russian messaging was ambiguous in so far as what Russian grievances actually were and what would satisfy the Kremlin, what was not in question was the expert power of the Russian armed forces. On conspicuous display was the modern hardware and the new tactical organisation of an armed force that had been substantially reformed since 2008.[2] It was believed that if Russia decided to launch a large-scale invasion of Ukraine it would be a short, one-sided affair.

---

[1] Collins, Harry and Robert Evans. *Rethinking Expertise*. Chicago: University of Chicago Press, 2007, 13–35.

[2] Renz, B., *Russia's Military Revival*. Cambridge: Polity Press, 2018.

In the event the invasion of 24 February was a dismal failure. The expertise in the operational art and the technological and tactical changes supposed to have radically altered the effectiveness of the Russian military proved illusory. On the ground, in the air, and at sea the expertise of Russian forces was far more limited in combat than initially anticipated. This came only six months after the withdrawal of Allied forces from Afghanistan had also shown that highly developed, expensive military expertise could not prevent humiliation and disaster. In the world of the military, as in civil society, the authority of the experts was undermined.

During the previous ten years, the technocratic authority of experts, which reached its apogee in the managed economies of the period between 1945 and 1968, faced rapid decline. The faltering economic growth of the late 1960s accentuated divisions between Keynesian and free market economic experts. The consistently recurring incidence of major industrial disasters, from oil spillages and accidents at sea, aircraft crashes and civil engineering failures, to the near catastrophic disaster at Three Mile Island New Hampshire in 1979 and the actual nuclear disaster at Chernobyl in 1986, undermined public faith in an infallibility of scientific and technological expertise. Alongside this, the new media made possible by the worldwide web opened almost unlimited channels of information for individuals to select their own narratives and versions of truth. Both the sophistication of deliberate misinformation campaigns and the lack of sophistication in conspiracy theories, combined to put even greater pressure on the credibility of experts.

While dependence upon scientific and technological progress remains at the very core of modern social expectations, and expertise continues to be developed, sub-divided and applied, the authority of experts is increasingly challenged. The pain felt by many societies in the wake of the 2008 financial clash left many unhappy with both the predictive and palliative capabilities of economic and political experts. The fact that scientific and technological knowledge often progresses incrementally, with research periodically throwing up only conditional, partial, and contradictory results, is understood within scientific communities, but does not comfort those in society whose belief lies in either rigid scientific certainties or anti-science ideology. It undermines the authority of the experts by blurring the difference between scientific knowledge and the 'common sense' knowledge of society at large. Climate change denial is given equal credence with climate science. Vaccine denial has equality with immunology. The loss of patience with experts is an integral part of the rise of populism worldwide. Common sense formulae, emotional and rhetorical flourishes often carry greater weight than complex, nuanced arguments in political contests and the former achieves a greater and faster spread of popular endorsement and reinforcement. In civil society it has taken a major epidemiological crisis, that might have far-reaching consequences, to put the expert back at the centre of policy making, but it is far from complete.

There is, of course, nothing new in this. The tension between experts and political, democratic, leadership is as old as the Greek city states.[3] How to incorporate experts and the decision as to which experts would be invited to be 'at the top' (but on no account 'on top') is a consistent theme as societies adjust to their evolving needs for expertise.

The military have suffered a similar crisis of popular political confidence. One of the original types of expertise required by societies was military expertise. This was embedded in the training of elites in most societies, uniting military and political expertise. In the Middle Ages, feudalism imposed military expertise (whether genuine, or assumed) as a social requirement of political leadership. As political and economic structures have changed, and warfare altered, so the need for practical military expertise in the social elites was overlaid with more symbolic and cultural attributes associated with chivalry.[4] At the same time, different forms of expertise had to be integrated within political leadership. In eighteenth-century Britain there was a close relationship between the landed ruling classes, and the military, clerical, legal, and commercial experts, which had been evolving over centuries.[5] The rapid pace of change in the nineteenth century required much faster accommodation with new experts from public health to manufacturing and engineering.[6]

Useful definitions of expertise have been provided by Harry Collins and Robert Evans. Within a taxonomy of types of expertise, their description of 'specialist tacit knowledge', obtained by intellectual endeavour and the experience of using it in live situations within a community of practice, is a good starting point for the type of expertise considered here.[7] It implies the ability to use the expertise appropriately in different situations. We will return to this in more detail shortly.

The negotiation of technical experts with the political leadership of a state has been the subject of a number of studies since the beginning of the twentieth

---

[3] Plato's concern in *The Republic* (c. 375 BCE) with how a democratic polity could control its expertly trained leaders has been constantly revisited throughout the centuries.

[4] In Italy, the decline of the military tradition was particularly noticeable. See Hanlon, Gregory, *The Twilight of a Military Tradition: Italian Aristocrats and European Conflicts, 1560–1800*. London: UCL Press, 1998.

[5] Corfield, Penelope J., *Power and the Professions in Britain, 1700–1850*. London: Routledge, 1995; Holmes, Geoffrey, *Augustan England : Professions, State and Society, 1680–1730*. London: Allen and Unwin, 1982.

[6] Macleod, R., ed. *Government and Expertise: Specialists, Administrators and Professionals, 1860–1910*. Cambridge: Cambridge University Press, 1988. For the Royal Navy's need to adapt to the requirements of a new steam navy at the end of the nineteenth century see, Davison, Robert L., *The Challenges of Command: The Royal Navy's Executive Branch Officers, 1880–1919*. Aldershot: Ashgate, 2011.

[7] Collins, Harry, and Evans, Robert, *Rethinking Expertise*.

century, particularly those concerned with professions or professionalism.[8] The institutionalisation, or legal protection, of specific, technical expertise, provided the means of codifying expert knowledge, channelling it through accepted individuals and thus making it available to society at large, usually endorsed by political authority.

Naval expertise is a particularly interesting form of knowledge and practice. Commanding ships, squadrons, or fleets requires a highly specialised from of knowledge. Effective navigation requires detailed intellectual engagement with physics, astronomy, metrology, and mathematics. It also requires practical experience of how ships move in water, and the impact of water and wind on vessels. Experience of the capability of different types of ships in various water conditions, the mechanics of the propulsion and the effectiveness of the weapons systems are also important. Further experience is needed of how crews of ships respond in different situations, which will have an impact on what can be done with the aggregated human endeavour on the ship.

Moving a ship safely in different conditions is but one aspect of this expertise. Ultimately, a warship is intended to impose the will of one society upon another. To achieve this it requires a different range of skills relating to the weapons systems, the robustness of all the systems that make up the fighting ship. Knowledge of the enemy and ability to quickly interpret data in three dimensions, decide, and then to achieve decisive action is vital, but only possible with both understanding of principles and a deep experience of the ships, the crews, and the enemy. The sheer intensity of this expertise is most famously illustrated by the 'Perisher' course for submarine command in the Royal Navy.[9]

Collins and Evans presented an interesting way of looking at this specialist expertise. It is possible to build up a working knowledge of a subject through reading and research using the ubiquitous tools of literacy, numeracy, generic analytical skills, and the like, that any member of society might possess. However, without experience that immerses the individual deeply in the practice, he or she will never reach a point of being able to utilise that expertise as a skilled practitioner. This deep level of expertise might also enable an individual to use it to inform judgements in life outside of the narrow confines of the expertise. This might be to judge other specialists in different, but related, social locations (transmuted expertise). It might be the ability to judge

---

[8] Ritzer, George, 'Professionalization, Bureaucratization and Rationalization: The Views of Max Weber'. *Social Forces* 53, no. 4 (1975): 627–634; Ash, Eric H., ed. *Expertise: Practical Knowledge and the Early Modern State*. Washington DC: Osiris, 2010; Burrage, Michael and Rolf Torstendahl, eds. *Professions in Theory and History: Rethinking the Study of the Professions*. London: Sage, 1990.

[9] Hennessy, Peter and James Jinks. *The Silent Deep: The Royal Navy Submarine Service since 1945*. London: Allen Lane, 8–43, 2015.

experts in their own field that are more skilled, equally skilled or less than they are (technical connoisseurship).[10] Finally, it might be that the expert can use expertise in one context to inform decisions in a completely different one (referred expertise).

This is important in our study because of the nature of naval expertise and political authority. The naval expert and the political expert achieve their expertise in very different contexts. The naval expert gains their expertise in applying themselves to activity at sea. They can become highly skilled experts able to command and influence the world they inhabit. Within the context of maritime organisation and warfare they can have significant 'transmuted expertise', judging the performance of peers in other navies and other specialisms. They will also have considerable 'technical connoisseurship' in their own specialism. However, all this naturally takes them away from their home society. It puts them on the fringes of the land-based networks of power and influence that are at the very centre of the experience of the political expert. It can disconnect them from the interests and priorities of large sections of the population. Very few societies have a deep concern for the maritime/naval dimension of their social, political, and economic lives. The recurrent lament that society suffers from 'sea blindness' is partly both cause and effect of the relative isolation of naval expertise. There are many other competing experts, whose interests and assumptions are more deeply entrenched in the public mind. Few people have a personal connection with the sea, or an interest in the significance of naval affairs in a globally connected world.

This raises an important question; how do societies (and their political experts/leaders) develop their understanding of naval and maritime affairs? An obvious answer is that they turn to their naval experts, but if those experts are only marginally influential or understood this does not bode well for informed decision-making. To take Great Britain as an example in the last quarter of the nineteenth century, British society had imbued about 200 years of political and economic dialogue that put maritime and naval affairs at the centre of state decision-making. As the challenges to its assumed naval supremacy grew up to 1914, so political society accepted and built upon those maritime traditions. This does not mean that the 'navalism' of the period was either hegemonic, or that decisions based upon it were always sound, but it did mean that professional naval expertise was listened to at the highest level.[11]

---

[10] However, Collins and Evans conclude that it is only really possible to judge someone whose expertise is less than that of the judge.

[11] Marder, Arthur J., *The Anatomy of British Sea Power: A History of British Naval Policy in the Pre-Dreadnought Era, 1880–1905*. New York: Alfred A. Knopf, 1940; Semmel, Bernard, *Liberalism and Naval Strategy: Ideology, Interest, and Sea Power during the Pax Britannica*. London: Allen and Unwin, 1986.

The situation changed between 1910 and 1918. Britain's decision to engage on the Western Front led to a mass conscript army. The significance of the economic blockade of Germany, although ultimately successful, had less traction with public opinion than the trauma caused by the massive battles in France. The failure of the Royal Navy to win another Trafalgar against the German High Seas Fleet, was a considerable political burden. The authority of naval experts never recovered. Although the sea played a far more visible role in the outcome of the Second World War, the Cold War confrontation between NATO and the Warsaw Pact across the Central Front in Europe and an American nuclear umbrella, left less space for public engagement with specifically maritime and naval policy. The Falklands War (1982) occurred at a time when there was serious concern that the political support for an oceanic navy outside the NATO area was on the point of disappearing.[12] The experience of that war went some way to refocusing attention on naval options, but after the Cold War ended in 1991 the visibility of naval expertise in debates about Britain's future faded once again.

Today, the evidence of growing geo-political tensions between the United States and challenger states like China and, to a lesser degree, Russia, is forcing Britain, and all states, to think more clearly about how they manage their naval resources. The ability of North Korea and Iran to act as disrupters in key geographical areas is also increasing public perceptions of the potential threats. The question of how the authority of naval expertise is integrated into political authority is therefore likely to be as important as ever, and it is to this question that these essays might have something to say. For naval expertise to have a significant political impact it is necessary for those naval experts to exercise that referent power indicated by Collins and Evans. They must be able to convince the political actors of conclusions informed by their expertise. It is not easy if the nature of their expertise is foreign to most of those other actors, and the way they acquire it (at sea) places them outside the normal, day-to-day networks of influence and power. A familiar trope in naval histories and novels is to juxtapose the bluff seamen who know what must be done against the ignorant, self-serving (if not corrupt) politicians who make it impossible to achieve. While comforting to the seamen and a good narrative device to engage the reader, it is too simplistic as an explanation for such an important and persistent question.

To date, it is a question that has not received as much as attention it deserves. It is a subject in the study of strategy, but so often the strategist is assumed to be at the top of decision-making system. It is a natural aspect of the study of leadership at that level, but is usually subsumed into the generic exhortation to 'manage upwards'. There are some possible reasons for this.

---

[12] Hastings, Max, and Simon Jenkins, *The Battle for the Falklands*. London: Pan, 24–25, 1997.

The first is, perhaps, because of the weight of attention that is given to the story of the heroic leader or leader of genius, who, almost by definition, is the successful leader. Almost all western studies of military leadership revolve around the performance of leaders – how good or bad they were, or what strengths and weaknesses they displayed. There is very good reason for doing this. Whether they be early histories designed to illustrate the genius or moral superiority of one individual or society over another, or more modern, social scientific, studies, of leader behaviours, the purpose is usually the same – to help people in formal leadership roles carry out their tasks more effectively. The traditional way of doing this is for the reader to be presented with role models to emulate. Furthermore, there is a natural focus for readers and historians on the individuals who come to encapsulate the 'brain' of societies in conflict. Decisions are made by human beings and carried out by them. The leaders themselves play an important role. The evidence that survives is drawn up by them and is usually expressed in terms of their own understanding of events. There is a natural desire to enhance their own role in success, and exploring the experience of the leader in a particular situation is a satisfying way to connect the reader to the decisions and dramas of past conflicts.[13] The history of the successful leader provides the human drama and the easiest way of translating the lessons of the past into the mind of the current aspirant leader. It is a natural lens through which the narrative of war can be understood and made useful. However, success and failure are important variables in all these histories or case studies. When the victors exclusively write the history, then the historian must be cautious. Winston Churchill's famous statement that history would be kind to him because he intended to write that history, is applicable, to one degree or another, to all leaders. With success the attributes of the leader tend to obscure the structural and contingent factors that influenced the situation, but when studying leadership decisions from the perspective of the loser those factors become far more prominent. Often a great deal more is learned about a situation when studied from the viewpoint of the loser.[14]

---

[13] A good discussion of a set of decisions and how various actors claimed or allowed their role to be assumed, can be found in relation to the development of the tank in the First World War. See, Harris, J.P., *Men, Ideas and Tanks: British Military Thought and Armoured Forces, 1903–1939*. War, Armed Forces and Society. Edited by Beckett, I.F.W. Manchester: Manchester University Press, 4–39, 1995.

[14] Schivelbusch, Wolfgang. *The Culture of Defeat: On National Trauma, Mourning and Recovery*. London: Granta, 4–8, 2003. For an interesting example of how the defeated German military integrated their interpretation of the war on the Eastern Front, 1941–1945 into American popular understanding of that conflict, see, Smelser, Ronald, and Edward J. Davies, *The Myth of the Eastern Front: The Nazi-Soviet War in American Popular Culture*. Cambridge: Cambridge University Press, 2008.

A second reason might lie in the cross-over between the study of civilian and military leadership. There is a constant inter-change between studies aimed at the military and those aimed at civilian leaders. The ethical, moral, intellectual, and emotional dimensions have strong parallels. The achievement of the task objective is central to both. Leadership, generally, is often seen as a generic problem-solving activity, demanding a set of intellectual calculations. Rational choice theory has underpinned much leadership literature. The task of the leader is to evaluate options with as much rigour as possible and apply the one with the greatest probability of success.[15] It has commonly been likened to a game of chess. The mind of the opponent was unknown, but all the pieces and all the rules were known. The options could be evaluated and planned within known constraints. Whoever plays the better game wins.

Others have been dissatisfied with this, particularly in the context of military leadership. One of the distinguishing features of military leadership is that it is overtly directed towards defeating an enemy, or at least convincing a potential enemy that conflict is an unwise option. It is not the same as trying to fulfil a market demand or creating a new demand better than others might do (deterrence). It comes far closer to a zero-sum situation for the societies concerned. The capitalist free market has its weaknesses, but achieving long-term economic growth is not one of them. For the CEOs of companies engaged in aggressive market competition it may feel that life or death is at stake, but this competition itself is, in many cases, extremely healthy for society. This cannot be said of military leadership. The failure of military leadership can be catastrophic for societies, from the individuals serving in the forces to entire social systems. In military conflicts all participants are likely to walk away damaged, but it is highly unlikely that all will benefit. The greater the benefit for one side usually means the greater loss for the other and the annihilation of the entire social and economic fabric of society is seldom unthinkable. In military conflicts it is quite common for the rules to change during events and the pressures imposed upon societies to throw up entirely unexpected situations. Some have likened this form of leadership to a game of poker, where the role of chance and the importance of playing the opponent not the cards emphasise the contingent nature of any situation.[16]

Thus, the dominant means of studying leadership, through focus on the performance of the individual, particularly those successful leaders, in their own command environments, and the assumption that the generic techniques

---

[15] Kepner, Charles H. and Benjamin B. Tregoe, *The New Rational Manager*. London: John Martin, 1981. However, for an examination of the limits of rationality under pressure, see Payne, Kenneth, *The Psychology of Strategy: Exploring Rationality in the Vietnam War*. Oxford: Oxford University Press, 2015.

[16] Conrad, J., *Gambling and War: Risk, Reward, and Chance in International Conflict*. Annapolis, Naval Institute Press, 2017.

of leadership transfer across all organisational contexts, means less attention has been paid to how the specialist expertise of leaders works within their host societies.

A third reason may lie in the study of strategy. National strategy is where decisions concerning the deployment of scarce national resources have to be made. The decision-makers, possessing both political authority and expertise are the essential leadership element. They must conceive of the long-term trajectories of potential investment decisions, make decisions upon highly ambiguous data or flimsy projections. They need to be capable of responding to unknown future shocks. They must be able to mobilise all the other actors that can to turn a decision into a functioning policy and plan. All this must be done within the context of understanding of how an enemy might react. If any of this is inadequate, then it will reduce the prospect of a successful outcome. The more complex the machinery of war and society, the more difficult the task becomes. It is highly unlikely that the political leadership in any state will possess all the expertise to make the best possible judgements in all contexts. It is understood that in most conflicts the side that makes the fewest mistakes is the one most likely to emerge successful. Avoiding mistakes depends on the extent and value of specialist expertise that the political authorities can incorporate into their decision-making process. How they access different expertise and the authority they give to technical experts, are vital elements in the strategic behaviour of states.

During the twentieth century the incorporation of technical expertise into strategic decision-making accelerated tremendously. How military and naval expertise was captured within services, codified and made available to the political leadership of states has now got a substantial literature.[17] The demands that total war and the narrowness of the margin between success and failure in the first half of the twentieth century left diminishing space for inefficiency or ineffectiveness. By 1945 the consequences of failure were starkly apparent in the devastation of Europe and Japan. Science, technology, social sciences, and the arts were co-opted as never before into massive national efforts.

However, today the student of strategy is faced with a perplexing vision. It is not the lack of literature on strategy or strategic leadership that is the

---

[17] A few examples are, Gibbs, Norman H., *The Origins of Imperial Defence*. Oxford: Clarendon Press, 1955; d'Ombrain, N.J. 'The Imperial General Staff and the Military Policy of a 'Continental Strategy' during the 1911 International Crisis'. *Military Affairs* 34, no. 3 (1970): 88–93; French, David and Brian Holden Reid, eds. *The British General Staff: Reform and Innovation, 1890–1939*. London: Frank Cass, 2002; Goerlitz, Walter. *History of the German General Staff*. Boulder: Westview Press, 1985; Podsoblyaev, Evgenii F., Francis King, and John Biggart. 'The Russian Naval General Staff and the Evolution of Naval Policy, 1904–1914'. *Journal of Military History* 66, no. 1 (2002): 37–69.

problem but its sheer volume. As with the subject of leadership, military and civilian strategic studies have become conflated, with a good deal of mutual benefit. Strategy has become a key word in organisation studies.[18] Strategy is perceived as being at the pinnacle of organisational power and to be a strategic leader is to be perceived as the key driver of organisational success. In the Anglophone world the word *strategy* has an emotional power that other words in the management or leadership lexicon do not. It stands out as a primary force that determines the fate of all who live and work in organisations. This prominence has led to massive growth in the literature, from the scientific, through all the social sciences (including history) to cultural studies. Yet at the same time, there is a constant and even growing concern about how strategic leadership works or might be made to work. This is being stimulated at least in part by major geostrategic and economic shifts and the increasingly complex responses by states to the issues of sovereignty and security that they pose.

As levels of strategy became increasingly differentiated (for example grand, national, theatre, maritime, air or land) and the technologies (often adapted from civilian uses) for analysing their impact and costs improved, so the definitions of strategy and the role of strategic leaders has become more varied and open to exploration. The result is an impressive volume of literature, shedding light on important aspects of strategic leadership. The vital relationship between the political authorities and the technical experts has certainly been noticed and the question of leadership deeply considered.[19] Whether it was the struggle between the 'Frock Coats and Brass Hats' in the British Cabinet and Committee of Imperial Defence during 1917–1918; the Imperial General Staff and Winston Churchill in the 1940s, President Truman and General MacArthur during the Korean War, or Robert McNamara and the Joint Chiefs of Staff in the 1960s, the issue constantly re-presented itself.

However, the means by which experts of different types have their expertise integrated into the political decision-making framework and the reasons why this does or does not happen has received less attention. For naval officers this poses a distinct problem for the reasons discussed above. The distance between naval expertise and that of others within the decision-making framework can be enormous. The priorities of the political leadership can be influenced by a multitude of factors and actors, whose influence upon the decisions can be unknown to the naval expert.

---

[18] Outside of the military, the academic study of strategy is fairly new. See Bracker, Jeffrey, 'The Historical Development of the Strategic Management Concept'. *Academy of Management Review* 6, no. 2 (1980): 210–224.

[19] One only has to look at the index to the U.S. Naval War College Review to see how seriously leadership and strategy are studied. See https://digital-commons.usnwc.edu/do/search (accessed 2 May 2020).

Similarly, the political leadership often has very little knowledge of the practicalities of naval matters. This can work to the advantage of the service experts in a crisis as the political leadership might have little appetite for intervening in operational matters. However, it is a distinct disadvantage at the strategic level when matters of long-lead time investment strategies for equipment programmes have to be agreed and sustained over many budget cycles. Much depends on hypothesising threats spanning a long time period rather than demonstrating responses to known threats. For example, the melting of the high Arctic ice, the development of uncrewed vehicles (at sea, in the air and on land), and the growth of cyber-warfare are just a few varied aspects of a shifting environment for which long-term strategic planning is required, but every year immediate political realities force adjustments to budgets, and priorities. Thus, strategic decisions are, by their nature, extremely expensive and fragile and are often abandoned long before fruition. Decisions to which organisations are committed, but are not carried through, have massive sunk costs and irrecoverable forgone alternatives. What makes this long-term perspective even more problematic is that at no point in the life cycle is success or failure readily demonstrable – deterrence is a concept that it difficult to prove. This requires the expert to argue solidly from the known data (which is shared knowledge of the decision-making group), deploying their accumulated expertise to present what can be inferred from it to an unknown but probable future situation, in a manner in which it is possible for the political authorities to understand and accept. It is a hard task for any expert at any time.

Historically, the ability of navies to ensure a long-term focus on their needs by political leadership has been very patchy. Other priorities intrude with regularity, extending investment cycles, diminishing the practical expertise of seamen, and even sacrificing whole areas of expertise.[20] Even states which are supposedly 'seapower' states, find this extremely difficult.[21]

As has been noted, this is not a new phenomenon, but it is under-researched. This collection of essays results from an international project undertaken with the support of the Spanish ministry of defence to examine the issues relating to the higher command of navies. There was no intention to pose a single question or to test any specific proposition. The ambition was simply to generate a reasonably broad chronological and international perspective from historians who chose their own foci for study. Nevertheless, as happens

---

[20] Erikson, A.S., L.J. Goldstein, and C. Lord, eds. *China Goes to Sea: Maritime Transformation in Comparative Historical Perspective*. Annapolis: Naval Institute Press, 2009.

[21] Lambert, Andrew. *Seapower States: Maritime Culture, Continental Empires, and the Conflict That Made the Modern World*. New Haven: Yale University Press, 2018.

in many of these permissive contexts, a degree of convergence emerged in some of the essays. They indicated that the higher level of naval command had very different experiences in their interface with the sources of political authority, which had significant consequences both for navies and the societies they served. It is these essays that are the subject of this collection.

France is examined by Dr Alan James and Professor Olivier Chaline from the sixteenth to the end of eighteenth centuries. The consistent penetration of naval expertise into French decision-making was extremely limited. From the earlier period at least until the death of Louis XIV in 1715, the importance of the French navy as an organ of domestic royal government outweighed its value as a military/diplomatic tool. Naval officers might be given great latitude in their operational decision-making, but their ability to influence policy was extremely limited. The navy was important as a tool for consolidating domestic centralisation of state power, and as a symbol of the monarch's prestige at home and abroad. Appointments to the senior posts were made with this very much in mind. Absolute loyalty to the monarch, solid support for the Roman Catholic Church, and a noble status adequate to represent the king were essential elements in these officers, rather than a demonstration of deep naval expertise.[22] Their capability to inform the monarch or council of state of the practicality of policy was of lesser value. The quality of plans and decisions depended very much upon the ability of the ministers of marine, who had access to the council of state. As Professor Chaline has shown elsewhere, the inability of naval expertise to influence deeply French political authority was accompanied by its mirror effect – the heavy influence of domestic political authority upon operations at sea.[23]

A further complication for French naval plans in the eighteenth century was, in many cases, their dependence on Spanish collaboration to achieve a basic numerical parity with the British Royal Navy. This required understanding at the very highest levels of state and an ability to translate joint intentions into effective joint naval action. This capability, dependent as it was on a range of ministers from the two monarchies, seldom developed beyond a

---

[22] As Professor Surreaux has shown, these officers could be highly experienced, demonstrating all the qualities in battle and command that might be wished. Their appointments to senior command could be well deserved. However, their influence at the highest levels of policy remained limited. See Surreaux, S., 'The Reputation of the Vice-Admiral of France'. In Harding, R. and Guimerá, A., eds., *Naval Leadership in the Atlantic World*. London: University of Westminster Press, pp. 35–47, 2017. DOI: https://doi.org/10.16997/books2.d.License: CC-BY-NC-ND 4.0.

[23] Chaline, O. 'Admiral Louis Guillouet, Comte d'Orvilliers (1710–1792): A Style of Command in the Age of the American War'. In Harding, R. and Guimerá, A., eds, *Naval Leadership in the Atlantic World*. London: University of Westminster Press, pp. 73–84, 2017. DOI: https://doi.org/10.16997/books2.d.License: CC-BY-NC-ND 4.0.

superficial willingness jointly to disrupt the operations of the Royal Navy. While alliance warfare was, and is, a very common phenomenon, the way navies operated together and their influence on policy making and political authorities in the early modern world is currently a subject that is in need of much more investigation.

Although France and Spain developed close diplomatic and naval interests during the eighteenth century, the relationship between naval expertise and political authority developed very differently. In French historiography, opinions of the Spanish navy are generally poor.[24] Yet the ability of the Spanish navy to develop through the combination of professional and political expertise was far more noticeable than in France. The task for the Spanish monarchy was colossal. The Spanish Bourbon monarchy had to create a national navy after 1713 in place of the largely collapsed regional and functional squadrons that it had inherited from the Habsburgs. Thus, an accumulated experience of a navy with an embedded officer corps and extensive independent expertise was not immediately available to Spanish policymaking. However, Professor Ivan Valdez-Bubnov shows that throughout the century strategic thinking about the navy evolved via a productive mix of naval and civilian experts. Statesmen and administrators, like José Patiño, Bernardo de Tinajero, and the Count de Aranda; economists such as Jerónimo de Uztáriz, and naval officers such as Antonio de Gaztañeta, José Navarro, and Enrique Macdonnell, managed to influence the development of the navy to the point that by the 1790s Spanish warships, operations, and naval policy were, for the size of the fleet, equal to any in Europe. There appears to have been space within the political authority to allow maritime interests and expertise to have an impact on policy. This was certainly owing to the clear dependence of the Spanish state on the resources of the Spanish empire in America.

The advantages and the limits of the Spanish monarchy's ability to exploit the expertise of naval officers is demonstrated by Dr Guimerá's study of the leadership of the secretary of state, the Count de Floridablanca and the secretary of the navy, Antonio Valdés. The two men guided foreign and colonial policy and the development of the navy between 1783 and 1792. Floridablanca created a decision-making process in the *Junta de Estado* that enabled the monarchy to respond to the needs of the empire at its greatest extent. With Valdés' expertise, their efforts maximised an understanding of maritime dimension in government and facilitated the development of a large and effective navy. It was, however, the final brilliant flourish of Spanish naval power. The limitations of committed and informed leadership became apparent as the foundations of Spanish policy began to crumble with the French Revolution in 1789 and the dismissal of Floridablanca in 1792. It is a

---

[24] Guimerá, Agustín and Olivier Chaline, eds. *La real armada: la marine des Bourbons d'Espagne au xviiie siècle*. Paris: PUPS, pp. 9–15, 2018.

case study of how naval power is influenced by a combination of the great structural changes of international politics and the micro-politics of individuals operating within a state organisation.

The catastrophe of the wars 1793–1815 dealt that Spanish navy a devastating blow. Savaged by the Royal Navy at the peak of its power between 1795 and 1808 and enervated by the crumbling of the administrative and fiscal apparatus of the monarchy in the face of the French invasion of 1807/8, the navy was in no condition to deal effectively with the independence movements in South and Central America from 1810. The instability of the restored Bourbons and the loss of the resources of the Americas saw the navy dwindle in significance to the political authority and interests in Madrid. The influence of the navy and the development of its expertise was largely limited to the Philippines and the Caribbean islands, combatting pirates, smugglers, and insurrection. Dr Agustín Rodríguez shows how the authorities in Madrid were aware of the limitations on the reach of Spanish naval power in the 1850s and 1860s. This frustrated some senior officers, causing a major crisis with Peru and Chile in the summer of 1862. On the other hand, the crisis gave some, like Castro Méndez Núñez, a chance to shine, impressing both the Royal and United States Navies on the spot. His use of force, his fine diplomatic judgement and action to secure the honour of the Spanish flag, impressed the authorities in Madrid. Without being close to the centre of power and without spectacular naval victories under his belt, Méndez Núñez, became a force within the political system in Madrid. Promoted to vice-admiral in 1866 and feted as a hero when he returned to Spain in 1868, he became the subject of popular hero worship. While he had been away, the revolt that overthrew Queen Isabel II had split the army, but the navy and Méndez Núñez remained neutral. Both the revolutionaries and the queen wanted his support. Although he accepted the vice presidency of the admiralty, a task within his professional competence, he refused the offer of becoming regent while the revolutionaries sought a new monarch. His authority was such that his death in August 1869 was accompanied by rumours of assassination. Here was a case of naval expertise being taken into the heart of political authority. That expertise was not purely technical, although it had been fashioned in battle and long campaigns. He was a public hero, wounded in action and famed for his defence of Spain's honour. The complexity of his campaigns had helped hone his political judgement and he returned to Spain at a time when his fame, political astuteness, and his isolation from the events that led to the revolution, made him stand out as a man of honour to both sides.

The permeability of naval expertise and political authority in Spain continued into the twentieth century. The prestige of the navy in the last quarter of the nineteenth century suffered badly with the disaster of the Spanish-American War of 1898 and recovery was slow. A new disruption occurred when the monarchy was overthrown at the end of 1931. The navy adapted to the new republic but its political leadership slid into confusion as ministers and ministries came and went in quick succession. However, before the demise of the republic, it was a civilian administrator and politician, José Giral Pereira, who gave the navy new confidence and a realistic naval strategy. Lieutenant Colonel Dr Adolfo Morales Trueba shows how this occurred through Giral's willingness to learn. A republican idealist, Giral had no naval experience before joining the naval ministry in 1931, but he brought to the task a clear understanding of the needs of the republic and, working with professional experts in the navy, developed an understanding of how the navy could adapt to provide the maritime force needed. His initial plans roused opposition among republican politicians and naval professionals alike as he challenged the assumptions of both. However, by February 1936, when he was appointed minister of the navy, he had earned the respect of naval officers and politicians and created a realistic strategic plan. The outbreak of the civil war in July meant that the plans were never implemented, but Giral had demonstrated again that the Spanish political system had the flexibility to combine naval and political authority to create realistic strategic plans

The question of integrating professional expertise with political authority was no less important in the development of the navies of Great Britain and the United States. At first sight there is a much closer association of naval expertise with the political authority in these states. The navalist ideology which had been evolving in Britain since the end of the sixteenth century did a great deal to make political authority receptive to the advice and recommendations of professional officers. By the early eighteenth century Great Britain was, self-consciously, a naval power. That self-identification did not begin to weaken until the First World War. However, this did not mean that there was a consistent understanding of knowledge or expertise between professional and political experts. There were quite short periods in which the understanding was very close. For example between 1757 and 1763, 1779–1783 and between 1793 and 1815. By 1763 it is possible that the influence of naval expertise over political authority was too strong. Even William Pitt the Elder, the greatest advocate of naval influence between 1756 and 1760, was concerned that it was being pushed too far and threatening the wider strategic interest of Britain.[25] At other times, the ability of naval experts to influence political authority was greatly diminished. Richard Harding shows that over a relatively short period, 1739–1747, the ability of naval experts to 'frame' the decisions of the British ministries declined rapidly as confidence in the Royal Navy dwindled. In the British case there was no other specialist 'expertise', offering an alternative policy that could fill the gap and so that decline was not fatal nor long-lasting.

---

[25] Cobbett, William, ed. *Parliamentary History of England from the Earliest Period to Year 1803,* Vol. 15 (1753–1765), 9 Dec. 1763, London: Hansard, pp. 1260–1267, 1813.

Although naval ideology remained deeply entrenched in British political culture throughout the nineteenth century, it did not exercise a hegemonic influence.[26] By the end of the century there were additional concerns. The traditional French and Russian threats were augmented by the growing German and United States navies. The changing technologies of steam, shell guns, and torpedoes had markedly changed ships and tactical possibilities. The lack of operational experience in intensive naval warfare left the Royal Navy with questions that ranged from the strategic impact of naval warfare to the use new weapons. Professor Andrew Lambert shows how Sir Julian Stafford Corbett forged a partnership with the navy that enabled him to present explanations to sailors and statesmen about the strategic role of navies in contemporary conditions. The Royal Navy was not equipped to do this from the expertise it had developed among naval officers. Corbett, a lawyer by training and a man of wide literary and cultural interests, was well-connected, informed, and erudite. He was almost fifty before he began the serious task of educating naval officers and the political authorities. His works remains important for understanding the role of sea power today. In Corbett the Royal Navy had found a champion of sea power who could influence the development of strategic expertise within the service and wrote clearly enough for the non-specialists within the political establishment to understand the arguments. However, as Professor Lambert points out, too few people read Corbett. This illustrates the problem of the transfer of expertise very well. Corbett was writing at a time when the certainties of naval power in Britain were under challenge – it was the point at which Corbett was most needed, but at the same time it was the point when he was least likely to be read. Other interests and expertise were jostling to provide the answers, explanations, and visions for the future. He did not manage to influence, significantly, Britain's conduct of the First World War. In 1918 there were still senior political figures who did not understand what he was saying and Corbett died in 1922, before he was able to complete the official history of the war at sea in which he could have presented his ideas and illustrated them in the light of events.

In the United States the growing navy also faced the problem of influencing political authorities. Unlike Britain, with its centuries of navalist ideology to support the Royal Navy, the United States Navy was a new institution in a new republic. In the early years, the lack of experience in operating large squadrons or fleets and a strong republican distrust of professional military elites, militated against the development of institutional expertise and its acceptance by the political authorities. Professor John Hattendorf shows how, over the course of 200 years, the US Navy (USN) evolved the hierarchies, structures, corporate ethics, systems, and educational curriculum to become a

---

[26] Semmel, Bernard. *Liberalism and Naval Strategy: Ideology, Interest, and Sea Power during the Pax Britannica.* London: Allen and Unwin, 1986.

powerful institution within the state. The teaching of history to inform strategy and operations and latterly the formal study of leadership though the social sciences, closely links the navy with civilian education in these matters. Shared understanding of concepts and discourses, provided a means for relatively easy exchange of expertise and thus influence. Although always evolving as circumstances changed, the USN has proved adept in integrating civilian expertise into its own operational practices where necessary. It led to problems, as Robert MacNamara's tenure as secretary of defence (1961–1968) during the Vietnam War demonstrated. But it also led to major successes like Admiral Hyman Rickover's influence at Capitol Hill, which did so much to establish the nuclear propulsion programmes for submarines and aircraft carriers.

1

The Evolution of French Naval Leadership: Defining the Admiralty of France from the Sixteenth to the Eighteenth Century

ALAN JAMES

It is easy to conclude that over the course of the sixteenth and seventeenth centuries France did not develop the naval leadership needed to compete effectively with Britain in the eighteenth, and this despite the many outstanding individual exceptions and successes that can be identified along the way. This relative weakness, it seems, was due to a series of deep contradictions within the French navy. Separate Mediterranean and Atlantic coasts, for example, presented practical problems of coordination and command, but also quite distinct cultures of leadership: one sea where traditions of noble, military command stretched back centuries and the other where any such traditions had to be invented. A gulf could also be said to have existed between the maritime periphery and the centre in Paris or Versailles, separated not just geographically but also by contrasting maritime and continental strategic outlooks. Similarly, it was difficult to integrate a typically jealous, privileged, and Catholic nobility with the body of active and able seamen in coastal communities, a great many of whom were Huguenots. Thus, the conflict within the naval hierarchy (traditionally said to be divided between the noble *officiers rouges* and the *officiers bleus* of the lower orders) was made all the more intractable by the wider confessional division in France. If some of these contradictions now seem less stark than they were once believed to be, they nevertheless still contribute to the perception that the navy suffered from a debilitating imbalance due to the separation of civil and military authority. The history of the navy was dominated by a succession of high-profile and powerful ministers of state which appears to have come at the cost of strong naval leadership and command. The admiralty of France seems irrelevant in comparison. That this was a larger political failure in France is reinforced by the popular image of an ineffective or uninterested monarchy acting as something of an emblem of this wider structural dysfunction. This civil-military division needs to be considered more carefully, however. Far from just the effect of serial mismanagement, it was the product of careful attempts to manage the balance between another, far more relevant, contradiction. Historically, the navy was shaped by its twin functions as an aspect of governance and as a military arm of royal power. It is in the evolution of the admiralty from the sixteenth century that we can identify the attempts by the crown to resolve this tension, an approach to naval leadership that was more consistent and coherent than is usually credited.

Problems associated with this separation of powers were at their most acute during the reign of Louis XIV. According to Étienne Taillemite, a *règlement* of 15 October 1707 set out definitively the emasculated and now almost entirely honorific role reserved for the admiral of France in contrast to the vast powers and responsibilities of the *secrétaires d'état de la marine*. The admiral was effectively limited to the command of operations whenever it was to be granted by the king. For Taillemite, this marked the end of a long process of strangulation of the admiralty, and it represented a complete victory for Pontchartrain and, by extension, for the king. The vision of the navy as a bureaucratic, modern institution of state had decisively won over the anachronistic forces of noble, military leadership. Specifically, this was the defeat of one final, last gasp attempt by the admiral of France, the comte de Toulouse, to claw back for the office some real authority and the practical military and administrative leadership of the navy. For Taillemite, this was a damaging victory. The effect was that neither here, nor indeed in any other legislation, was there any guidance on military command; there was no instruction about the practical matter of fighting war at sea.[1] For some reason, over time, effective naval command had been squeezed and eventually legislated out of existence.

This was a key moment according to Jamel Ostwald, too, although he takes a rather different approach. In his important study of siege warfare on land, he located a fundamental shift in the balance between two tendencies within the military leadership of France as a whole which he linked to the career of Sébastien Le Prestre de Vauban. The first of these was embodied by Vauban himself as the foremost military engineer of his day with his systematic and largely successful approach to conducting sieges: orderly, rational, calculated war with its emphasis on 'efficiency'. The other was a preference among impatient generals for headlong, offensive war, or martial 'vigour'. Eventually, as Vauban lost royal support, and especially after his death in 1707, these generals had their way, affecting the conduct of war for a century or more to France's ultimate detriment.[2]

---

[1] Étienne Taillemite, *L'Histoire ignorée de la marine française* (Paris: Perrin, 2003), pp. 151–152.
[2] Jamel Ostwald, *Vauban under Siege: Engineering Efficiency and Martial Vigor in the War of the Spanish Succession* (Leiden: Brill, 2007).

We can see how this also maps onto naval strategy, at least in the sense that there was a shift at this time from the careful, large-scale construction, organisation, and tactical deployment of fleets, the so-called 'guerre d'escadre', to a more piecemeal reliance on privateering, occasional attacks on enemy trade, and individual acts of heroism. This, too, was regrettable and damaging to French naval interests, even according to sympathetic interpretations which acknowledge the financial and military pressures that pushed France in this direction.[3] Although Benjamin Darnell is quite correct to caution against the traditional assumption that there was a simple, binary strategic choice in France between this and the very costly investment in formal battle fleets that had driven the growth of the navy up to the mid-1690s, as he says, with the collapse of the navy and the financial system that supported it, a 'guerre de course' was fully embraced in France from 1707–1708.[4]

From this perspective, however, Vauban's career makes a curious fulcrum on which the balance in naval strategy can be said to have tipped. In this case, it seems that from his death in 1707, far from declining, Vauban's influence on the navy actually grew, becoming decisive, for he had been the mouthpiece of the value of privateering over formal battle fleets.[5] Applying the lens of Ostwald's interpretation to the sea is also problematic in other respects, for not just the trajectory of Vauban's influence but his very priorities seem to be reversed. Ironically, what was being superseded by 1707 largely included precisely what Ostwald might call 'Vaubanian efficiency'. To deploy large fleets effectively in war required just the sort of practiced tactical precision and measured, disciplined manoeuvres that Père Hoste famously outlined with his *évolutions navales* that recall the detail and calculation of Vauban's meticulous siegecraft on land.[6] Perhaps this reveals nothing more than Vauban's personal, relative indifference to naval warfare. Yet it is not just Vauban that does not fit. To some extent, Ostwald's perceived shift from 'efficiency' to 'vigour' itself is also reversed in the naval context. After all, there was evident efficiency in the later emphasis on privateering, in the sense that the royal treasury could save large sums of money on the deployment of great battle fleets, one of the

---

[3] G.W. Symcox, *The Crisis of French Sea Power, 1688–1697: From the Guerre d'Escadre to the Guerre de Course* (The Hague: Martinus Nijhoff, 1974).

[4] B. Darnell, 'Reconsidering the *Guerre de Course* under Louis XIV: Naval Policy and Strategic Downsizing in an Era of Fiscal Overextension', in *Strategy and the Sea*, eds, N.A.M. Rodger, J. Ross Dancy, B. Darnell, and E. Wilson (Woodbridge: Boydell, 2016), p. 48.

[5] Michèle Virol, *Vauban: de la gloire du roi au service de l'état* (Paris: Champ Vallon, 2003), pp. 116–120.

[6] Paul Hoste, père, *L'Art des armées navales, ou traicté des évolutions navales* (Lyon: Anisson et Posuel, 1697).

main purposes of which had, in theory at least, been the aggressive pursuit of decisive battle and the headlong pursuit of victory.

Questions remain, therefore, about the significance of 1707 to naval leadership, and it seems fitting to revisit the matter of civil-military relations and their effect on the conduct of war at sea in France. To the extent that there was an aggressive determination in naval operations, this came in the 1660s, at least, from the admiral (or, rather, the grand master of navigation), the duc de Beaufort, who assumed command of operations against the Ottomans in Crete. Thereafter, however, it came from the *secrétaires d'état*, especially, as Jean-Philippe Cénat has shown, from 1672 to 1692 when there was a period of *stratégie du cabinet* during which time Seignelay and Pontchartrain, in particular, had a determining influence on strategy.[7] Notably, of course, at the Battle of Beachy Head in 1690, it was Seignelay who was famously disappointed and pressed for more dramatic results from the victory and Admiral Tourville who earned a reputation for caution and maintaining order.[8] Thus, not only does Ostwald's shift from 'efficiency' to 'vigour' as embodied by Vauban seem not to apply fully in a naval context, it is difficult to ascribe any such tendencies in the dual, adversarial way that Taillemite treats them.

Nevertheless, there is still a common theme within French naval history of the strained relationship between ministers or *secrétaires*, on one hand, and the noble, military leadership or the experienced commanders on the other, with the former judged much more favourably, on the whole, than the latter. Indeed, the fortunes of the navy are often seen as synonymous with the careers of the ministers of state in Paris while the admirals and captains of the navy themselves seem largely inconsequential. Michel Vergé-Franceschi, for example, tells us that the admirals of France in the sixteenth century offered no naval leadership at all. They were simply noblemen at court with no interest in the sea and no influence on it whatsoever. The admiralty was just an office.[9] In contrast, ministers of state from Sully onward, or the later *secrétaires d'état de la marine*, tend to be lauded. Their growing powers and their grand reforms, particularly those of Colbert from the 1660s, are often commented upon and commended.

---

[7] Jean-Philippe Cénat, *Le Roi stratège: Louis XIV et la direction de la guerre, 1661–1715* (Rennes: Presses Universitaires de Rennes, 2010).

[8] Alan James, 'La Bataille du Cap Béveziers (1690): une glorieuse victoire pour le roi stratège', in *La Bataille: du fait d'armes au combat idéologique, XIe–XIXe siècle*, eds, Ariane Boltanski, Yann Lagadec, and Franck Mercier (Rennes: Presses Universitaires de Rennes, 2015), pp. 205–218.

[9] Michel Vergé-Franceschi, 'Les Amiraux de France: 1492–1592 – treize terriens', in *La France et la mer au siècle des grandes découvertes'*, eds, Philippe Masson and Michel Vergé-Franceschi (Paris : Tallandier, 1993), pp. 177–191.

Without question, these changes are, indeed, signs of the navy at its most institutionally ambitious. Yet an emphasis on these very successes inevitably draws attention to personal, or even structural, failures in political leadership. Taillemite is not alone in identifying the greatest limitation of these architects of the modern navy in the failure to develop an effective naval command. As long ago as 1965, Henri Legohérel identified Cardinal Richelieu's failure, as the first of the new grand-masters of navigation and commerce, to regularise the finances of the navy and to integrate them into the growing institution.[10] Worse, the administration of the ports and arsenals of the kingdom, and even the command of the different regional squadrons, was divided awkwardly and arbitrarily between civil and military authorities, a problem which it is said crippled the navy for decades.[11] Despite his reputation as the father of the modern French navy, under Richelieu, the fleet was beset with squabbling over seniority and rank. Sometimes conflicts between officers even got violent. In other words, the administrative, civilian authority grew in the seventeenth century but, it would seem, without allowing the sufficient development of an effective military leadership.

Curiously, however, in any such considerations of the evolution of the French navy, historians tend not to emphasise the role of the monarchy. This is surprising given that the reputation of any king, and of France more generally, depended on the successful conduct of war. As Cénat reminds us, for Louis XIV especially it was always important to be seen to be in control of the direction of war, and from 1692 he took a more direct lead with greater consultation between him, the ministers, and the admirals. For Daniel Dessert, the most excoriating critic of the navy, Louis XIV was actually an active part of the problem. He was guilty of neglect. His ministers of state were effectively independent, free to interfere with strategy, to dominate the finances of the navy and its offices to make themselves hugely wealthy and politically powerful. Their corrupt and inept interference made any real naval leadership or effective command at sea impossible.[12] Even historians who have tried to come to his rescue and to be positive about Louis XIV, such as François Bluche, tend to argue only that his interest and investment in the navy was genuine.[13] John Lynn, too, has underlined the importance of the navy to the king as an integral part of the military forces at his disposal, underscoring his

---

[10] Henri Legohérel, *Les Trésoriers généraux de la marine (1517–1788)* (Paris: Cujas, 1965).

[11] Alain Berbouche, *L'Histoire de La Royale: du Moyen-Âge au règne de Louis XIV* (St Malo: Pascal Galodé, 2011), pp. 158–163.

[12] Daniel Dessert, *La Royale: vaisseaux et marins du Roi-Soleil* (Paris: Fayard, 1996), pp. 17–21.

[13] François Bluche, *Louis XIV*, trans. Mark Greengrass (New York: Franklin Watts, 1990), pp. 225–228.

interest and political investment in naval warfare.[14] Yet despite Guy Rowlands' refreshingly perceptive study which concludes that Louis XIV managed 'on the whole ... to enforce a degree of good order' within the naval command, rarely is there any challenge to the impression that Louis XIV's personal strategic influence was much more than the well-meaning delegation of authority.[15] There is some truth in this, of course, for no one would doubt that the king shared the military values of the day and recognised that war was won or lost on land. Nevertheless, according to Cénat's otherwise largely sympathetic assessment, there was still a failure of political leadership in the navy. The problem, he says, was precisely that, even as Louis XIV took more direct control of warfare, he did not provide the leadership that was necessary at sea. Those in command were left with too much freedom. This is the source of French naval weakness in the War of the Spanish Succession.[16]

Certainly, like his predecessors, Louis XIV never really took the navy to heart or had to rely on it to build a governing consensus in the way that Charles II or James II did in England.[17] Indeed, in some ways, he seems to have displayed utter contempt for naval command. This is especially so in 1669, for example, when he named his illegitimate, two-year old son, the comte de Vermandois, to the newly re-constituted charge of admiral of France. At the very same time, of course, he handed greatly expanded powers over the navy to his minister, Jean-Baptiste Colbert. Vermandois died a few years later and was replaced in 1694 as admiral by another illegitimate son, the five-year old, comte de Toulouse, who would remain admiral for the rest of the reign. This display of apparently complete indifference to command contrasts very oddly, however, with the determined concentration of powers on those ministers of state who could force the emergence of the great fleets and arsenals of the kingdom. Certainly, the very nature of naval warfare, with its port structures, its lengthy preparations, and vast cost meant that it required bureaucratic support on a scale that would always guarantee a defining role for *secrétaires d'état*, as Cénat suggests. Nevertheless, such apparent extremes in the priorities of Louis XIV still need to be reconciled; it is not sufficient simply to dismiss this growing civil, administrative authority as a mere passing concession by

[14] John Lynn, *The Wars of Louis XIV, 1667–1714* (Abingdon, 2013); Dominique Lacroix-Lintner, 'La Formation navale de Louis XIV: un aspect meconnu de la personalité du roi', *Chronique d'Histoire Maritime* (forthcoming).

[15] Guy Rowlands, 'The King's Two Arms: French Amphibious Warfare in the Mediterranean under Louis XIV, 1664 to 1697', in *Amphibious Warfare, 1000–1700: Commerce, State Formation and European Expansion*, eds, D.J.B. Trim and Mark Charles Fissel (Leiden: Brill, 2006), p. 310.

[16] Cénat, *Roi stratège*, p. 349.

[17] J.D. Davies, *Kings of the Sea: Charles II, James II and the Royal Navy* (Barnsley: Seaforth, 2017).

the king in a passive adherence to a shared vision of a bureaucratic navy without any concern for operational effectiveness.

It could be said that the relationship between the monarchy and the naval leadership is the least well understood element of French strategy and that this contributes as much as anything to its presentation as chronically contested and incoherent. The picture has been confused by the conviction that there was an unwillingness in France to address its deep, structural problems. In contrast, the influential sociologist, Norbert Elias, saw Britain's relative success over France precisely in its ability to reconcile its own contrasts. Long-term success he equated rather too straightforwardly to overcoming the social and political barriers to absorbing talent from lower social orders in a conflict in the British navy.[18] Yet, as J.D. Davies' work on the Restoration navy has demonstrated, the situation was more complex than any apparent clash between 'gentlemen and tarpaulins'. These divisions and categories are too stark to describe the leadership of the Royal Navy usefully. Social boundaries bled into each other. Moreover, it was not just the embrace of the talent from below that was the secret to the relative success of English naval leadership but also of the adventurous noble spirit.[19] Unfortunately, despite a number of studies of the disparate social origins of French naval officers, of the efforts to introduce naval education in France, or growing professionalism, and so on, there has been no equivalent reassessment of the French navy as an engineered political or social success or as any kind of wider, shared endeavour.[20] Positive assessments of French leadership are still mostly limited to studies of individuals, careers that display bravery and success in war at sea, navigational skill, or good judgement, or they focus on exceptional administrators like Colbert.[21] These all provide hints of a hidden potential that was never fully realised because the French navy was perennially undermined by its contradictions and the inability or unwillingness to integrate the talents and resources available to it. Relative to Britain, the civilian authority and central administration of the French navy grew but was too distant and even uninformed about naval matters. Again, this is an indictment of leadership at the very top of French

---

[18] Elias, Norbert, *The Genesis of the Naval Profession* (Dublin: University of Dublin Press, 2007).

[19] J.D. Davies, *Gentlemen and Tarpaulins: The Officers and Men of the Restoration Navy* (Oxford: Oxford University Press, 1991).

[20] Roberto Barazzutti, 'Étude comparative des officiers généraux aux Provinces-Unies, en France et en Angleterre à l'époque de Louis XIV (1643–1715)', *Revue d'Histoire Maritime* 12 (2010), 167–192; Michel Vergé-Franceschi, *Marine et éducation sous l'ancien régime* (Paris: CNRS, 1991); Michel Vergé-Franceschi, 'Les Officiers généraux de la marine royale en 1715', *Revue Historique* 273, 1 (1985), 131–157.

[21] See, for example, Michel Vergé-Franceschi, *Abraham Duquesne: Huguenot et marine du Roi-Soleil* (Paris: France-Empire, 1992).

society. The consensus appears to be that the administration of the French navy was too *dirigiste*, with the royal council imposing its policy decisions on a reluctant maritime population and even to the frustration of its warrior nobility. In other words, absolutist France could build a navy, but it could never evolve naturally with the interests of its subjects. That appears to be the essential difference with Britain.

It is all too easy, however, to overlook the integration of noble interests with naval warfare in France. Indeed, even more than in England, the French nobility was a crucial, even defining, feature of the navy and its prospects for success. Debates about civil-military relations with respect to the French navy simply cannot afford to lose sight of this nor of the active, direct role of the monarchy in achieving a workable balance. Far from acting as an impediment to long-term naval success, the French monarchy was always intimately associated with the navy to the point where maintaining that association defined its very purpose. This involved the careful management of the admiralty. Indeed, although the office of admiral of France is rarely considered to have been a key element of the navy, its authority was always carefully nurtured. It was essential for the admiral to be seen to be an extension of the king's personal stature and reputation. In this respect, he needed to be occupying a valuable military office of the highest order. He also needed to try to ensure effective government over a growing and active maritime sector, for the admiralty was traditionally also, indeed primarily, a judicial office. Balancing these two imperatives was, in fact, one of the greatest challenges of the early modern French navy.

In this respect, the crown was not well-served by the medieval legacy of French maritime government. The coastal provinces of France were a jumble of different jurisdictions, local authorities, claims of independence, and overlapping and contradictory systems of government. The admiralty of France was, therefore, a heavily contested jurisdiction. Even just the separate legal existence of the admiralties of Brittany, Guyenne, and of the Levant made sure of this. Moreover, where the authority of the admiral of France was actually legally recognised, it was invariably distant and notional, at best.[22] Nevertheless, it remained an important office from the perspective of the crown. It was an established charge with a long pedigree which by its very existence acknowledged the theoretical reach of the French monarchy over land and water. Despite the lack of a permanent fleet in the sixteenth century, therefore, for this reason the admiral of France was one of the *grands offices* of the realm, a role that put it among the elite, along with constable and chancellor and other officers of the royal military household. This embodiment

---

[22] Alan James, 'Les Amirautés à l'époque de Richelieu', in *Pouvoirs et littoraux du XVe au XXe siècle*, eds, Gérard Le Bouëdec and François Chappé (Rennes: Presses Universitaires de Rennes, 2000), pp. 145–150.

of the personal authority of the king and his military reputation was reserved for the highest-ranking nobility to occupy; it was among the highest possible services for a loyal nobleman to fulfil on behalf of his king. As such, the office of admiral should be thought of less in terms of naval command and more as a legal extension of the king's authority. More than that, the admiralty was a judicial office which, in theory at least, oversaw the court system that administered justice on the maritime periphery of the realm with respect to all legal matters arising from the use of the sea.

Far from an institutional irrelevance, then, the enforcement of this legal jurisdiction became a matter of some urgency in the sixteenth century, for the lack of any practical system of maritime government was dangerous. Many coastal communities had adopted the Calvinist 'heresy' and become centres of armed resistance. The ability of these Huguenots to use naval power and their overseas initiatives and international connections with Calvinists abroad, in the Low Countries and in England, meant that imposing royal authority on the maritime periphery of France was interesting not just for its own sake.[23] It became a matter on which the survival of the monarchy itself, and of France as a Catholic kingdom, depended. The potential domestic ramifications of royal weakness were brought home early in the wars when the Huguenots invited English forces to occupy Le Havre in 1562.[24] That this drove the crown's subsequent response to naval leadership seems borne out by the events a decade later around the St Bartholomew's Day massacres of 1572. Although the naval aspects of this event are never acknowledged, it is worth remembering that, at this vulnerable and desperate time for the crown, it was the public assassination of the Huguenot admiral of France, Gaspard de Coligny, that sparked the widespread violence. Of course, it would be an exaggeration to say that Coligny was killed because the crown wanted to have a new admiral, but a new admiral it certainly did need. The massacres were followed immediately by a combined operation of Mediterranean galleys and Atlantic warships in the first of the sieges of the Huguenot stronghold, and active port, of La Rochelle. That this was the first major naval operation since the wars with England of the 1540s says a lot about the crown's approach to sea power and the importance with which it was held. Born out of civil disorder and driven by the direct threat that this posed to the crown, the modern navy, and with it an invigorated admiralty, remained instruments of governance and part of the reconstruction of domestic royal authority.

---

[23] D.J.B. Trim, 'Transnational Calvinist Co-operation and "Mastery of the Sea" in the Late Sixteenth Century', in *Ideologies of Western Naval Power, c.1500–1815*, eds, J.D. Davies, Alan James, and Gijs Rommelse (Abingdon: Routledge, 2019).

[24] Tom Glasgow, 'The Navy in the Le Havre Expedition, 1562–64', *Mariner's Mirror*, 54 (1968), 281–296.

Though rarely mentioned in the context of the wider Wars of Religion, naval leadership was actually one of the key battlegrounds. For his part, in 1582 Henri III chose a close personal favourite from court, Anne de Joyeuse, to become admiral of France, and in a manner that would be echoed throughout the early modern period he granted him lucrative personal rights and privileges and encouraged their enforcement and collection. This political investment in the self-interest of a powerful and politically reliable client was part of a desperate contest against the centrifugal effect of local traditions and the lingering complexity of legal practices in maritime France. More ominously, it was also a contest against other leading noble figures and political forces that threatened to tear the kingdom apart, including many of the most powerful names in the Wars of Religion. For example, two of the most high-ranking Huguenot nobles, the prince de Condé and Henry of Navarre (who would later become Henri IV of France), both claimed the admiralty of Guyenne and used it to build the political independence and financial support of the Huguenots in the wars. Likewise, the leading Catholic leader, the duc de Guise, used the admiralty in Normandy to consolidate not just his position there and his ambitions to become admiral of France but his leadership of the new Catholic League, which was quickly becoming the main destabilising and driving force of the next phase of the wars.[25]

For this reason, leadership of the navy in France took on certain defining characteristics, with long-lasting effects. Above all, an effective admiral had to demonstrate unquestionable loyalty to the king. He also had to embody the essentially Catholic nature of the navy, and he had to have sufficient noble status to hold high office and to represent the monarchy and enforce its authority. This is not a sign of indifference to the sea or to the operational effectiveness of fleets in royal service but rather of the crucial political function of the navy in France. To be sure, admirals also had to take advice from experienced seamen on practical matters, and they could recommend nominations to the crown for active command. Yet throughout the seventeenth century, the navy remained primarily an instrument of governance though one that had to embody the military reputation of the monarchy. Admirals had two functions, therefore: to invigorate and complement what would remain an essentially judicial body and royal jurisdiction; and, militarily, to lead or to advise the king about naval campaigns at sea. Although Cardinal Richelieu is frequently credited for his modernising vision for the navy and for the expansion of French overseas trade and colonies, it was not any great reforming programme that made him the logical choice to hold the newly created and vastly expanded office of grand-master of navigation from 1626 or that made him successful. It was his recognition of this duality in the navy and his ability to embrace all that

---

[25] Alan James, *The Navy and Government in Early Modern France, 1572–1661* (Woodbridge: Boydell, 2004), pp. 11–54.

it represented. A cardinal of the Catholic church and a noble dedicated to the service of Louis XIII, he was entrusted to oversee all aspects of the navy and, in turn, to use it to build his political authority and wealth. Indeed, more than anyone before him, Richelieu used the iconography of the navy and the sea in the political construction of his personal stature. As he invested financially and politically in it, so he was able to regularise local maritime government, enough at least to create a platform to build a formidable instrument of war to take on Spanish power at sea.

If historians have been impressed with Richelieu's immediate successes and his vision, his legacy has been relatively harshly judged. A decline in the size and effectiveness of the navy after his death in 1642 is often presented as a sign that his institutional innovations did not go far enough. His reputation is only really sustained on the grounds that he was later held up as an inspiration by Colbert for his much more vigorous and ambitious naval reforms from the 1660s and beyond. Yet Richelieu's contribution to the history of the navy needs to be considered less from this institutional or material point of view. Indeed, much more can be learned from his approach to active naval leadership. Command of the Mediterranean galleys, for example, was always exercised by the traditional office of general of the galleys. Richelieu owned this office but left it entirely unreformed. Traditionally coveted and exercised by the nobility for military reputation and standing, it served Richelieu's purposes well just as he found it. He took advantage by expanding the fleet and grooming one of his nephews, du Pont-Courlay, for the office. With respect to the growing Atlantic warship fleets, the same financial, political, and dynastic interests drove Richelieu to improve the reputation of naval leadership there. Arguably, his most significant innovation for the navy was to groom another nephew, the duc de Maillé-Brézé, to command naval operations and to bequeath to him the new office of grand-master. Just as a marshal's baton might represent the highest ambition of the traditional military nobility on land, Richelieu created something of an equivalent at sea by investing the highest naval office of the realm with real command of operations. His ambition was most certainly not to create a modern, bureaucratic institution. He wished to expand the navy, and by combining automatic command of the king's fleets with the highest naval office, to build on sixteenth-century developments, creating a prestigious and lucrative office that would advance the dynastic interests of his family and, specifically, of his nephew.[26]

This personal, dynastic interest in the growth of the navy is something that Louis XIV would later replicate himself. In 1669, he dissolved the office of grand master of navigation and re-created that of admiral of France. The

---

[26] James, *Navy and Government*, 92–107; James, 'Une Époque sans amiral: les grands-maîtres de la navigation, 1626–1669', *Revue d'Histoire Maritime*, 19 (2014), 109–118.

impression that this was a retrograde step relative to the well-known innovations of his naval minister, Colbert, seems to be confirmed by his appointment to the role of his infant son. Yet, Louis XIV was simply taking advantage of the growing reputation of naval leadership for his own dynastic purposes. The rising status of naval command made it possible for him to refashion the admiralty as a military office of the very highest rank, one that would advance the interests of the Bourbon monarchy and, at the same time, to ensure that the navy remained a direct extension of his personal reputation.[27] In this sense, Louis XIV was building on Richelieu's successes, and in naming legitimised princes of the blood to the admiralty he was firmly within the long tradition of the evolution of French naval leadership. It was not an attempt to trivialise the admiralty in order to give Colbert a free hand. The admiralty would continue to protect his navy's essentially Catholic and royal nature and ensure that any successes it might achieve would reflect directly on the king's reputation.

In many respects, the comte de Toulouse was probably truest to Richelieu's legacy. As admiral of France, he tasted command at sea at the battle of Vélez-Málaga in 1704, pushed for wider powers, and indeed was finally able to assume an influential role on the royal council, though only after 1715. The focus of Richelieu's efforts, after all, had been the symbiotic growth of both the distinct civil and military leadership of the navy. Thus, Toulouse revealed an enduring feature of naval power in France. It had always been a vehicle of political invention. Indeed, contrary to common perceptions, naval office had always attracted the highest nobility. Likewise, in the sixteenth century, the Huguenots had used naval warfare in their effort to establish a legal, political and military existence within France. The crown responded in kind, most spectacularly through Richelieu's later development of his legendary authority as principal minister. Now, it had become a vehicle of self-definition for the Sun King himself. From the perspective of the court, a key function of the admiralty had always been to express and to reinforce the authority of France's warrior kings, and from 1669 it did this more directly than ever by advancing the personal dynastic interests of Louis XIV.

This was in no way inconsistent with Louis XIV's recognition of the need for a firm ministerial or bureaucratic hand to oversee the administrative development of his growing navy. Indeed, the civil authority, that is to say the effective governance of the maritime periphery, and the personal, military prestige of high office had always been recognised as two essential, mutually dependent aspects of French naval success. There was no desire, however, to continue to combine them ever more closely and to invest broad civil and military power in one office, for that could now actually potentially undermine

[27] Alan James, 'Colbert and "La Royale": Dynastic Ambitions and Imperial Ideals in France', in J.D. Davies, Alan James, and Gijs Rommelse, eds, *Ideologies of Western Naval Power, c.1500–1815* (Abingdon: Routledge, 2019).

the future sense of the crown's ownership and direction of the navy. After all, Toulouse, it should be remembered, had not covered himself in glory in 1704.[28] Yet, by confirming the basis of the Admiral's standing solely in terms of the potential for future glory in naval warfare, Louis XIV not only left the door open for what Ostwald would call naval 'vigour' while at the same time ensuring careful, thoughtful, and 'efficient' administration and direction of the institution, but he was fitting within a long pattern of French policy. The admiralty had always been a military office requiring status and personal influence as an extension of the personal authority of the king. It was also a judicial jurisdiction. Development of the former had always been necessary for the proper functioning of the latter. It is easy to overlook the fact, therefore, that throughout the sixteenth and seventeenth centuries the reputation and status of the admiral (or grand master of navigation) was among the preoccupations of the state and the key to naval reform. In 1707, Louis XIV was taking this to its logical conclusion in the development of his 'dynastic state'.[29]

Effective, practical naval leadership, therefore, was not absent-mindedly side-lined in 1707, as Taillemite seems to suggest. Even less, however, was it allowed to come to dominate naval strategy and lead to a culture of martial vigour in the eighteenth century at sea as Ostwald's model might imply were it to be applied to the sea. Rather, in a legal sense it was isolated, or rarefied, and used as the basis for the formal re-creation of the admiralty of France. In many respects, this was a return to, or rather the fullest expression of, a traditional approach to naval leadership. Rather ironically, of course, Louis XIV's success at guaranteeing the close association of the monarchy with the navy and with control of operations and maritime government, in this way, might well have been a contributory factor to the damaging isolation of the navy in the royal council in the eighteenth century that is described by Olivier Chaline.[30] By widening the gap between civil and military authority in the navy, perhaps a step had been taken toward undermining the long-term influence of the *secrétaires d'état de la marine,* leaving the navy without a powerful enough voice in the royal council to allow it to meet fully the growing strategic demands of the eighteenth century.

---

[28] Dessert, *La Royale*, pp. 234–235.

[29] For the concept of the 'dynastic state', see Guy Rowlands, *The Dynastic State and the Army under Louis XIV: Royal Service and Private Interest, 1661–1701* (Cambridge: Cambridge University Press, 2002).

[30] See his chapter in this volume.

2

The Makers of Spanish Naval Strategy in the Eighteenth Century: Strategy, Tactics, and Shipbuilding Policy[1]

IVAN VALDEZ-BUBNOV

During the eighteenth century, the Spanish Bourbon naval system evolved in two well-defined political and administrative phases, roughly divided by the outcome of the Seven Years War.[2] This evolution, however, has seldom been understood from the perspective of strategy. The purpose of this article is to outline the evolution of Spanish naval strategy from the writings of four authors who have rarely been studied from this perspective, or who are practically unknown as strategic thinkers. The four plans described in this essay illustrate the evolution of Spanish naval thinking during both periods, showing not only the main objectives of Spanish foreign policy, but also the tasks that naval forces were expected to fulfil, their interaction with land forces, their relation to merchants and privateers, and the relation between naval strategy and shipbuilding policy.

In order to understand the origins of Spanish Bourbon naval strategic thought, is it necessary to consider the situation of Spanish naval forces during the late Spanish Habsburg period.[3] During the second half of the seventeenth

---

[1] This chapter incorporates results from two previous publications from its author: Valdez-Bubnov, I., 'Pensamiento táctico y liderazgo estratégico: la evolución de la doctrina naval española entre los siglos XVII y XVIII', in Guimerá, A. (ed), *Liderazgo estratégico en España, 1475–2018*, Madrid, CSIC/Instituto Universitario General Gutiérrez Mellado, 2019, pp. 39–63; and 'Spanish Naval Strategy and the United States, 1763–1819', *The Mariner's Mirror*, 101 (2015): 4–20.

[2] See Blanco Núñez, J.M., *La armada española en la primera mitad del siglo XVIII*, Madrid, IZAR Construcciones Navales, 2001; and *La armada española en la segunda mitad del siglo XVIII* (Madrid: IZAR Construcciones Navales, 2004).

[3] On this subject, see: Storrs, C., *The Resilience of the Spanish Monarchy, 1665–1700* (Oxford: Oxford University Press, 2006).

century, the main naval threat to the empire came from the rising power of Louis XIV's France.[4] After having simultaneously fought the Dutch Revolt (1566–1648) and the Thirty Years War (1618–1648), the Spanish monarchy still had to combat the French armies until the Peace of the Pyrenees was signed in 1659. This, however, proved to be only a brief respite, and Franco-Spanish hostilities resumed during 1667–1668 (War of the Devolution), 1672–1678 (Franco-Dutch War), 1683–1684 (War of the Reunions), and 1689–1697 (War of the League of Augsburg). In this same period, the French monarchy followed a programme of mercantilist expansion, aimed at seizing a share of international commerce, which, in turn, led to confrontation with the English and the Dutch. These emerging maritime powers, on the other hand, fought three naval conflicts (1651–1654, 1665–1667, and 1672–1674) that led to important transformations in the European practice of war at sea.[5] The traditional armed merchantman, improvised as a warship and used as an infantry rather than an artillery platform, became obsolete in the face of the specialised man-of-war, larger, strongly built, and primarily armed with heavy broadside cannon. The traditional tactics inherited from galley warfare, which favoured line abreast formations and the use of manoeuvre and gunfire as preparation for boarding and infantry combat, gave way to a new tactical principles based on sustained artillery fire and line-ahead formations.[6] In all, this led to a greater degree of state intervention in the building, financing, and maintenance of battlefleets, and to the construction of complex, permanent, and state-owned technological infrastructures.[7]

During the second half of the seventeenth century, the Spanish Habsburg naval system remained based on different regional squadrons, each one with its own administration and sources of finance. The monarchy operated them directly in the Mediterranean, the North Sea, and the Atlantic. Other squadrons, maintained by the Spanish American vice-royalties, operated in the Caribbean, along the Pacific coasts of the American continent, and in the South Pacific from the Philippines. Apart from specific purpose-built warships built and operated by the crown, the provision and operation of most squadrons was contracted with specialised entrepreneurs, while private merchant ships were

[4] Lemineur, J.C., 'La marine de Louis XIV. Une marine nouvelle de conception française', in Acerra, M. and José Merino (eds.), *L'invention du vaisseau de ligne, 1450–1700* (París: SPM, 1997).

[5] Tunstall, B., *Naval Warfare in the Age of Sail. The Evolution of Fighting Tactics, 1680–1815* (London: Conway Maritime Press, 1990).

[6] Tracy, N., 'Naval Tactics', en Gardiner, R. (ed.), *The Line of Battle. The Sailing Warship 1650–1840* (London: Conway Maritime Press), 1992.

[7] Palmer, M.A.J., 'The 'Military Revolution' Afloat: The Era of the Anglo-Dutch Wars and the Transition to Modern Warfare at Sea', in *War in History*, 4 (1997): 123–149.

frequently pressed into royal service by temporary, remunerated seizures known as *embargos*. In order to systematise these procedures, the crown standardised linear and volumetric systems of measurement, imposed universal methods for calculating the tonnage of ships, and set specific tariffs for the compensation of ship owners. It also passed a universal technological legislation, aimed at ensuring that all ships built by Spanish subjects had uniform characteristics, mainly the potential to be used either as merchantmen, in private service, or as men-of-war, in the regional squadrons.[8] But the shipbuilding regulations also existed in order to limit the size of the ships, in order to ensure that they could sail the relatively shallow fluvial waters leading to Seville, the main port of Spain's transatlantic and the only authorised base for the merchant fleets of the Indies' run. This protected Seville's quasi-monopoly against rising rival interest groups, mainly based in the maritime port of Cadiz, which had been allowed to receive the largest merchant ships, as well as the treasure galleons returning from Spanish America. By the 1670s, the danger presented by the specialised warships of rival powers was clearly perceived, and influential Spanish naval thinkers strongly advocated for technological reform. This, however, proved difficult to achieve, since the influence of Seville's interest group, wary of the possible transfer of the administrative and fiscal institutions of transatlantic commerce to Cadiz, strived to maintain the core of the existing shipbuilding legislation.[9]

This situation began to change rapidly after 1700. The heirless death of the last Habsburg king led to the transfer of the Spanish crown to the French house of Bourbon. Louis XIV's grandson, Philip of Anjou, was crowned as Philip V, and the supporters of the Habsburg pretender summoned international help. A powerful coalition, comprising Austria, England, and the Dutch was formed against the Spanish Bourbon king and France. The ensuing War of the Spanish Succession (1700–1714) signalled the transfer of French administrative models to Bourbon Spain, and the final triumph of Philip V's cause led to a complete re-organisation of the state. In 1714, most of the traditional regional squadrons of the Habsburg naval system were abolished, and a new centralised ministry of the navy was created. New corporations and schools for naval officers were established, and work was begun on a new, state-owned, naval infrastructure in Peninsular Spain.[10] This allowed comparatively greater

---

[8] Valdez-Bubnov, I., *Poder naval y modernización del estado: política de construcción naval española (siglos XVI–XVIII)* (Mexico-Madrid, Bonilla Artigas/ Iberoamericana Vervuert, 2011), pp. 70–84.

[9] Valdez-Bubnov, I., 'War, Trade and Technology: The Politics of Spanish Shipbuilding Legislation, 1607–1728', *International Journal of Maritime History*, 21, (2009): 75–102.

[10] Torres Sánchez, R., *Military Entrepreneurs and the Spanish Contractor State in the Eighteenth Century* (Oxford, University Press, 2016).

levels of state intervention in the shipbuilding industry, and in 1721–1722, new technological legislation, authored by Antonio de Gaztañeta, substituted the old Habsburg shipbuilding regulations. This eliminated the traditional limitations to the size of Atlantic ships, which, in turn, had been made possible by the previous transfer, in 1717, of the administrative and fiscal institutions of transatlantic trade from Seville to Cadiz. In all, by the mid-1720s, the defining characteristics of the Bourbon naval system had been established. Important continuities with old Habsburg institutions and practices remained, however, particularly in the relatively limited numbers of academic naval officers in comparison with those trained in the merchant marine and the privateers.[11] Another important continuity remained in shipbuilding: the Gaztañeta legislation was conceived, just as the Habsburg shipbuilding regulations, to ensure that all ships built by Spanish subjects were suitable to serve private merchantmen or as royal men-of-war. In this sense, the Gaztañeta designs were not line-of-battle ships, directly equivalent to those built by Spain's naval rivals because of the experience of the Anglo-Dutch Wars. Rather, they were a development of the technological criteria that had defined shipbuilding under the Habsburg regime.[12]

The strategic doctrine of the new Spanish Bourbon naval system was defined by the Navarrese economist Gerónimo de Uztáriz, in his work *Theórica y práctica de comercio y de marina* (1724).[13] This was a long and erudite treatise advocating the Spanish adoption of French Colbertian mercantilism, and has been seen by specialised scholarship as a blueprint for the most important economic policies developed by Philip V's government.[14] Uztáriz advocated strong royal support to Spanish manufactures, a protectionist fiscal policy, and greater participation in international trade. But equally important, he developed a complex and sophisticated definition of Spanish naval strategy at an imperial and international level.[15] It remains the only comprehensive and explicit strategic discourse dealing with the nature, objectives, and reach of Spanish naval power for the first half of the eighteenth century, based on the interaction between merchants, privateers, and the state-owned battlefleet.

For Uztáriz, the main purpose of Spanish navy was to protect the mercantile routes of the empire from the battlefleets of the monarchy's rivals. From

[11] Ortega del Cerro, P., 'La profesionalización de la oficialidad naval española, 1750–1800: aproximación a sus destellos desde las sombras', *Vegueta*, 16 (2016): 221–244.

[12] Uztáriz, G., *Theórica y práctica de comercio y de marina*, 1724.

[13] Castillo, A., *Spanish Mercantilism Gerónimo de Uztáriz. Economist* (New York: Add Press, 1930); Fernández Durán, R., *Gerónimo de Uztáriz (1670–1732): una política económica para Felipe V* (Madrid: Minerva, 1999).

[14] Castillo, *Spanish Mercantilism*.

[15] See Valdez-Bubnov, 2019.

this perspective, the warship core built or purchased during the 10 years that followed the end of the War of Spanish Succession was meant to deter naval attacks in three main theatres: the Atlantic, the Caribbean, and the Mediterranean. In the first one, the main role of the Spanish navy was to detach a few escort vessels for each voyage of the Indies' merchant fleets, in number sufficient to deter isolated enemy privateers. In the Caribbean, on the other hand, this task was to be entrusted to a remnant of the Habsburg naval system: the Armada de Barlovento, a naval force financed by the Mexican exchequer, based in Havana and Veracruz. This Spanish American squadron was also expected to persecute and punish privateers and smugglers who operated from English and Dutch possessions in the Caribbean. For these purposes, the then practically non-existent Armada de Barlovento was to be provided with four medium-sized warships and two small frigates. These ideas were not new, and show that Uztáriz was familiar with the different projects for the revival of Spanish naval power produced during the aftermath of the War of Succession, namely the 1712 Cuban project 'Memoir by Juan de Monségur and Tinagero-Gaztañeta 1712 Cuban project'.[16]

In the Mediterranean, on the other hand, frigates were to be deployed to contain the Barbary corsairs, particularly those from Rabat-Salé and the North African dependencies of the Ottoman empire. Another remnant of the Habsburg naval system, the galley squadrons operating from the coasts of southern Spain, were to be employed in a similar fashion. Uztáriz also suggested maintaining a constant pressure against these maritime regions by keeping a regular naval presence to deter Ottoman intervention in European conflicts, to protect Spanish lines of communication, and to land troops whenever needed. Also, he suggested promoting Spanish privateering against Muslim commerce, in order to obtain a favourable balance in the exchange of prisoners common in that area.[17]

According to Uztáriz, the central Mediterranean required a different course of action. The interests of the Spanish royal family in the Italian Peninsula called for future military intervention, and the use of naval power to project military force could reduce the number of troops needed by half in relation to a purely land campaign. A surprise landing offered great tactical advantages, and the use of sea lanes for the transport of troops and supplies provided a remarkable economy of cost in relation to the transfer of large numbers of men by continental routes. In his view, an army of 100,000 or even 200,000 men operating in Italy was worthless without naval support. Moreover, a strong

---

[16] Uztáriz, p. 239. See Valdez-Bubnov, I., 'De Monségur a Uztáriz. El origen de las reformas navales de Felipe V', in María del Pilar Martínez López-Cano, *Historia del pensamiento económico. Testimonios, proyectos y polémicas* (Mexico: UNAM-Instituto Mora, 2009), pp. 68–90.

[17] Ibid., p. 240.

Spanish battlefleet in the Mediterranean could prevent any foreign design against Spanish dynastic claims in Italy.[18]

To attain these objectives, Uztáriz believed the navy needed 50 line-of-battleships, ranging from 50 to 100 guns. This number included several 60-gun two-deckers meant to serve as escorts of the Indies' fleets, and smaller 50-gun two-deckers to support privateering and for the repression of smugglers in the Caribbean. In the Mediterranean, this core of line-of-battleships was to be supported by 16 frigates from 10 to 40 guns to be used against the North African dependencies of the Ottoman empire. Eight galleys were to be kept in Spanish Mediterranean ports for the same purpose. This force of 50 line-of-battle ships, 16 frigates, and eight galleys was not meant to be kept in permanent readiness. Uztáriz believed most of them could be kept disarmed in their respective ports, with only the number of units required for concrete tasks to be fitted out at specific moments.[19]

This information is important, for it reveals the tactical and strategic purpose of Gaztañeta's 1720–1722 shipbuilding legislation.[20] Uztáriz explicitly stated that the types of ships best suited for his definition of naval strategy were the two-decked ships of 30, 40, 50, and 60 guns, that is, from the medium-size frigate to the small 50-gun ship of the line. The larger 60-gun type, on the other hand, was conceived for the protection of the new centre of gravity of Spanish transatlantic trade: the deep-water, oceanic port of Cadiz, which had substituted Seville in that role in 1717. Uztáriz also stated the need to build larger line-of-battleships of 70 and 80 guns, meant to constitute the core of a battlefleet to be fitted out only during wartime, and kept disarmed during peacetime for deterrence.

The preponderance of the smaller 50- and 60-gun types, on the other hand, was linked to the importance he attributed to privateering and anti-contraband duties. He believed that both types could be leased to private entrepreneurs to stimulate them to engage in these activities. Uztáriz was aware that the heavy expense of manning and fitting out large ships could prevent private entrepreneurs from collaborating with the navy in this fashion. To overcome this potential obstacle, he called to adopt the procedures described in the French 1689 naval Ordonnance, Title. 3, Book 22, which limited to one third the proportion of the prizes' value due to the royal exchequer, delivering another third of these earnings to shipowners and investors, and one third for the officers and crews. This interaction between private initiative and the State

---

[18] Ibid.

[19] Ibid. pp. 241–242.

[20] Valdez-Bubnov, I., 'Navios para un imperio global: la construcción naval y la Matrícula de Mar en España, América y Filipinas durante el largo siglo XVIII (1670–1834)', *Espacio, Tiempo y Forma*, Serie IV, Historia Moderna, 32 (2109), p. 136.

could stimulate the participation of merchants in naval warfare, the training of crews and officers, the punishment of enemies and economic rivals, and the general growth of sea power, while simultaneously enriching the monarchy.[21]

These ideas show that Uztáriz's definition of Spanish naval strategy was strongly influenced by the transformation of the French naval system that occurred during the 1690s. The naval defeats of Barfleur-La Hogue, the bad harvests of 1692–1693, and the heavy costs imposed by the battlefleet strategy developed by Colbert after the Anglo-Dutch Wars, prompted his successor, the marquis of Seignelay, to fully implement the privateering strategy described in the 1689 naval Ordonnance.[22] Uztáriz was aware of the economic importance of these changes, and he firmly believed that the last French efforts at battlefleet strategy during the War of Spanish Succession had confirmed the advantages of the *guerre de course*. In fact, he stated that the unfortunate experience of the battle of Velez-Málaga (1704), in which the French and English battlefleets bombarded each other for days using line-ahead tactics with great bloodshed and little strategic results, proved the wisdom of Seignelay's reforms.[23]

Uztáriz's interpretation of the French *guerre de course* strategy led him to develop clear-cut ideas regarding shipbuilding policy. His discourse on strategy and tactics preceded a strong critique on the production of three-decked line-of-battle ships, based on two lines of argumentation: their high operational costs, and the difficulty of using them for anything other than a battlefleet strategy based on line-of-battle tactics. He criticised the large number of ships of more than 80 guns still present in the French navy of his day, as well the preponderance of 80-, 90-, and 100-gun three-deckers in the British navy, consolidating his previous argument in favour of the production of medium and large two-deckers for the navy of Spain. This, however, did not lead him to utterly proscribe the idea of producing some large three-deckers, which he considered relevant as symbols of royal prestige. He suggested to build one 100-gun vessel to serve as flagship – called *almiranta* in Spanish fashion – as well as two other large three-deckers of 90 and 86 guns respectively, to serve in the supporting role of *capitanas*. The traditional configuration of Spanish Atlantic battle squadrons comprised only one *almiranta* and one *capitana* in any given battle squadron, and Uztáriz's inclusion of a second *capitana* has no precedent in Spanish tactical legislation or practice. This innovation was directly linked to the appropriation of another French principle: the separation of command in three divisions. Uztáriz called these *Vanguardia, Cuerpo de*

---

[21] Uztáriz, p. 245.

[22] Pilgrim, D., 'The Colbert-Seignelay Naval Reforms and the Beginnings of the War of the League of Habsburg', *French Historical Studies*, 9 (1975): 235–262.

[23] Uztáriz, p. 272.

Batalla, and *Retaguardia,* and observed that other nations put them under the command of an admiral, a vice-admiral, and a rear-admiral.[24]

The line-of-battle ship core proposed by Uztáriz as the minimum required by the Spanish monarchy to keep control of its imperial sea lanes consisted of 17 large two-deckers. This comprised eight 70-gun ships and nine 80-gun ships, plus the already mentioned two *almirantas* of 86 and 90 guns, and the sole 100-gun three-decker. Ten more 60-gun ships were to be deployed as escort of the Indies' fleets, supported by four 50- to 54-gun ships, and the already mentioned 16 frigates for Atlantic and Caribbean service.[25] Finally, three more frigates of 40, 30, and 20 guns were to be deployed for various Atlantic duties, while the Armada de Barlovento was to be provided with three more ships of 60, 54, and 50 guns, supported by three frigates of 40, 30, and 20 guns.[26]

These paragraphs represent the only existing discourse on Spanish naval strategy and its relation to shipbuilding policy for the first half of the eighteenth century. Uztáriz's proposals were followed almost *avant la lettre* to guide warship production during the two decades that followed the first edition of the *Théorica y práctica,* both in the traditional private shipyards and in the new, state-owned shipyards of Cadiz, Ferrol, and Cartagena. His masterful interpretation of the interaction of the *guerre d'escadre* and the *guerre the course* in a Hispanic context, as well as his adaptation of French legislation, became the main guidelines for the definition of Spanish Bourbon naval doctrine at least until the mid-1760s.

During the 1730s and 1740s, there was a growing French influence in Spain's naval system. Gaztañeta's death in 1728 led to the rise of French master shipwrights in the state-owned shipyards and to the adoption of contemporary French tendencies in naval shipbuilding. Two-decked ship designs were lengthened by the increase of the main battery by one gunport, with 80-gun ships reaching 15 gunports per main broadside; 70-gun ships, 14 per main broadside, and 13 gunports per main broadside in 60-gun-ships.[27] Only one three-decker was built: the 114-gun *Real Felipe,* launched from Guarnizo in 1732.[28] In all, the strengthening of the various two-decked types, and the almost total disappearance of the three-decked type point towards an increased emphasis on the defensive criteria defined by Uztáriz. This illustrates the profound connection between naval strategy and shipbuilding policy in a specifically Spanish context.

---

[24] Ibid.
[25] Ibid., p. 273.
[26] Ibid., p. 275.
[27] Valdez-Bubnov, *Poder naval y modernización del Estado,* pp. 222–226.
[28] González-Aller Hierro, J. I., 'El navío de tres puentes en la armada española', *Revista de Historia Naval,* 9 (1985): 45–76.

The Mediterranean policy followed by Philip V's government after the War of the Quadruple Alliance (1718–1719) was aimed towards recovering Spanish influence in the Italian Peninsula, by promoting the accession of the offspring from his second marriage to regional thrones. This coincided with the worsening of Anglo-Spanish relations generated by the English participation in Spain's transatlantic trade allowed by the Treaty of Utrecht (1713). Also, the death in 1736 of Joseph Patiño –Spain's leading naval reformer – led to the 1737 creation of a new governing *junta* for the Ministry of Navy: the *Almirantazgo*.[29]

In 1738, a new plan for the configuration of the Spanish navy was defined, together with changes in shipbuilding administration designed to reach high production and maintenance goals. The main criterion behind these measures was the possibility of renewed naval conflict with Great Britain in the Mediterranean and Caribbean theatres. This configuration included one three-decked flagship, two 80-gun two-deckers, 12 70-gun ships and 17 60-gun ships, supported by 10 50-gun ships. Four 40-gun frigates were added, together with two 30-gun and four 20-gun smaller types. Four packet boats and four mortar ships – called *bombardas* in Spanish fashion – were also added. Detailed calculations of the necessary shipbuilding quotas required to reach these numbers were also made.[30]

This configuration presented some important differences with the one proposed by Uztáriz in 1724. The heaviest ship types – those corresponding to the *capitanas* and *almirantas* in Uztáriz's configuration – were significantly reduced, while the number of large, 70 and 60-gun two-deckers was increased. The number of 50-gun types was reduced by half, and that of frigates by one third. These figures are indicative of the evolution of Spanish naval doctrine between the 1720s and the |1740s. In all, they can be seen as a radicalisation of the defensive criteria outlined by Uztáriz in his *Théorica y práctica*, which had already departed from the battlefleet strategies derived from the Anglo-Dutch Wars and Colbert's shipbuilding programmes, towards an increased embrace the de-centralised approach to naval warfare defined by Seignelay's reforms in France.

These ideas, however, began to change during the 1739–1748 war. In February 1744, a Spanish squadron returning from Italy under the command of Juan Joseph Navarro de Viana y Búfalo was intercepted by a British force in the

---

[29] Guirao de Vierna, A. 'Notas para un estudio del Almirantazgo', *Revista de Historia Naval*, 4 (1984): 83–100; Domínguez Nafría, J.C., 'Perfiles institucionales del Almirantazgo en España', *Cuadernos monográficos del Instituto de Historia y Cultura Naval*, 42 (2003): 13–56.

[30] Museo Naval de Madrid (MNM), Ms. 1467, doc. 1, fols. 1–26 y Ms. 472, fols. 39–51: 'Reglamento general de la Marina, o pie fixo de ella, en que se expresa la calidad y cantidad de buques de guerra de que se ha de componer la Armada de España...'

proximity of Cape Sicié, near the French port of Toulon.[31] The Spanish convoy was composed of the only Spanish three-decked ship of the line, the *Real Phelipe*, one 80-gun ship, one 70, three 60s, and seven armed merchantmen recently recruited according to the procedures still envisaged by Gaztañeta's legislation. The British squadron, on the other hand, was composed of 17 line-of-battle ships, 13 of which were three-deckers. The combat was violent, and Navarro fell wounded, but only one Spanish ship was lost to the British: the armed merchantman *El Poder*, which was recaptured by the Spanish only to sink later.

This experience negatively shaped Navarro's perception of the current strategic paradigm and its corresponding shipbuilding policy. In 1747, he addressed a long memoir to the Council of State, under the title *Varios puntos de gobierno,* in which he criticised the high proportion of two-decked ships in the Spanish navy. In contrast, he proposed a fleet configuration composed of a core of 24 three-decked ships of the line of 100 or more guns, while reducing the number of 70-gun two-deckers to half of that number. Moreover, he also suggested to increase the firepower of the main line-of-battle ships by augmenting the weight of ball of the guns of the second battery to 24 *libras* (Spanish pounds) instead of only 18. The upperworks were to be fitted with guns of 12 *libras* weight of ball. The types destined to the protection of trade in the Mediterranean and the Caribbean were to be reduced to a lesser but undefined number of frigates. Also, he stated the need to have 10 fireships, 10 *bombardas*, 12 xebecs, and 24 smaller vessels for reconnaissance and liaison duties.[32]

Navarro's argument for the adoption of an aggressive battlefleet strategy and a shipbuilding policy based on the production of heavier ships of the line was shaped by his combat experience. Nevertheless, he also had a previous academic formation based on French naval tactics. During his early years as professor at the recently created Naval Academy in Cadiz, Navarro begun a translation of the classic French interpretation of the tactical and strategic paradigm derived from the Anglo-Dutch Wars, the treatise *L'Art des armeés navales*, published by the Jesuit priest Paul Hoste in 1697. Therefore, the possibility that Navarro's

---

[31] See Vargas Ponce, J., *Vida de D. Juan Josef Navarro* (Madrid: Imprenta Real, 1808); Martínez Ruiz, E., 'El Marqués de la Victoria y la política naval española', *Cuadernos monográficos del Instituto de Historia y Cultura Naval*, 28 (1996): 7–20; Blanco Núñez, J.M., 'El marqués de la Victoria y la táctica naval', *Cuadernos monográficos del Instituto de Historia y Cultura Naval*, 28 (1996): 35–50; O'Donnell, H., *El primer marqués de la Victoria, personaje silenciado en la reforma dieciochesca de la Armada* (Madrid: Real Academia de La Historia, 2004); and 'El Marqués de la Victoria, una opinión discordante con la política naval de Ensenada', *Anuario de Estudios Atlánticos*, (2008), 13–41.

[32] Real Academia de La Historia, Ms 9/2061.

command experience consolidated ideas he previously assimilated as a scholar must be considered. In any case, his views on tactics and strategy developed consistently in the same direction during the 20 years that followed the Battle of Cape Sicié. In effect, as the Seven Years War (1759–1763) was coming to an end, Navarro again made a proposal for the reform of the Spanish navy, this time to the new king Carlos III. He presented it as a continuation of an old technical debate dating from the late seventeenth century regarding the tactical efficiency of medium versus large-sized ships.[33]

The discourse began with a severe criticism of the high proportion of medium-sized ships in the Spanish navy, stating that in combat they were more of a hindrance that an advantage, being useless and incapable of making any contribution to victory, even when interpolated between larger ships in the line of battle. He went on to clarify that he did not intend to wholly exclude 50 to 60-gun ships, frigates, and smaller ships from the navy. Rather, he wanted to prove with logical arguments that a force of larger ships formed in line of battle (a squadron from six to eight ships), would always be stronger and more powerful than an equivalent or larger force composed of medium-sized vessels.[34] From there, he launched a direct criticism of the current naval doctrine, stating that a 70-gun ship, armed with a main battery of 24 *libras* weight of ball, a second battery of 18 *libras*, and of 8 *libras* in the upperworks, would always be inferior in firepower when compared to a 90-gun three-decked ship. Moreover, the three-decker would also be better equipped to withstand the broadsides of its enemy than the 70-gun two-decker, being more strongly built, with heavier timbers and taller masts. He also derided the higher proportion of smaller guns present in the armament configuration of medium-sized ships, stating that the bow and stern chasers were good for nothing when formed in line of battle. In all, he praised the larger proportion of heavy guns equipping the larger ship.[35]

Navarro went on to discuss the rate of fire in relation to the total number of guns, stating that a well-served cannon, properly refreshed after every five shots, could fire 10 times within an hour. This meant that a 90-gun ship, with a broadside of about 45 cannons could shoot 450 balls per hour. If a 70-gun ship could only count on 30 effective cannons per broadside, what would be the outcome, he asked rhetorically, in a combat with a three-decker lasting for three to four hours?[36] He concluded this reflection by stating that France had recently lost her colonial empire due to the lack of a competent navy, being

---

[33] MNM, Ms. 608-5, Ms. 600; Ms. 601; Ms. 602, and Ms. 604.
[34] MNM, Ms. 608-5.
[35] Ibid.
[36] Ibid.

reduced to watch the sad spectacle of her strongholds and possessions being insulted and severed from the Motherland.[37]

This time, Navarro's message was stronger than it had been in 1747: there had to be a greater proportion of three-deckers, rather than two-deckers, in the composition of the Spanish navy. As Uztáriz did in his time, Navarro defined his ideas on shipbuilding policy according to the different theatres in which the navy had to operate. The core of line-of-battle ships deployed in European waters was to be composed of 18 90-gun three-deckers, mounting broadsides of 24, 24, and 12 *libras* weight of ball, without the poop; six 80-gun ships, built preferably with three decks and capable of firing a broadside of 24, 24, and 8 *libras* weight of ball; 24 two-decked ships of 70 and 60 guns, divided evenly, mounting batteries of 24, 18, and 8 *libras* weight of ball, and 18, 12, and 8, respectively. He added 12 heavy frigates of 40 to 50 guns, mounting batteries of 18 and 8 libras weight of ball. For the protection of trade in the Mediterranean and the Atlantic, he added 12 frigates, two *bombardas*, 24 22- to 30-gun xebecs, 24 large fluyts, six lateen ships, and two hospital ships.[38] Finally, he also addressed the king directly, recommending him to keep a powerful and offensively oriented navy, supported by a well-supplied permanent infrastructure, in order to avoid the useless expense represented by the other alternatives. In his view, this was the only way to prevent insults from other naval powers and protect the Spanish empire.[39]

Navarro's proposals demonstrate that the transition from the defensive doctrine present in Uztáriz's 1724 *Théorica y práctica* to the battlefleet strategy formally adopted by the Bourbon powers after the Seven Years War had an important Spanish precedent in the strategic and tactical ideas of Juan José Navarro.[40] Although he might have been influenced by Hoste's works on the nature of the late seventeenth-century French *guerre d'escadre*, his command experience at the Battle of Cape Sicié was decisive in shaping his perception of the combat effectiveness of two and three-decked ships of the line, the tactical use of the line of battle, and the configuration of the Spanish battlefleet. As already mentioned, his proposals can also be seen as a continuation of the late-seventeenth century debate on the tactical efficiency of medium and large ships. This discussion had been eclipsed during the creation of the Spanish Bourbon naval system by the imposition of a strategic doctrine implicitly defined by Gaztañeta's shipbuilding legislation and explicitly stated by Gerónimo de Uztáriz's writings on economic policy and grand strategy.

[37] Ibid.
[38] Ibid.
[39] MNM, Ms. 608-5.
[40] Scott, H.M., 'The Importance of Bourbon Naval Reconstruction to the Strategy of Choiseul after the Seven Years' War', *The International History Review*, 1 (1979): 16–35.

It can be stated that the Uztáriz/Gaztañeta strategic and technological paradigm, despite the relevant changes in shipbuilding policy that took place after 1730, lasted until the middle of the eighteenth century. In this sense, Navarro's doctrine precedes in almost 20 years the French turn towards a battlefleet strategy, under the leadership of Choiseul, and adopted in Spain as a result of the joint foreign policy of the Third Family Compact, leading to the re-construction of the Spanish navy around a strong core of very large three-decked line-of-battleships. The Spanish 70-gun two-decker began to be superseded by new, more heavily armed 74-gun ships of French inspiration, whereas the 60-gun ships were replaced by the larger 'French' 64.

The naval forces of the Bourbon alliance were put to the test during their joint intervention in the North American War of Independence (1778–1783). The first strategic plan for the use of the Spanish navy in an all-out conflict with the British was written in 1777 by Pedro Pablo Abarca de Bolea y Ximénez de Urrea, count of Aranda, under the title *Idea de un plan entre ofensivo y defensivo formado a solicitud de Vergennes*.[41] This plan is important for the history of Spanish strategic thinking because it shows a more complex interaction of the specialised battlefleet built after the Seven Years War with an all-out *guerre de course* conceived as an offensive expedient, thus incorporating the main principles defined by Uztáriz and Navarro into a unified conception of naval warfare.

Aranda's idea was to use the Bourbon battlefleets in direct coordination with privateers from all maritime regions of the Bourbon empires. This required strong royal support for private armaments in the Iberian Peninsula and Spanish America. He believed that the rebels would sooner or later become allies of the Bourbon powers, and wanted to open all Spanish and French ports to them, in America and Europe. He also expected that an eventual Franco-Spanish intervention would increase the number of American privateers raiding British commerce, thus making the *guerre de course* a major strategic expedient.

Aranda anticipated that the British naval response to the Bourbon privateering offensive would be to resort to the ancient system of convoys. This, in his view, was the key to the effective use of naval power, for it gave the Spanish and French fleets the opportunity to attack the concentrated merchant ships. For this purpose, the heavy cruisers and 74-gun two-deckers were to be sent against them, while a core of heavy Spanish and French line-of-battle ships was to be kept in readiness, to strike at the British naval forces as soon as they attempted to protect the convoys. Aranda believed that this would force the British government to keep very large numbers of warships in readiness, at least 160 of all types, imposing a significant strain on its finances. Moreover, he expected that the large number of sailors drafted into the Royal Navy

---

[41] Valdez-Bubnov, I., 'Spanish Naval Strategy and the United States, 1763–1819.' Mariner's Mirror, 101 (2015): 5.

would reduce the numbers available for recruitment in the British privateering industry, and also make it more difficult to staff the merchant fleets.

In order to attain these objectives, Aranda calculated that the Bourbon fleets needed to fit out 80 line-of-battle ships and 60 frigates. Thirty-five battleships and 24 frigates were to be stationed in Ferrol and Brest; and 14 battleships and 14 frigates between Cadiz, Cartagena, and Toulon. Also, he wanted at least 20 line-of-battle ships and 12 frigates stationed in American waters. These were to be used as cruising squadrons, while keeping a number of heavier line-of-battle ships concentrated and ready to strike at British lines of communication, or directly at the main British fleet. Aranda's plan also had a global dimension, since he also expected several frigates to be stationed in the Indian Ocean, and to use the Spanish naval forces deployed in the Southern Pacific to reinforce the divisions stationed at Ferrol or Cadiz. The land forces of both countries, on the other hand, were to be used in support of the naval war, protecting dockyards and ports, with 20,000 men in northern Spain, 8,000 around Gibraltar, and around 60,000 stationed on the French coasts. The troops deployed in France were to be used as an invasion threat, forcing the British to concentrate large forces in the English Channel and diverting them from action in other naval theatres.

Aranda's all naval, blue-water strategy, directed against British commerce and naval forces is relevant from the point of view of the evolution of Spanish naval strategy, but it was never put into practice. When hostilities erupted, in 1778 and 1779, the new Spanish first minister, the count of Floridablanca, expected to use the Bourbon fleets to protect an amphibious landing in the British Isles, but this proved impossible due to logistical problems. Successful amphibious operations were undertaken in Minorca, Florida, Campeche, and Honduras, while the blockade and siege of Gibraltar failed.[42] After the war, the shipbuilding policy outlined by Juan José Navarro was not altered, and Spain's imperial shipyards continued to produce large and powerful three-deckers,

---

[42] Ibid., 5–7. See Graham, G., *Empire of the North Atlantic: The Maritime Struggle for North America* (Toronto: Toronto University Press, 1950); Batista, J., *La estrategia española en América durante el Siglo de las Luces* (Madrid: MAPFRE, 1992); Ruigómez de Hernández, M.P., *El gobierno español del despotismo ilustrado ante la independencia de los Estados Unidos* (Madrid: Ministerio de Asuntos Exteriores, 1978); Hernández Franco, J., *La gestión política y el pensamiento reformista del Conde de Floridablanca* (Murcia: Ediciones de la Universidad, 2008); Martínez Shaw, C., 'Participación de la armada española en la guerra de Independencia de los Estados Unidos', *Revista de Historia Naval*, 10 (1985): 75–80; Alzina Torrente, J., *Una guerra romántica, 1778–1783: España, Francia e Inglaterra en la mar* (Madrid: Ministerio de Defensa, 2006); Rodríguez González, A.R., 'Les objectifs de la marine espagnole', in O. Chaline, P. Bonnichon, and C. Vergennes (eds), *Les Marines de la guerre d'Independance américaine (1763–1783)* (Paris: I. L'instrument naval, 2013), pp. 129–150.

74- and 64-gun ships, and different types of heavy and medium-sized frigates and cruisers. The Spanish navy soon reached its apogee in terms of the number of ships in service, and warship production continued without interruption until 1798.

Nevertheless, the international situation of the Spanish Empire became progressively more complex. On the one hand, the outbreak of the French Revolution created an unexpected ideological and military situation, and Spain temporarily aligned itself with Great Britain during the War of the First Coalition. On the other, the newly independent United States began to pressure for the right to navigate the Mississippi river, in order to get mercantile access to the Gulf of Mexico. Moreover, there was a constant American demographic pressure into Spanish North American territories, and there were serious filibustering attempts, launched from United States territory, aimed at overthrowing Spanish rule in Florida. Thus, by the end of the eighteenth century, the containment of Anglo-American expansion into the Gulf of Mexico and the Caribbean became one of the basic goals of Spanish foreign policy, thus protecting Spain's commercial monopoly with its colonies, and the territorial integrity of the empire.[43]

In 1800, the new Spanish prime minister, Manuel de Godoy, attempted to resolve these problems by ceding the large North American territory of Louisiana to France, a Spanish ally once again after the 1797 Treaty of San Ildefonso. But Spain's strategic situation began to deteriorate rapidly. From 1798 to 1800, France and the United States fought the Quasi-War, an undeclared naval conflict that led to the capture of large numbers of American ships. Many French privateers operated from Spanish American ports, and Spanish American privateers took active part in the offensive. In 1803, after the slave revolts in Saint-Domingue closed the main outlet for French produce from Louisiana, Napoleon decided to sell that territory to the United States, and in 1804, a British naval attack forced Spain to enter the War of the Third Coalition on Napoleon's side.[44]

---

[43] Griffin, C.C., *The United States and the Disruption of the Spanish Empire, 1810–1822: A Study of the Relations of the United States with Spain and with the Rebel Spanish colonies* (New York: Octagon Books, 1937); Cussik, J.G., *The Other War of 1812: The Patriot War and the American Invasion of Spanish Florida* (Athens: University of Georgia Press, 2007).

[44] Bonnel, U., *La France, les États-Unis et la guerre de course* (París: NEL, 1959); Crowhurst, P., *The French War on Trade. Privateering, 1793–1815* (Aldershot: Scholar Press, 1989); De Conde, A., *The Quasi-War: The Politics and Diplomacy of the Undeclared War with France, 1797–1801* (New York: Scribner, 1966); Palmer, M.A., *Stoddert's War: Naval Operations during the Quasi-War with France, 1798–1801* (Annapolis: Naval Institute Press, 1987); Hill, P.P., *Napoleon's Troublesome Americans. Franco-American Relations, 1804–1815* (Washington DC: Potomac Books, 2005);

These events had an impact on the evolution of Spanish strategic thought, leading to the development of more complex ideas for the combined use of military and naval power. It can be stated that the expansion of the United States into Spanish territory forced an integration of maritime and land strategy in a way it had not been expressed before. In 1804, Enrique Reynaldo Macdonnell y de Gondé, a brigadier in the Spanish navy, proposed a detailed strategy for a full-scale naval war against the United States. The context and details of Macdonnell's plan are already well known by specialised historiography, and they will only be outlined here.[45] The purpose of the following section is to examine the extent to which Macdonells' ideas on strategy reveal a change in relation to those set forth during the second half of the eighteenth century.

Macdonnell's plan started with a detailed geographical and hydrographical description of the United Sates. This introduction was followed by a description of the political system of the country, stressing what he perceived as a political rift between Northern and Southern states, which could possibly lead to secession. He believed the American economy was weak, with imports surpassing exports, a large national debt, and a high annual deficit. This, in his view, was the cause of North American contraband into the Spanish colonies. He then proceeded to give an unimpressed account of its land forces, followed by a more respectful description of the navy. He described their heavy frigates, and compared them favourably with Spanish ships of equivalent rate. He also gave a detailed assessment of the shipbuilding potential of the republic, showing that it could rapidly become a naval threat to the Spanish empire. He nevertheless pointed out that the most fearsome aspect of the United States was not its armed forces, but rather, its growing population, massing at the frontiers of the kingdom of Mexico, and their uncontainable impulse to migrate.

Macdonnell thought that despite all their weaknesses the United States was going to grow powerful and rich. He predicted the Anglo-American population would expand to the West and, in two decades, the United States would threaten Mexico. He concluded that it was necessary to declare war immediately, while the Americans were still underdeveloped and Spain had a clear military and naval superiority. The main political objectives of the conflict would be to close the Mississippi river to United States' navigation, and to prevent their further expansion into Spain's North American territories.

The plan comprised combined land and sea operations, in a campaign season lasting from February to June. The land campaign was to start with the creation of an arsenal in St Augustine, East Florida, designed to supply

---

Lambert, A. *The Challenge: Britain against America in the Naval War of 1812* (London: Faber & Faber, 2012).

[45] The constants of Macdonnell's plan are described in detail in Valdez-Bubnov, 2015, pp. 9–19. The following paragraphs summarise the contents of this publication.

an invasion army of 8,000 to 12,000 men. The attack was to start with an amphibious landing in San Marcos, Apalaches Bay, from where the Spanish armies were to move along the rivers San Juan and Nassau, to occupy the state of Georgia, and then attack New Orleans. At the same time, Nueva Madrid would be used to launch a guerrilla campaign into Indiana, Kentucky, and Tennessee, with the help of local Indian tribes. Once Georgia was conquered, the land forces were to proceed to the conquest of South Carolina and then, if needed, of North Carolina too.

The second part of the manuscript described the naval campaign. Like Aranda, Macdonnell was aware that a conflict with the United States would necessarily have a global reach. He started by establishing a first line of operations, which he called the 'stationary line' or 'line of first position', from Puerto Rico to Havana, where it divided in two, one going to Veracruz, and the other to St Augustine, Florida, where the arsenal for the invasion army was to be established. He then traced a second line, composed of what he called alternatively 'lines of movement' or 'spheres of activity'. It connected New England, around Cape Cod, close to Boston, Pennsylvania, between the river Delaware and Chesapeake Bay, and the Carolinas, around Charleston, and its adjacent coasts. American merchant shipping in these areas was to be intercepted by Spanish cruising squadrons, composed of one ship of the line and two frigates. Other cruisers, based in Ferrol, Cadiz, Cartagena, and Algeciras were to patrol the Atlantic and Mediterranean trade routes used by American merchants. Squadrons were also to be sent to patrol the trade routes from Manila to Canton, and from Coromandel to Malabar. To complete this, two more cruiser squadrons were to operate, one from Havana to the Florida Keys, and another from Santo Domingo to the port of Baracoa. A division composed of two line-of-battle ships and four frigates was to attack the enemy frigates deployed against Tripoli and other Barbary nations.

In the last phase of the plan, all Spanish naval forces were to concentrate and, in three divisions, form a 'third line of movement', or 'line of blockade'. The first division was to blockade the coasts of New England, especially around Cape Cod. The second division, from New York to Cape Henry, and the third one, from Cape Fear to Savannah. From here, the three divisions were form a 'fourth line', or 'line of attack'. They were to unite and attack the North American coasts, shelling ports, landing infantry parties, and burning dockyards and ships. In Macdonnell's view, this step, together with the completion of the land campaign, would compel the United States government to an armistice.

The project ended with the conditions of the peace treaty. These basically consisted of closing the Mississippi to United States navigation, from the Ohio to the Gulf of Mexico, establishing a new frontier line, from the Atlantic to the Mississippi, and closing the Pacific to American navigation, from California to Cape Horn. Also, United States whaling in the River Plate was to be terminated, and all Patagonia was to be closed to its shipping.

There is evidence showing that Macdonnell's project was taken seriously by prime minister Manuel Godoy, but political considerations prevented its implementation. Godoy had been the main influence behind the Louisiana cession to France, and the idea of starting a war to repair the consequences of that deed might have seemed risky from the perspective of court politics. Moreover, in the same year that Macdonnell delivered the manuscript (1804), Spanish frigates carrying bullion were attacked by the British, forcing Spain to enter the War of the Third Coalition on Napoleon's side. The following year, an important part of the Spanish navy was destroyed at the battle of Trafalgar. Three years later, in 1808, the French army occupied Spain, starting the Spanish War of Independence. All this coincided with a less aggressive stance taken by the United States government, due to its growing maritime frictions with Great Britain, now a Spanish ally in the war against Napoleon. In 1810 revolution erupted both in Mexico and South America, and the insurgent privateers found useful allies in the merchants of the United States, who purchased their prizes and provided logistical support.

The frontier problems with the United States resumed after Napoleon's definitive fall, in 1815. By then, Spanish royalist forces had nearly completed the defeat of Spanish American revolutionary armies, but the insurgent fleets remained active, and a civil war between Spanish and Anglo-American settlers raged in Florida. Moreover, in 1816, an invasion army comprising many volunteers from the United States landed in New Spain's northern provinces.[46] In this new context Joseph Vázquez de Figueroa, secretary of the navy of the restored Spanish king, Ferdinand VII, ordered Macdonnell to produce an updated version of the plan, according to the new political situation and proportionate to Spain's existing naval resources.[47] Macdonnell delivered the second version of the plan in September 1816. The author now stated that the menace posed by the United States was far greater than in 1804, and that open conflict was inevitable. He believed that the United States army comprised 10,000 regulars, not counting militias, and were deployed against the British, near Canada, and the other half in the vicinity of New Orleans. He believed their naval forces counted two ships of the line, 12 to 13 frigates,

---

[46] García Baquero, A., *Comercio colonial y guerras revolucionarias: la decadencia económica de Cádiz a raíz de la emancipación Americana* (Sevilla: EEHA, 1972); Gámez Duarte, F., *Del uno al otro confín: España y la lucha contra el corso insurgente hispanoamericano, 1812–1828* (Cadiz: Dipuación, 2008); Grafenstein Gareis, J. von, 'Insurgencia y contrainsurgencia en el golfo de México, 1812–1820', in V. Guedea, M. Chust et al., *La Independencia de México y el proceso autonomista novohispano, 1808–1824* (México: UNAM-Instituto Mora, 2001).

[47] For this section of the plan, see Valdez-Bubnov, 2015, pp. 14–19.

and an undetermined number of smaller vessels. In the event of a war these forces could capture the ports of Panzacola (Pensacola) and San Marcos de Apalache, and launch a damaging *guerre de course* against Spanish shipping.

The new version of the plan was proportionate to what Macdonnell believed were Spain's existing naval forces, and was different from the 1804 version. The first step of the land war was to fortify all the frontier outposts of New Spain's Internal Provinces; the ports and bays of Florida, especially Panzacola, and to place gun and mortar batteries to prevent their use by American privateers. The second step was to reinforce the garrisons of Puerto Rico and Cuba. The third step was to capture Mobile, in order to use it as a first base for the landing of military supplies. A second base was to be established at Pontchartrain Lake. A third base was to be placed in Natchitoches. Once all this had been achieved, land forces stemming from all three points were to attack New Orleans. Macdonnell warned that, if New Orleans was not captured, and Panzacola was lost, then the Spanish frontier would recede back to Cuba, implying the loss of the Gulf of Mexico.

Again, Macdonnell described the naval war in a second, separate section. The first objective of the Spanish navy was to protect Spanish shipping from enemy privateers. He believed that four up-gunned frigates would be sufficient to escort the Cadiz convoys, and expected to compel Spanish merchants into arming six privateers of 30 to 40 guns, and six of 12 to 20. These would escort the convoys sailing to the Antilles and the Mediterranean. He also wanted to use the rest of the Spanish navy to launch an intense *guerre de course*, which he believed would have devastating effects against the economy of the United States. To maintain control of the Gulf of Mexico, two line-of-battle ships and two frigates were to be stationed in Havana; two more frigates in Panzacola, and two more in Nassau. From these points, cruisers were to sail according to the lines of operation he proposed in the 1804 plan. If two more line-of-battle ships could be fitted out, they were to be stationed in the New England coast, to harass American trade and attract the attention of the enemy naval forces. He believed that this new version of the plan for land and naval warfare could be carried out with five regiments of foot, one of horse, two to four line-of-battle ships, and 10 frigates.

Vázquez de Figueroa concluded that there were not sufficient forces to carry out Macdonnell's second plan. Until the Spanish navy could be rebuilt, he considered that the best course of action was to appease the United States government, and try to contain their migrants. Moreover, the North American strategy had to compete with other plans, promoted by the powerful financial interests that had supported the military solutions attempted both by the regency and Ferdinand VII's government. In the end, the idea of a war against the United States was abandoned and superseded by a diplomatic focus, while a strong naval and military expedition against the last strongholds of Spanish American insurgency began to be prepared.

Macdonnell's plan represents a landmark in the history of Spanish naval strategy, not only for its complex integration of land and sea operations. This combination had naturally been expressed and undertaken before in various forms, as the global reach of Uztáriz and Aranda's plans clearly demonstrate, and as many previous Spanish combined arms operations from different epochs also do. Macdonnell's plan took these principles to a higher level of integration between the battlefleet, the privateers, and the land forces. But the real innovation in his thinking derived from his explicit attempt to express strategic principles from a scientific perspective. In effect, the author utilised a scientific, geometrical nomenclature for his principles, and attempted to present the whole plan as the practical application of abstract, scientific notions. This method was inspired, as he acknowledged, by the published works of Henry Lloyd. In a historical study of the Seven Years War land campaigns (*History of the Late War in Germany,* 1766), Lloyd had tried to establish a method to plan military operations according to geography, the enemy's strategic points, and the lines along which armies could move, which he called 'lines of operation'. Macdonnell used Lloyd's terminology to present the planning of the naval campaign against the United States as a 'new method' to devise naval strategy in a scientific manner.

Macdonnell stated that his 'new method' had the virtue of establishing 'fixed and permanent principles' for the conduct of naval operations. He claimed he had derived these philosophical ideas while reflecting on strategy, or the 'sublime part of naval warfare', after careful study of the Spanish intervention in the 1779–1783 war. Then, he claimed, he read Lloyd, being impressed by his idea of 'lines of operation' in land warfare. Thus, he borrowed Lloyd's nomenclature and was stimulated to create a 'scientific method' for the planning of naval operations, based on the search for permanent and invariable principles that could be systematically applied to strategy. Macdonnell's words deserve to be quoted again:

> I foresee, in the horizon of what is possible, the emergence of a New Science, which has always existed, but has never been properly understood. This is the Science of Naval Strategy, or the sublime part of War at Sea.

In other words, Macdonnell, in adapting Lloyd's method to the study of naval warfare, had attempted to create a scientific approach to strategy, as later naval historians tried to do. In fact, the works of Lloyd inspired one of the most influential military thinkers, Baron Antoine-Henri de Jomini, into deriving fixed, unchanging strategic principles from the study of military history. It might be worth pointing out that Jomini's work, in turn, influenced the great American naval philosopher, Alfred Thayer Mahan, in his definition of the permanent principles of maritime strategy that constitute the framework of his *Influence of Sea Power Upon History* series. Thus, Macdonnell's ideas represent an early and rare example of the merging of science, history, and strategy that was to define navalist thinking in the late nineteenth and early twentieth centuries.[48]

It can be concluded that the transition from a mainly defensive conception of naval power, characteristic of the first half of the eighteenth century, to a full-fledged battlefleet strategy in the second, had a direct impact on shipbuilding policy and warship design. In this sense, it is important to emphasise that the principles defined by the first author analysed here, Gerónimo de Uztáriz, indicate a structural continuity with the objectives and technological policies of seventeenth-century Habsburg naval strategy. On the other hand, Navarro's implicit criticism of Uztáriz's principles, foreshadowed the joint policies followed in the French and Spanish naval systems after the Seven Years' War, and demonstrated that the transition between strategic, tactical, and technological paradigms had a distinctively Spanish root. Aranda's project for a Franco-Spanish naval campaign in support of the independence of the United States clearly demonstrates that, despite the strong emphasis on the production of heavy line-of-battle ships that epitomised this period of Spanish shipbuilding history, the use of various types of cruisers and the support of privateering entrepreneurs remained a very important component of Spanish naval thinking. Finally, Macdonnell's project shows the degree of sophistication that Spanish strategic and tactical culture had reached by the early nineteenth century, combining land and sea operations in the form of amphibious landings, blockades, coastal bombardment, *guerre de course* and battlefleet action in thoroughly synchronised operations. There is another important innovation in Macdonnell's thinking: his ideas on the total nature of warfare. He envisaged systematic destruction as the means to achieve the political ends required by Spain's relationship with the United States. He explicitly recommended imposing heavy contributions on the American population and destroying what could not be seized by the advancing Spanish armies, in order to 'ruin the country for many years'. In summary, Maconnell's writings are important because they show the emergence of some of the defining characteristics of nineteenth- and twentieth-century Western strategic culture: the idea that warfare can be understood and directed by scientific means, the acceptance of total war, and the integration of military and political objectives in the planning and conduct of actual operations. From this perspective, it can be stated that Maconnell's work foreshadowed by several decades the main ideas developed by the great military and naval strategic thinkers of later periods.

---

[48] See Paret, P., Gordon A. Craig, and Felix Gilbert, *Makers of Modern Strategy: From Machiavelli to the Nuclear Age* (Oxford: Oxford University Press, 1986); Sumida, J., *Inventing Grand Strategy and Teaching Command: The Classic Works of Alfred Thayer Mahan Reconsidered* (New York: Johns Hopkins University Press, 1997).

3

Naval Strategic Leadership in Britain, 1739–1748: Political Leaders and Professional Knowledge

RICHARD HARDING

The War that Britain fought between 1739 and 1748 has not been considered one in which the strategic, operational, or tactical abilities of its statesmen and military leaders blossomed. In London, Sir Robert Walpole, the duke of Newcastle, the earl of Carteret and almost all their colleagues in the highest positions of state, are usually seen as ill-informed, misguided, and fractious. On the battlefields the likes of the duke of Cumberland, the earl of Stair, Sir John Cope, Henry Hawley, seem to have little grasp of the broader purpose of their campaigns. At sea, Edward Vernon, Thomas Matthews, Charles Knowles, Henry Medley, and John Byng were unable to make good use of Britain's greatest strategic advantage – sea power. At best the war, which for Britain ended with the *status quo ante,* was solid training for those lights were going to burn brightly eight years later in the Seven Years War – most obviously, the secretary of state for the Southern Department, William Pitt, but also the illustrious commanders, George Anson, Jean-Louis Ligonier, Edward Hawke, Edward Boscawen, Jeffrey Amherst, and James Wolfe.

The transformation of Britain's performance in the two wars has long been associated with the emergence of this new generation of leaders. That they played important roles in the victories is undeniable, but locating the causes of success almost exclusively in the characters of the leaders, throws much else into the shade.[1]

---

[1] The image of Pitt as the sublime author of an inspired global strategy, attracting the great military talents to him and faultlessly directing its execution does not carry the same weight as it did in the early years of the twentieth century, but it still features as the dominant factor in popular histories of the Seven Years War. Perhaps the most influential historian in this respect was J.S. Corbett, whose, *England in the Seven Years War*. 2 vols. London: Longman Green, 1907, set the standard for analysis in his day.

This chapter will focus less on the performance of individual leaders than on the social process of leadership itself. This way of looking at leadership shows that it is not rigidly hierarchical, nor bureaucratically determined. Nor are its outputs the product of a purely scientific rational process. It is not confined to formal organisational 'commanders' nor the preserve of a single brain. Leadership at all levels is a social process that exists between people – the leaders and the led – who are in a constant process of renegotiating that relationship and may be changing roles at any time. Even the output of the strategy formulation process – strategic policy – is only one step in actual performance of the organisation. Policy requires implementation and interpretation throughout the organisation with all the attendant filters of competence, comprehension, and control – each of which is subject to local leadership interventions. This is before and during the exposure of policy to the reality of operations and the enemy's reactions. While the old truism that strategy seldom survives the first contact with the enemy remains entirely valid, it may also be true that in many cases strategy does not survive the implementation process.

This emphasis on leadership as a process is not new.[2] Over the last thirty years, the concept of leadership has been heavily researched from many perspectives and occasionally, the results have influenced thinking about historical events. For example, several ideas based on decision-making have provided some interesting insights. Work on investment decisions in the 1970s, particularly on the concept of risk, led the development of Prospect Theory. This was found to have use in international relations and, over time, it provided some fruitful insights into historical leadership situations.[3] The principal contention of Prospect Theory is that individual decision-makers fear the loss of what they already possess more than they desire to make further gains. Thus, they will take greater risks and pay higher prices to avoid losses than they will to secure more gains. In the international arena this could have an important impact on deterrence. Deterrent measures are more likely to be effective against someone who is acting to make a gain than one who is trying to avoid losses. Aggressive opportunists, therefore, should be more easily deterred by the threat of military reaction than leaders who are in real fear of losing national power or prestige. Wars will, therefore, be more common, longer and savage between powers defending what they perceive to be the status quo than between those seeking some sort of new gain.

---

[2] For example see, Grint, Keith, *Fuzzy Management: Contemporary Ideas and Practices at Work*. Oxford: Oxford University Press, 1997.

[3] Farnham, Barbara, ed., *Avoiding Losses/Taking Risks: Prospect Theory and International Conflict*. Michigan: University of Michigan Press, 1994. Professor Geoffrey Parker found this concept useful in his analysis of the strategy of Philip II of Spain. See Parker, Geoffrey. *The Grand Strategy of Philip II*. New Haven: Yale University Press, 2000, p. 283.

There are, of course, many exceptions that can be cited. For example, the War of American Independence (1775–1783) does not entirely fit this explanation. For Britain there is no doubt that this war was about preventing the loss of a colonial empire, but before the French entered the war in 1778, British opinion was ambivalent about using force. To some the British government was trying to impose an innovation (taxation without representation), which was a direct attack on traditional liberties of Englishmen overseas.[4] That changed as the stakes became far higher with Bourbon intervention – invasion of the home islands and the loss of the crucial West Indian islands then became far more significant than the loss of the Thirteen Colonies. However, what is important is the perception of the combatants. If the leaders 'frame' their decisions as defensive it produces a different perception of the purpose and significance of war than if they frame their decisions as a policy of aggressive expansion. Therefore, the question of how decisions are framed, and by whom, becomes important and interesting. A second important issue is who decides what are 'losses' and what are 'gains'. They could be material, for example, territory or economic privileges, and they could be symbolic, such as honour, prestige. The relative importance given to these factors by any society is dependent upon the balance of influence or leadership of individuals or groups who champion them.

The framing of any decision, or set of decisions is, therefore, the important context within which decision-makers, or leaders, work. Within most nation states there are formally recognised decision-makers, or strategic leaders. They are expected to make decisions – theirs is the choice of action. However, they do not work in a vacuum on an abstract chessboard. Their understanding of the situation, the threats, the opportunities, and the policy options is influenced by a great many other actors who provide information about how society in general would view and respond to those decisions. These are people who influence the framing of the decisions. Some will have great technical knowledge, such as the military or administrative advisors. Others such as domestic politicians and foreign ambassadors, will have strongly held views that reflect competing pressures in the wider political system. The existence of a press or other media can reflect, channel, magnify, or expose opinions from all sorts of interests and communities. All these actors will influence what is considered important to society – the value of the potential losses and gains in any conflict. None of this is fixed, but will alter as different actors achieve influence at any given point. Deeply held ideological axioms, current concerns, and even random events, such as the death of a monarch, a diplomatic revolution elsewhere in the world, or even a particularly violent weather event, such as a storm, could suddenly shift the frame of the decision

---

[4] Sainsbury, John, *Disaffected Patriots: London Supporters of Revolutionary America, 1769–1782*. Kingston: McGill-Queen's University Press, 1987, pp. 22–54.

and thus the options available. Leaders may strive to exert a hegemonic control over the framing of decisions, but this is seldom possible in the long term. Slogans, representing ideological commitment, such as the 'the international order', 'the balance of power', 'manifest destiny', 'natural borders', or 'the right side of history' serve to create a frame that is resistant to challenge, but the turbulence of circumstances, especially those unleashed by war, have a tendency to undermine the force of rhetorical devices and ideological axioms.

In this context, strategic leadership exists not so much in the policy decisions themselves, but in influences that provide the frame for a decision. This way of looking at the strategic decision-making process can be presented as a diagram (Figure 1):

Decision parameters (perceptions of possibility)	Decision influencers	Definition of the strategic space and objective	Decision-makers' strategic framing choice
Political culture Domestic politics Economic performance Institutional performance International conditions	Institutions Ad hoc actors External shocks	Strategic threats Opportunities Objectives Range of choices	Offensive or defensive

Figure 1. The Strategic Framing Process

It starts with decision parameters – the perceived bounds of possibility either for losses or gains and the values are put on them. These will be identified within society and articulated, through expressions of a deep political culture, to the more immediate events of domestic politics, economic performance, institutional adaptability, and international conditions. The judgements are likely to be varied, contested, and in a state of flux. On top of these the sudden, unexpected external shocks can always upset and adjust all these perceptions.

Those which become the dominant decision influences that lead to the framing of strategic objectives and options will be determined by the power of social actors within the political system at any given time. Institutions, with their assumptions and operations already deeply embedded in the national system, will be particularly powerful. Naval, military, administrative, legislative, executive, legal, and economic institutions have privileged status in society and are all able to make powerful, and not necessarily compatible, cases. Ad hoc actors may appear on the scene occasionally and have significant influence. For example, the West India merchant lobby in the late 1730s, was not as institutionally embedded as it was to become, but became extremely important in the decisions that led to war with Spain in 1739.[5] Similar merchant lobbying groups were significant in the critical period between 1754 and 1757. External shocks also have the potential to shift the frame. The death of the Emperor Charles VI in October 1740 and the Prussian invasion of Silesia in December shifted British calculations regarding the war with Spain. Similar re-calculations occurred during the War of Spanish Succession when the Emperor Joseph I died in April 1711.[6] Natural events such as the weather and disease could also be important in a world that was highly vulnerable to both. Operations in the West Indies were usually predicated on the necessity to move rapidly before disease inevitably diminished the numbers and vitality of non-immune expeditionary forces. The frustrations with long delays caused by bad weather were common throughout the century among ministers whose reputations dependent upon success.

These influences and perceptions continually adjusted and developed. The threats, opportunities, the possible objectives and range of options available to the decision-makers change. However, once the choice was made it had to be converted into policy and action. Seldom can the decision-makers do this themselves. They had to rely upon the institutions and actors that influenced the framing of the situation. To do anything other than that which makes sense to those influencers would be to risk decisions being altered, amended, and negated by these important groups and individuals in the process of implementation. Their support provided the political and professional weight behind the decisions. Prospect Theory fits the behaviour of many governments in the way they explain or present policy. If people are more inclined to support decisive military action when they feel that the state is on the verge of losing something valuable, it will be more difficult to get support for action if is presented as an unadulterated plundering operation. It is probably no coincidence that the history of imperial expansions, often articulated by aggressive, optimistic rhetoric, are also accompanied by dire warnings of imminent decline or catastrophe if the expansionist option is neglected.[7]

Seen in this light, strategic decision-making has two important features. The first is that the reality seldom conforms to an idealised model of a rational,

---

[5] O'Shaughnessy, A.J. 'The Formation of a Commercial Lobby: The West India Interest. British Colonial Policy and the American Revolution'. *Historical Journal* 40, no. 1 (1997).

[6] Hattendorf, J.B., *England in the War of the Spanish Succession: A Study of the English View and Conduct of Grand Strategy, 1702–1712*. New York: Garland Publishing, 1987, pp. 238–245.

[7] Anon, *A Letter from a Merchant to a Member of Parliament Relating to the Danger Great Britain Is in of Losing Her Trade by the Great Increase of the Naval Power of Spain*. London 1718.

intellectual exercise of a single mind (whether individual or corporate) focused upon defined problems. Decisions embody the influences of many actors which are rational, ideological, and emotional. Second, it suggests that strategy implementation is equally diffused. Whatever the formal decision-making machinery of state, the key influencers may be located anywhere in the political system. Their influence may be fleeting, but as timing is critical in any situation, that influence may well exceed any long-term leverage they may hold. Nonetheless, while strategic policy flows from inception to execution through their areas of influence its power and direction will be affected.

During the wars from 1739 to 1763 one of the most important influences in framing decisions was the Royal Navy. Its influence was at least two-fold. The first was the professional expertise that it could put into the decision-making process. How far did the knowledge of professional seamen inform the decisions? How far was that knowledge transferred to the decision-makers in terms of understanding what they were being told and being able to act upon it? The second was the image of the Royal Navy held by the politically active population. How far did their belief in what the Royal Navy was, or could do, underpin the pressure the public put on the decision-makers? Finally, how far did the professional knowledge of experienced seamen and the public perception of the Royal Navy influence the implementation of those strategic decisions?

The traditional view of British ministerial decision-making during this period has generally been extremely negative. The two individuals who dominated the ministry, Sir Robert Walpole and the duke of Newcastle, have been characterised as indecisive, unsteady and ignorant.[8] Much of this is based upon the powerful narrative of the contemporary political opposition to Walpole and the Old Corps Whigs. It was reinforced for later generations, who were able to see the strong contrast with the ministry of William Pitt the Elder between 1757 and 1761. Pitt's strategic vision and ministerial leadership were presented as inspired and decisive. It is well-known that Pitt's political survival depended upon his public image. Pit depended on public support as a counterweight to his lack of influence within the king's closet and he was highly successful in the manipulation of the newspaper and pamphlet literature to present his image and promote his popularity.[9] The images of patriotism,

---

[8] Richmond, H.W., *Statesmen and Sea Power*. Oxford: Clarendon Press, 1946, p. 112; Williams, Basil, *Carteret and Newcastle: A Contrast in Contemporaries*. Cambridge: Cambridge University Press, 1943, p. 114; Langford, Paul, *The Eighteenth Century, 1688–1815*. Oxford: Oxford University Press, 1976, p. 115.

[9] Langford, Paul, 'William Pitt and Public Opinion, 1757'. *English Historical Review* 88 (1973); Peters, Marie, 'The Myth of William Pitt, Earl of Chatham, Great Imperialist Part I: Pitt and Imperial Expansion 1738–1763'. *The Journal of Imperial and Commonwealth History* 21, no. 1 (1993): 31–74.

vision, and leadership were tightly woven in a manner that successfully framed the problems and the narrative of the late 1750s. The role of the press in its antipathy to Walpole and support for Pitt is an established historiographical element of the middle decades of the eighteenth century, but its impact on the framing of strategic decisions of the 1730s and 1740s has been less fully explored.[10] During the peak of its influence in the late 1730s and again the mid-1750s, it proselytised the mission of the Royal Navy as the weapon that could decisively reverse the decline of British fortunes and this had a great impact on how the problems and the responses of government were framed. Between 1688 and 1714 the British public and representatives in Parliament developed a stronger understanding of their navy and its capabilities. The wars of 1689–1697, and 1701–1713 produced many events and forced many explanations that enhanced public understanding of their navy.[11] The press campaigns against Spain in the 1730s added further weight to significance of naval opinion.

By the early summer of 1739 the decision parameters concerning Anglo-Spanish relations had aligned to make options extremely narrow. The convoluted evolution of Anglo-Spanish diplomatic relations between 1715 and 1738 cannot be described here, but a few general comments can be made.[12] The interference by Spanish coastguards in British West Indian trade was not just an affront to honour and an unacceptable burden on merchants, but a direct threat to Britain's future. If Spain managed to disrupt this trade it would soon be taken over by France. Already, by the late 1720s, French sugars were driving British sugar out of the lucrative European re-export trade.[13] It might only be a matter of time before British trade was swamped by French colonial produce. To Spain, these anxieties were merely a cover to trade illegally with her colonies and if this were permitted it would not be long before Britain would engulf that trade and effectively divert the vital

---

[10] Harris, Robert, *A Patriot Press: National Politics and the London Press in the 1740s*. Oxford: Oxford University Press, 1995; Peters, Marie, *Pitt and Popularity: The Patriot Minister and London Opinion During the Seven Years War*. Oxford: Clarendon Press, 1980.

[11] Johnston, J.A. 'Parliament and the Navy, 1688–1714', PhD thesis, University of Sheffield, 1968; Denman, Timothy J., 'The Political Debate over Strategy, 1689–1712'. Unpublished PhD thesis, University of Cambridge, 1985.

[12] The best modern study of the diplomacy leading to the war is Woodfine, Philip, *Britannia's Glories: The Walpole Ministry and the 1739 War with Spain*. Woodbridge: Boydell Press, 1998.

[13] Butel, Paul, 'France, the Antilles and Europe in the Seventeenth and Eighteenth Centuries: Renewals of Foreign Trade'. In *The Rise of Merchant Empires: Long-Distance Trade in the Early Modern World, 1350–1750*, edited by James D. Tracy. Cambridge: Cambridge University Press, 1990, pp. 152–173.

trans-Atlantic bullion flow.[14] Both monarchies perceived themselves as being under existential attack.

By 1738 several diplomatic initiatives had failed to resolve the points of contention with Spain and a growing section of British political opinion was proclaiming that it would only be resolved by force. That force was at hand in the shape of the Royal Navy. This argument shifted the framing of the problem from a diplomatic to a military one which possessed an internal logic that made it difficult for the decision-makers to resist. For over twenty years there was a popular belief that British naval power was second to none. If it were true that Britain possessed overwhelming naval superiority then she had nothing to fear from Spain and had an easy and effective means of resolving the dispute. Direct action by seizure of territory in Spanish America, and a commercial blockade of her ports would rapidly force Spain to terms. The enthusiasts for war could point to the repeated failure of negotiations and, in contrast, they could also point to a long history of naval success, going back to the days of the Anglo-Spanish war of 1585–1604 and Cromwell's seizure of Jamaica in 1655. They also linked the opportunities of war to the mythological cultural identity of Britain as a natural maritime power that could not fail to defeat at sea the land-focused monarchies of Europe.[15] Thus, by 1739 the parameters within which a decision would be made were powerfully in favour of war – war was necessary and it would be easily won. There was an urgent existential threat that could quickly and easily be solved. This dominant narrative did not emanate from the formal strategic leaders. Rather it came from within the public political debates of the time. Of course the decision-makers could adopt any policy that they desired, but any other strategic decision would demand the building of a counter narrative to support continued negotiation, reframing the problem again as a diplomatic one. Over the years, Walpole had failed to win the pamphlet and press debates, despite the best efforts of his brother Horace. By 1739 it is highly questionable if it was possible for Walpole and his colleagues to reframe the problem to avoid war, but, in any event, it would have taken time which they no longer had. Crucially, there were by then many within the decision-making group, including the king, the secretary of state for the Southern Department, the duke of Newcastle, and the first lord of the admiralty, Sir Charles Wager, who now believed that the military option was the only reasonable and politically feasible one. Eventually, even Sir Robert Walpole was reluctantly forced to agree. Whether, objectively, anything had

---

[14] Sperling, John G., *The South Sea Company: An Historical Essay and Bibliographical Finding List*. Boston: Harvard Graduate School of Business Administration, 1962.

[15] Anon., *The Present State of Europe Explaining the Interests, Connections, Political and Commercial Views of Its Several Powers*, 5th ed. London: Longman, 1757, pp. 505–508.

changed in Britain's economic or diplomatic environment to make immediate action essential did not matter. The belief that Britain's future was on a knife edge and that the problem could be easily solved by a different, bellicose, policy was all that counted to impose a framework on the decision options.

At the fringes of the opposition attacks on Walpole there were assertion that he was a traitor, in league with the Bourbon monarchies to undermine Britain. This was uncomfortable, but had no great traction with the majority opinion either inside or outside of Parliament. What was far more damaging was the belief that Walpole's ministry had not stood up to the reviving power of those monarchies. British neutrality during the War of Polish Succession (1733–1738) had left Austria exposed to French and Spanish pressure on the Rhine and in Italy and although the war had ended in 1738 without a significant change in the European balance of power, it reinforced the idea that the ministry 'were mere Blunderers in politicks'.[16] Similarly, tolerating the insults of Spain for decades left the impression that the ministry would 'not be talked into Wars and Fighting, nor will they be guilty of the Effusion of Catholick Blood to satisfy their turbulent Humour'.[17]

Furthermore, there was the perception that the international conditions were right for war with Spain. Britain's allies, Portugal and the United Provinces would remain neutral, but it was believed so would France. Spain would be forced to face British naval power alone and public opinion could hardly believe that Madrid could stand the hammer blows to her trade and colonies that this power would rapidly inflict. To wait would be to risk France taking a more active part. It was here that the naval opinion played a part. In the summer of 1738, the first lord of the admiralty, Sir Charles Wager, had an assessment that the optimum time to strike had arrived.[18]

From the latter part of 1737 diplomatic and political events reinforced the narrative of unacceptable and pointless British subservience to Spanish insolence. The articulation of the frustration in the pamphlet and newspaper press was increasingly influential in framing a looming crises for Britain. With the failure of Spain to pay the £95,000 stipulated in the Convention of the Pardo in June 1739, the ministry was left without a credible counter narrative for the future and war was accepted by the ministry.

This was a major turn-around from the early 1730s. In 1732, Britain appeared to have stable and strong strategic frame. Under Sir Robert Walpole's administration Britain had lost an alliance with France in the late 1720s, but successfully

---

[16] Walpole, Horace, *A Letter to the Craftsman, Upon the Change of Affairs in Europe by the War That Is Begun against the Emperour*. London: J. Roberts, 1734, p. 4.

[17] Anon., *The Ministerial Virtue: Or Long-Suffering Extolled in a Great Man*. London: J. Purser, 1738, p. iii.

[18] B.L., Add. Ms 19036 (Wager Papers). Forces of France.

followed a broadly neutral policy in relation to central European affairs, underpinned by a conservative fiscal policy. The institutional decision-makers, the monarch, and the ministry had a common understanding of foreign policy issues. The key interests – those things that, if they were lost would seem catastrophic to contemporaries – were the Protestant succession, the protection of British trade, the exclusion of France from Flanders, and the integrity of George II's electoral possessions in Hanover. These were understood and supported by a substantial majority in Parliament. The ministry was also effectively linked to the administrative and operational systems, such as the admiralty, the treasury, the diplomatic service and the board of Trade which provided information and advice on capabilities and threats.

Within this network the Royal Navy also held an important position. The navy held a special place in British political ideology. It was seen as the key bastion of the defence of domestic political liberties and national independence. The nation that depended on maritime commerce and colonial produce and the navy preserved this wealth and prosperity.[19] The navy had become an institution, with influence on social and political assumptions.[20] It was embedded deeply in state decision-making. Since the Hanoverian succession in 1714 the post of first lord of the admiralty was always held by a senior naval officer, who attended the Cabinet. Professional opinion was integrated into strategic decisions and policy. In 1739, when the question of war with Spain was being discussed, the first lord, Admiral Sir Charles Wager, was joined in Cabinet by the admiral of the fleet, Sir John Norris for detailed discussions of plans.[21]

A Whig hegemony since 1714 and Walpolian domination since 1721 appeared to have created a powerful strategic leadership position – a solid network of interest, an administrative system that was well connected to the decision-makers and in a position to provide relatively good domestic and foreign intelligence. However, as always, the ground was shifting and the strength of the formal influences on policy was eclipsed by bellicose influences, pushing the ministry to war, which was agreed in June 1739 and declared on 19 October that year.

What happened to national strategic leadership in this situation? Strategic decision-making still lay where it should, with the king in Cabinet, but they were not leading the framing of the problem. They were certainly a major part of that process and they constructed policy that responded to the framework of an urgent strategic threat, but the dominant narrative, that war was necessary

---

[19] Harding, Richard, 'Naval Ideology and Its Operational Impact in Eighteenth Century Britain'. In *Ideologies of Western Naval Power, C. 1500–1815*, edited by J.D. Davies, Alan James, and Gijs Rommelse. Abingdon: Routledge, 2020, pp. 262–279.

[20] North, Douglas C. 'Institutions'. *Journal of Economic Perspectives* 5, no. 1 (1991): 97–112.

[21] British Library, Add. Ms. 28132 (Journal of Sir John Norris, 1737–1740).

and easily winnable, came largely from the political opposition. It was in tune not just with a relatively small group of aggressive expansionist merchants, but with a far larger political community to whom the loss of maritime trade was worrying.

Accepting the war narrative allowed the ministry to recover the strategic leadership of war policy. It constructed the expeditionary force that was to be sent to the West Indies to take and hold an important part of Spain's American empire. The ministry could rejoice along with the opposition when, in March 1740, news arrived of Admiral Vernon's capture of Porto Bello in November 1739. Walpole was to remain under political pressure, but his final loss of power early in 1742 was not the direct result of trying to assert a leadership role that was contrary to the dominant strategic narrative.[22]

Long before Walpole's fall the situation was changing. By the summer of 1740 France nudged the narrative in a different direction. Cardinal Fleury's ambivalent attitude to the war had concerned ministers throughout 1739, and by July 1740 the British ministry had to plan to fight both the French and Spanish fleets if they joined. In September 1740 Fleury dramatically clarified the position by the despatch of the Brest and Toulon squadrons to the West Indies. The British ministry had to assume it was facing an imminent Franco-Spanish war and strategy had to be driven from that perspective. War had to be accepted if it occurred, but little could be done in the short term. There was no long-term plan to deal with the French threat. The leadership of strategy had again slipped the ministry's hands by the intervention of France. Strategy was being driven by events

As it happened war with France in the West Indies was avoided that autumn despite a minor clash at sea and it seemed that the strategy for bringing about a successful peace with Spain could be followed through. However there is no clear evidence in the surviving documents of how the ministry might have adapted policy if a war with France had broken out in the autumn of 1740. By early 1741 the situation had changed again. The death the Emperor Charles VI in October 1740 was followed by the Prussian invasion of Silesia in December and then the claim to the imperial throne by Charles Albert of Bavaria. He was supported by France and Spain whose price would no doubt be compensation at the expense of Habsburg domains.

This forced another fundamental shift in the strategic frame for Britain. Spain and France were advancing armies into Germany and Italy. This might have made the resolution of the British dispute simpler in that it distracted both powers from British objectives in the West Indies. However, Britain could not ignore events in Europe. Despite differences, Austria was seen as the balance to the Bourbon powers in Europe and anything that reduced

---

[22] Harding, Richard, *The Emergence of Britain's Global Naval Supremacy: The War of 1739–1748*. Woodbridge: Boydell and Brewer, 2010.

Austria was a threat to that balance. In the autumn of 1741 Austria appeared on the verge of collapse, and preventing this suddenly intruded as a major factor in the strategic framing process. King George, as elector of Hanover and king of Great Britain was determined to honour his treaty obligations to the Habsburgs and support their claim through Maria Theresa's husband, Francis Duke of Lorraine to the imperial throne. However, French forces in Germany posed a clear threat to the electorate. Neither Britain nor Austria could provide the military support Hanover needed and George decided that neutrality for his electorate was his only strategic option. Ultimately, for the king, the existential threat to his electorate outweighed other considerations. He carefully distinguished between his actions as elector and those as king of Great Britain. Astutely, he would not tie the British response to neutrality, but he did demand that British decision-making incorporated Hanoverian neutrality as a key strategic factor.

Clearly, George was playing the role of a strategic leader, but in doing so, he further fragmented the strategic framing process. Parliamentary opinion had no real problem with incorporating the defence of Austria into its strategic frame. Even the defence of Hanover was acceptable. However, as Britain geared up to support Austria in the Mediterranean and in Flanders, the announcement of Hanoverian neutrality created doubts in the minds of some that George really had British interests at heart. For over eighteen months this doubt persisted and with it pressure to ensure that British resources were not being diverted for the defence of purely electoral purposes. It was not until the Jacobite rising of 1745 that this complication began to fade.

In the meantime, the fragmentation within the framing process went from bad to worse. In February 1742 Walpole fell from office. This did not mean the wholesale removal of the administration. The duke of Newcastle, who had been secretary of state for the Southern Department for twenty-four years remained in office along with many of the Old Corps Whigs, but they had to make room new allies from the opposition, including earl Carteret, whose personal objective, despite having leveraged political power by championing the war with Spain, rapidly shifted to securing himself by championing the king's concern for Hanover. Newcastle and his friends, who had gone through the turmoil of 1738–1739, were aware that British commercial interests in America were framed as the existential strategic objective, also recognised that Hanover had to be protected, but were never reconciled to Carteret's view that resolving the key issues of the war lay in Germany. For the next four years, until the final removal of Carteret in February 1746 the infighting created by political and strategic differences contributed to a further fragmentation of the strategic framing process. The alienation of the ministry from the king was reaching breaking point in September 1745 when news of the Jacobite successes in Scotland forced them to focus on the ultimate strategic objective – survival of the dynasty.

Several other things contributed to the fragmentation of strategic framing. Sir Charles Wager, the first lord of the admiralty left office with Walpole. He was replaced by the earl of Winchelsea, a man of no naval experience and who acknowledged himself unsuited to the job. The admiral of the fleet, Sir John Norris, who had seen himself as Wager's successor, was increasingly alienated and unwilling to work with Winchelsea, until finally, in March 1744 he resigned. For the first time since October 1714, the Cabinet was left without a senior naval officer as a member of the decision-making group.

During this period public confidence in the Royal Navy and the expeditionary strategy also began to decline. Belief in the power and competence of the navy, was deeply embedded in British political culture and played an important part in framing the options in 1739. The West Indian expedition, which had been reinforced in 1741, finally returned home at the end of 1742 in ignominious failure. The navy proved unable to prevent Spanish and French naval operations in support of the Bourbons in Italy. In February 1744 the Brest squadron was off Dungeness to support a French invasion from Flanders. Bad weather rather than naval power seemed to have saved the day. Public confidence in the Royal Navy and the voice of naval leadership were fading away together.

This did not mean that other options could immediately emerge. The land campaigns also proved disappointing. Ensuring France was kept out of Flanders was a strategic objective that was generally shared as essential to British security. British resources to subsidise Austria and other powers to provide troops for Flanders and the movement of British troops into Flanders to encourage Austrian and Dutch participation, were largely uncontentious – in contrast to similar actions that might be construed purely to assist Hanover. The problem was that they proved ineffective. The campaign of 1743 diverted the Pragmatic Army to Germany. The campaign of 1744 was disappointing and that of 1745 was a disaster. The battle of Fontenoy (May 1745) ended any hope of decisively dislodging the French from Flanders. The next two years only reinforced this as Marshal de Saxe manoeuvred the French army towards the Dutch border. Antwerp fell in May 1746. By the end of the year, Mons, Liège, and Namur were in French hands, leaving only Maastricht as a major route connecting the allies in Flanders to the Imperial territories to the east. By the end of April 1747 the forts along the Scheldt estuary were in French hands and the great fortress town of Bergen-op-Zoom fell to the French in September.

From the perspective of strategic framing, the other great event of the period, the Jacobite rising of 1745/6 was less disruptive. In June 1745, a month before Prince Charles Edward Stuart landed in Scotland, Britain was on the defensive in every theatre. Strategic ambition had shrunk at least temporarily to the defence of the Hanoverian succession and the home islands. It was a shared priority that few in the political system would dispute. Strategic leadership options were now being framed by survival for a few months. During its course the rebellion caused a mighty scare which drove other priorities down the agenda, thereby reducing the fragmentation of strategic leadership.

However, once the rebellion was decisively crushed the fact remained that strategically Britain remained on the back foot, but it was clear that some of the fragmentation in the framing process was diminishing. The issue of trade to the Caribbean, which had dominated the narrative between 1738–1739, had largely evaporated. Indeed, far from being an existential factor in the equation, the resolution was left until two years after the major peace treaties, and then largely on basis of Britain giving up the *Asiento*, the contract to supply slaves to Spanish America, which was the cause of so many other commercial problems between the two powers. The defence of Austria, so important in 1741–1743, was sliding from the frame. Ensuring the integrity of Hanover that had fragmented the framing of the situation between 1741 and 1746 was now less contentious. The parliamentary and extra-parliamentary opposition which had so much influence on the leadership process from 1738 ceased to play a major role until long after the end of the war. Countering French operations in Flanders that had dominated the strategic context in 1742–1745 was still seen as vital, but increasingly recognised as being only possible through indirect means. Those indirect means, attacks on French trade and colonies had been part of policy since 1744. French trade to the Caribbean was severely distressed and Louisbourg had fallen in July 1745. This policy did not deliver a decisive advantage for a number of reasons. A Canadian expedition fell through in 1746 and the fall of Madras to the French in 1747 ended hopes there. Nevertheless, among the most influential actors in the strategic framing process, this indirect pressure remained the only realistic option.

Over the last full year of the war pressures intruding on the framing process continued, but were far less disruptive. The general election of 1747, which could have produced more issues, was a success for the ministry. The revolution at The Hague in 1747 assisted plans to keep the Dutch engaged in the war. The Royal Navy, whose strategic influence had declined dramatically between 1741 and 1745, was gradually re-establishing itself. At one stage in 1745 Vice Admiral Edward Vernon, a man far from universally trusted, was the only senior officer of serious influence with the ministry. The emergence of George Anson as a political and professional leader began the process of recovery which was far from complete when the war ended.

Throughout the war the formal strategic decision-making process was clear. It remained with the king in Cabinet and those institutional strategic leaders knew their responsibilities. However, it could not be claimed that they exercised decisive strategic leadership. It was not in the power of king or Cabinet to dominate the strategic framing process. They were important leadership actors, but their ability to frame the strategic purpose was contested, particularly with regard to Hanover. Similarly, those championing a naval war did not have it all their own way. They certainly could rely upon a broad consensus that British trade was vital to her security and wealth. They could also rely on the plausibility of the claim that it was under threat, not just from Spain, but more importantly, France. What they could not do was demonstrate that the Royal Navy could achieve decisive success against the Bourbon powers. The performance of the navy simply did not provide that evidence of decisive influence. Despite the energy put into the plan to capture Quebec in 1746 in order to force France to evacuate its conquests in Germany and Flanders it had to be called off. Nor could they demonstrate that Flanders would be secure without the Dutch and Austrian alliances. Finally, despite public disquiet, they could not demonstrate that the preservation of the king's Hanoverian electorate was not in British interests.

Between 1748 and 1756 there were important shifts in the conditions that influenced the strategic framing in Britain. The Diplomatic Revolution (1753–1756) changed the value of both Flanders and Austria in decision-making. Despite the fears of a Franco-Austrian Catholic domination of Europe, Flanders and the United Provinces were actually protected by the Austro-French agreements. The threat to Hanover remained real, but the alliance with Prussia proved effective over the course of the Seven Years War. Very important was Spain's neutrality in that war which greatly simplified the strategic problem for Britain.

However, among the most important of all these changes was the public perception of the Royal Navy. Public confidence was returning after the successful battles off Finisterre in May and October 1747. Although the post of first lord of the admiralty remained in the hands of noblemen, the duke of Bedford and the earl of Sandwich, Admiral George Anson, had joined the board in December 1744 and played an important role in re-connecting public political opinion, ministerial confidence, and policymaking. Anson was the hero who captured the fabulously rich Manila galleon, *Nuestra Senora de Covadonga* in June 1743 and after the completion of his circumnavigation of the world in June 1744, he was a naval officer who stood high in public esteem. On his return home he was quickly incorporated into the political system with a seat on the board of admiralty. His service on the board and at sea, together with that of a few other officers, started the process of re-establishing public belief. Nonetheless, it took a long time. Between 1755 and 1758 the navy had many successes, but nothing to demonstrate that it could make a decisive diplomatic impact on the overall balance of forces in the Seven Years War. The implications of the threat of invasion, the loss of Minorca, the invasion of Hanover, the disappointing results of raids on the coast of France, disappointments and defeats in North America, created enough concern to keep the British political classes behind the war, but by the middle of 1759 even

William Pitt was concerned how the war was to be continued another year with prospects of a successful peace.[23]

The last three months of 1759 made all the difference. The fall of Quebec and Hawke's victory at Quiberon Bay in September and November respectively opened the way for a series of spectacular victories and conquests between 1760 and 1762. The prospect of working towards a peace that avoided important losses was replaced by that of magnificent gains from Canada, the French and Spanish colonies in the West Indies, the coast of Africa, and the Indian sub-continent. This was expansion at the cost of other European powers on a scale never before seen. The enthusiasm for an aggressive, acquisitive, imperial war coincided with the accession of George III, who declared that he gloried in the name of Britain and had little concern for Hanover. Together, these events between 1759 to 1762 changed the frame for foreign policy strategy. The experience and capability of British political, military, administrative, and economic institutions seemed to open possibilities for empire that had not existed before. Debates now focused on how to consolidate that empire. In order to have peace what should be given back to Britain's enemies? What concessions should be made to placate Britain's European allies? William Pitt, and some others in the ministry, understood the close relationship between Britain's maritime success and the support given to European allies. British naval power worked best in conjunction with British financial, military, and diplomatic power to manage crises in Europe. However, others were convinced that the successes of 1759–1762 proved the long-held belief that Britain was a natural naval and maritime power and was better off avoiding European conflicts completely.[24] At the time it was difficult to prove either contention, and the euphoria did not last long. However, the idea that British naval power could have a decisive diplomatic impact on Europe – an idea which had existed for over a century – now seemed to have been demonstrated beyond contention. It informed British strategy ever since, playing a part in framing the debates and continues to have a resonance to the present day. Although it never exercised a hegemonic appeal to the British public, it was nonetheless, a deeply embedded ideological axiom that persisted throughout the nineteenth century, providing a stability to the framing of strategic questions. How that ideology lost its force at the beginning of the twentieth century, leading to a reframing of the questions and ultimately permitting Britain to engage as a

---

[23] Harding, R., 'British Maritime Strategy and Hanover, 1714–1763'. In *The Hanoverian Dimension in British History, 1714–1837*, edited by B. Sims and T. Riotte. Cambridge: Cambridge University Press, 2007, pp. 252–274.

[24] See for example, Mauduit, Israel. *Considerations on the Present German War*. London: John Wilkie, 1760.

continental power with a mass conscript army in the 1914–1918 war is one of the most important questions of that period.[25]

Does this history of decision-making in the war of 1739–1748 have any significance for today? The ministries of the period have been seen as weak and purposeless. They are contrasted negatively with the ministries led by the great war leaders, particularly that of the near contemporary William Pitt the Elder. But if viewed as a ministry responding to particular circumstances it might hint at something that is relevant. Strategic leadership was seldom monolithic or located in one place for long. The actors that were strong decision influences were in flux throughout the period. They created a frame for the essential question of the moment that shifted from a diplomatic resolution to long-running Anglo-Spanish discontents to one that described it as an existential naval/commercial issue that demanded naval action. This was overtaken by others that framed the key issues as Hanoverian domination, a rising French threat and even the preservation of the Hanoverian Succession. Those that framed the problem as soluble by military or naval means found they were proven wrong by events. Nevertheless, it was not obvious where or if alterative leaders and strategies would emerge. Throughout the war, interventions from allies and enemies continued to influence how the key strategic questions should be framed. These actors were unpredictable in their emergence and impact. Domestic and diplomatic actors fed into the decision-making process, many of which destabilised the formal decision-making body. That destabilisation, which was becoming apparent in late 1737 continued, more or less, until 1759, when for a short period both domestic and military influencers stood clearly around a strategy that generated victories around the world and preserved essential defences in Europe. This emerged gradually and by the end of 1761 was beginning to fragment again.

Perhaps this is the nature of strategic leadership. Challenges and shocks to long-range planning and long-held assumptions have always existed. The locus of strategic leadership is constantly shifting. The power of individual actors change as new issues and priorities enter the framing process. Formal strategic leaders accustomed to the chess board or poker analogies may feel dangerously exposed. Those hoping to reduce their engagement to the management of rational decisions may feel overwhelmed by the irrationality and the disturbing sight of strategic trajectories being established without any apparent leadership.

By 1739 the Royal Navy had become an important actor within the strategic framing process in Britain. It was institutionally embedded in the British state during the second half of the seventeenth century, and the wars ending in 1713 had increased the public understanding of the navy as a powerful

---

[25] Lambert, Andrew. *The British Way of War: Julian Corbett and the Battle for a National Strategy*. New Haven: Yale University Press, 2021.

weapon. Indeed public expectations of its potency were raised far higher than its operational capability. Nonetheless, the belief enhanced the power of the navy within the strategy framing process. It also gave professional naval opinion weight in the decision-making process. Professional knowledge in the form of officers like Sir Charles Wager and Sir John Norris was accessed by the executive decision-makers and shaped strategic policy. Between 1742 and 1745 the collapse of that access to professional knowledge with the resignation of Wager and then Norris, the emergence of the crisis in central Europe, the disappointing operational results and eventually the opening of the war with France, significantly diminished professional naval influence. However, these crises did not reframe the fundamental strategic question or provide attractive alternative policy. It took years to re-build the public and professional influence of the Royal Navy, but it had begun in 1745/6 and had achieved enough by 1748 to re-establish confidence. By the time of the accession of George III in October 1760 public support for the Royal Navy and professional expertise were again major influences on British decision-makers. Their influence waxed and waned over the decades, but it has remained a constant presence to the present day.

4

The Statesman and the Naval Leader: The Count of Floridablanca and Navy Minister Antonio Valdés, 1783–1792

AGUSTÍN GUIMERÁ

In 1783, after the signing of the Treaty of Versailles, which brought the American Revolution (1776–1783) to an end, the land area of Spain's possessions in the Americas was larger than at any other point in history. Covering more than 16 million square kilometers, the Spanish Empire included a large part of both the North American and the South American continents. It extended all the way from California in the north Pacific, through the powerful viceroyalties of New Spain and Peru, to Tierra del Fuego, and the viceroyalty of Río de la Plata in the south Atlantic, and included the provinces of New Mexico, Texas, Louisiana, and Florida; the viceroyalty of Nueva Granada and several captaincies general; and the large Caribbean islands of Cuba, Puerto Rico, and Santo Domingo, in addition to the archipelago of the Philippines.

However, in spite of all it had achieved, after the war this huge empire was faced with a number of challenges. Historians today point to the end of the reign of Carlos III (1759–1788) as the beginning of a period of crisis for the Spanish monarchy. The Bourbon Reforms, as they are known, were reaching their limits. This was due in part to factors internal to the Spanish monarchy.[1] But there was a later phase characterized by renewed attempts at reform. This is the period between 1783 and 1792, during the tenure of the

---

[1] López-Cordón, M.V. , "Entre Francia e Inglaterra. Intereses estratégicos y acuerdos políticos como antecedentes de Trafalgar," in *Trafalgar y el mundo atlántico*, ed. Guimerá, A., Ramos, A., and Butrón, G. (Madrid: Marcial Pons, 2004), pp. 19–60; Molas i Ribalta, P. and Agustín Guimerá Ravina (ed.), *La España de Carlos IV* (Madrid, 1991), pp. 141–167; and Seco Serrano, C., "La política exterior de Carlos IV," in *Historia de España fundada por Ramón Menéndez Pidal y dirigida por José María Jover Zamora. Tomo XXXI. La época de la Ilustración. Volumen 2. Las Indias y la política exterior* (Madrid: Espasa Calpe, 1988), pp. 449–732.

Count of Floridablanca as secretary of state – the most powerful position in the government – which coincides with the creation of a new political institution: the Junta de Estado (1787–1792), a council of state that functioned as a true cabinet.[2]

In the present chapter, I focus on the aspects of reform that involved the navy. I attempt to analyze the importance of the support given by Floridablanca to the secretary of the navy, Antonio Valdés (1783–1795), a naval commander who played a leading role in the junta.

In a society based on privilege, like Spain's in the eighteenth century, in which there was no separation between the public and private spheres, power networks were vital. This was true for the exercise of political governance as well as naval leadership. It is important to keep in mind that the court in Madrid, as the embodiment of the absolute monarchy, was the epicenter of power relations between the ruling elites in Spain and its overseas empire. It was like a force field controlled by powerful men who presided over extensive systems of patronage for securing posts, resources, honors, and sinecures: the empire "was governed not through institutions but rather through men."[3] To govern, therefore, also meant to manage private relationships. To govern was to negotiate even more than to give orders. Political and naval leaders thus moved in an unstable political space.

My hypothesis is that Floridablanca's and Valdés's close collaboration during the period 1783–1792 made it possible for Spain's Real Armada (Royal Navy) to perform more effectively than at any other point in the eighteenth century, to become more organized, and to grow its personnel, infrastructure, science, technology, war fleet, armaments, supplies, and other military resources to new levels. This enabled the navy to fulfill, to the utmost of its capabilities, its function within Spain's imperial strategy. It was to be a deterrent in order to safeguard and defend Spain's maritime empire. In other words, the expert – in this case, the naval commander – was heeded by the statesman.

José Moñino, count of Floridablanca (1728–1808), rose to the post of secretary of state (1777–1792) by virtue of his own merit, in contrast to other politicians of his day, who relied on their aristocratic connections. He was a member of a second rank noble family from Murcia and a Bachelor of Law.

---

[2] Bernal, A.M., *España, proyecto inacabado. Costes/beneficios del imperio* (Madrid: Marcial Pons, 2005); Delgado Ribas, J.M., "América en la teoría y praxis política de José Moñino y Redondo, Conde de Floridablanca," *Hacienda Pública Española*, 108–109 (1987); Delgado Ribas, J.M., *Dinámicas imperiales (1650–1796). España, América y Europa en el cambio institucional del sistema colonial español* (Barcelona: Ediciones Bellaterra, 2007); and *El reformismo borbónico: una visión interdisciplinar*, ed. Guimerá, A. (Madrid: Alianza Editorial, 1996).

[3] Imízcoz Beunza, J. M., "El entramado social y político," in *Historia de España en la Edad Moderna*, ed. Floristán, A. (Barcelona, 2004), p. 67.

His distinguished career in government was the result of both his personal qualities and his professional competence. His methodical mind, training and erudition in history and law, composure in any and all situations, and the calm and compelling style of his juridical writing caught the attention of the court. He rose through the administrative ranks, going from jurist to diplomat: he was appointed Alcalde de Casa y Corte (1763), Fiscal of the Council of Castile (1766), and ambassador to Rome (1772).

Rome was where he honed his skills in the delicate art of negotiation, where he learned to apply an admixture of secrecy, face-to-face conversation, and persistence in pressing his points, along with subtle reminders of the political and military power of the monarchy he was there to represent. A defender of the law of nations and a strict Catholic, he was convinced that politics should be guided by religion and moral rectitude, and he went to great lengths to make sure that the pacts he negotiated were complied with. While in Rome, he was able to convince the pope to approve the expulsion of the Jesuits – which the Spanish monarchy had decreed in 1767 – and for this he was granted the title of count. In conclusion, he was a paragon of moderate reform who carried forward the work done by his predecessors as secretaries of the navy.[4]

Antonio Valdés (1744–1816) also came from a second rank noble family, in his case from Asturias, whose members had held important public offices and belonged to the military orders of Calatrava and San Juan. Valdés himself was made a knight of the latter order at the age of thirteen. He had a brilliant career in the navy, with an exemplary combat record: he participated in both the heroic defense of the Castillo del Morro in Havana (1762) and the war against North African privateering. But his true genius was for administration: he was appointed shipyard inspector (1775–1777), fleet inspector (1775–1778), the director of the Artillery Factory of La Cabada in Santander (1781) and inspector general of the navy (1783), all positions that were usually held by much older men. He also rapidly rose through the ranks of the Real Armada, becoming vice admiral in 1782. Thus, he had acquired solid training as an administrator as well as a good understanding of the job of being a soldier and sailor.

Because of this exceptional background and experience, Pedro González de Castejón (1775–1783), secretary of the navy at the time, recommended to the king that Valdés be named as his successor. When he assumed the post

---

[4] Hernández Franco, J., *La gestión política y el pensamiento reformista del conde de Floridablanca* (Murcia, 1984); Hernández Franco, J., *Aspectos de la política exterior de España en la época de Floridablanca* (Murcia, 1992); and *Floridablanca, 1728–1808. La utopía reformadora* (Murcia: Fundación Cajamurcia, 2008).

in March 1783, Valdés was only 38 years old, a very young age to hold such an important political office.[5]

In the eighteenth century, for a mercantilist nation such as Spain to defend its empire – its colonial possessions and its monopoly over Spanish-American trade – and preserve the international balance of power, it needed a powerful military and an extensive diplomatic network, both of which required the efficient administrative and fiscal systems. As a result, the Spanish government had instituted an ambitious program of reforms known as the "Bourbon Reforms," which were adopted between approximately 1750 and 1795. In doing so, Spain followed the lead of other European powers seeking to improve their domestic circumstances as well as their security, given the increasingly difficult international context.

Despite the territorial gains that Spain had secured as a result of its participation in the American Revolutionary War, Floridablanca's government was faced with the same challenges as always. Two colossal powers threatened the borders of its empire and its maritime trade: Great Britain and France. The two powers had advantages over Spain in many areas: in population, agriculture, trade, manufacturing, finance, and so on. In the case of Great Britain, an unbridgeable divide separated institutions such as Parliament from the Spanish monarchy. Despite the defeats it had suffered in the American war, the British Royal Navy's superiority over the navies of the two Bourbon powers was unquestionable, especially in its capacity to outfit, man, and maintain large fleets in multiple theatres over long periods of time.

---

[5] Valdés was also secretary of Indies – in the section related to war, royal treasury, trade and shipping – in 1787–1790. See Franco Rubio, G.F., "Reformismo institucional y élites administrativas en la España del siglo XVIII: nuevos oficios, nueva burocracia. La Secretaría de Estado y del Despacho de Marina (1721–1808) ," in *La pluma, la mitra y la espada. Estudios de Historia Institucional en la Edad Moderna*, eds. Castellano, J.L., Dedieu, J.P., and López-Cordón Cortezo, M.V. (Madrid-Barcelona, 2000); Guimerá, A., "Estado, administración y liderazgo naval: Antonio Valdés y Lord Barham (1783–1808) ," in *Un estado militar: España, 1650–1820*, ed. González Enciso, A. (San Sebastián de los Reyes: Actas, 2012), pp. 181–209; Guimerá, A., "Defensa del liderazgo naval: el Secretario de Marina Antonio Valdés, según Alberto Sesma (1806) ," in *Herederas de Clío. Mujeres que han impulsado la historia*, eds. Franco Rubio, G. and Pérez Samper, M.A. (Seville: Mergablum, 2014), pp. 263–275; Guimerá, A. and García Fernández, N., "Un consenso estratégico: las Ordenanzas Navales de 1793," *Anuario de Estudios Atlánticos* 54–II (2008), 43–48; Perona Tomás, A., *Los orígenes del Ministerio de Marina. La Secretaría de Estado y del Despacho de Marina, 1714–1808* (Madrid: Ministerio de Defensa, 1998), pp. 270–312; Valdés Ozores, M., *El baylío don Antonio Valdés*, doctoral thesis (Madrid: Universidad Complutense de Madrid, 1989); and Valdés Ozores, M., *El baylío don Antonio Valdés. Un gobierno eficaz del siglo XVIII* (Madrid: Libroslibres, 2004).

Spain was the third most important naval power in Europe, but its navy was directly compromised by the structural problems confronting the monarchy.

Given these limitations, Floridablanca was obliged to follow in the footsteps of his predecessors, adopting an indirect strategy whose objective was to preserve its overseas empire and its colonial trade, in addition to recovering possessions in the Americas that it had lost if the opportunity presented itself. This meant, among other things, the preservation of the balance of power among European nations. These topics have been thoroughly studied elsewhere.[6]

In his 1787 directives to the Junta de Estado, Floridablanca opted for maintaining harmony with Great Britain, even if this harmony was characterized by a lack of trust, given the peculiarities of the British system of government – Parliament – and nation. It was therefore necessary to monitor its actions constantly. There were still unresolved issues between the two governments, such as sovereignty over Gibraltar, the threat posed by Jamaica to shipping and trade in the Gulf of Mexico, British logwood-cutting establishments in Honduras, and Great Britain's interest in using the San Juan River and Lake Nicaragua. The approach to be taken should include constant vigilance over these possessions in times of peace and, if war broke out, seizing them and expelling the British. As for Gibraltar, an exchange had been proposed of either the stronghold at Oran and its port, Mazalquivir, or the Spanish half of the island of Santo Domingo, but these negotiations were unsuccessful.

Great Britain, for its part, was interested in a trade agreement with Spain that would give it direct access to Spanish American markets, while offering few concessions to Spanish shipping and trade in Great Britain and its overseas possessions. But when the British pressed for a new trade agreement, Floridablanca continued to argue that concessions should be reciprocal and mutually beneficial.

Floridablanca argued that British attempts to establish commercial bases or fishing grounds in South America should be discouraged by building fortified ports in the Strait of Magellan and Tierra de Fuego, as well as developing the existing *Compañía Marítima* for fishing in the Southern Cone.[7]

---

[6] See note 4. The sources are the "Instrucción reservada" of Floridablanca to the Junta de Estado, 08.07.1787; and the "Memorial" to the king Carlos III, 10-10-1788, and Carlos IV, 6-11-1789; in Floridablanca, conde de, *Biblioteca de autores españoles… Obras originales del Conde de Floridablanca* (Madrid: Ediciones Atlas, 1952), pp. 214–272 and 307–350. See also Floridablanca's letters to the new secretary of state, February–April 1792, in Rumeu de Armas, A., *El testamento político del conde de Floridablanca* (Madrid: CSIC, 1962); and Floridablanca, conde de, *Escritos políticos. El memorial y la instrucción*, ed. Ruiz Alemán, J. (Murcia, 1983).

[7] Instrucción of Floridablanca to the Junta de Estado, 1787; Floridablanca, *Biblioteca de autores españoles…*, pp. 214–272, articles CLXIV–CLXVI, CCCXXXV–CCCLXIII,

The linchpin for Spanish foreign policy was an alliance with France. Just like his predecessors, Floridablanca considered this alliance to be a necessary counterweight to British naval superiority. But Spain's centuries-old relationship with its neighbor, which had been defined in the so-called *Pactes de Famille* (the last of which had been signed by Floridablanca in 1779), was also characterized by a lack of rapport and by distrust. Since France was both a preeminent European power and a neighbor of Spain, Floridablanca warned of French plans to secure commercial advantages for itself, to hobble Spain's economy, and ultimately to render the Spanish monarchy a subordinate power. He provided examples of France's duplicity and disloyalty in its dealings with the Spanish monarchy. For these reasons, he argued, Spain should not be dragged into a war as a subordinate; rather, any belligerent action should be a decision made jointly by the two powers. He concluded that France might be Spain's best ally, but it could also be its worst enemy.[8]

Given the Spanish monarchy's power status vis-à-vis Great Britain and France, Floridablanca pursued a multilateral diplomatic strategy by seeking out other European alliances, with emerging powers such as Russia and Prussia, with the Austrian Empire, and with neutral nations such as Denmark or Sweden. He implemented a system of armed neutrality with the maritime powers of northern Europe during Spain's involvement in the American Revolutionary War, with the goal of isolating Great Britain. Later, Floridablanca promoted the idea that the Italian states, France, and the Netherlands should join this system, which would effectively hem in Great Britain diplomatically, forcing it to negotiate.[9]

Generally speaking, Floridablanca widened Spain's diplomatic network abroad by creating new consulates and sending delegations. He also successfully negotiated peace agreements with former enemies such as the Ottoman Empire, Tripoli, and Tunis (1782), which for centuries had threatened Spanish shipping, trade, and fishing in the western Mediterranean. Algiers, a Barbary regency that had done serious harm to Spanish interests, is the most important example of this new peace policy. Floridablanca called forcefully for negotiations with Algiers after Spanish forces bombarded the stronghold in 1783–1784. He took the preliminary steps toward a peace treaty in 1785 and obtained

---

CLXIII, XCVIII–XCLX, CIV, CVI, CIX–CXIV, CXX, and CXXXIX–CXL; and Floridablanca's letters to the new secretary of state, February–April 1792, in Rumeu de Armas, A., *El testamento político*), pp. 82, 86–90, 98, and 102.

[8] Instrucción de Floridablanca, articles CCII, CCV and CCCII–CCCXXXIV; Floridablanca, conde de, *Biblioteca de autores españoles*, pp. 214–272.

[9] Instrucción de Floridablanca, article CCCLXXII; Floridablanca, conde de, *Biblioteca de autores españoles*, pp. 214–272; and Memorial de Floridablanca to the king Carlos III, 1788 (Ibid., 309).

ratification the following year.[10] Lastly, Floridablanca sought to check British influence in Portugal and to improve relations with the neighboring country. He lured the Portuguese monarchy with a trade agreement and the marriage of Infante Gabriel of Spain to Infanta Mariana Victoria of Portugal, a match devoid of any Spanish dynastic pretensions.

Floridablanca used the new Junta de Estado as a strategic tool to achieve these ends and, at the same time, to neutralize his political enemies, including the influential count of Aranda (1719–1798), who at the time was ambassador in Paris. It was Valdés who proposed the idea of the junta. Though there were precedents for this institution in the Spanish monarchy, it was now revived by the government, as Floridablanca himself explains:[11]

> ... once Don Antonio Valdés became minister of the navy, following the death of the Marquis of Castejón, he discovered that there were several obstacles to procurement of many kinds of materials, especially those relating to the Indies ... For this reason Valdés spoke to me on several occasions of the need for [all of] us to meet in order to clarify and to come to agreement on points of difference, to avoid the acrimony and dissension [that might arise] in written communications ... I perceived that the minister of the navy was quite right ...

The purpose of the new Junta de Estado was to make the actions taken by the government as unified and streamlined as possible, absorbing the former functions of the Council of State. The role assigned to the junta included dealing with general business, looking into conflicts between the functions of different departments or ministries – in cases where these conflicts had not been resolved already by lower-ranking councils – and to make decisions should an emergency arise in any of the monarchy's domains. It was a veritable laboratory of empire, a small governmental body that sought to control and

---

[10] See a general survey in Guimerá, A., "La Marine espagnole contre la piraterie nord-africaine (1750–1785)," in *La Piraterie au fil de l'histoire. Un défi pour l'état*, ed. Battesti, M. (Paris: PUPS 2014), pp. 331–345.

[11] Memorial to the king Carlos III, 1788; Floridablanca, *Biblioteca de Autores Españoles*, p. 343 and pp. 344–346. See Escudero, J.A., *Los orígenes del Consejo de Ministros en España. La Junta Suprema de Estado* (Madrid: Editora Nacional, 1979) 2 vols.; Escudero, J.A., *Administración y Estado en la España Moderna* (Valladolid: Junta de Castilla y León, 1999); Gil Cremades, "La Junta Suprema de Estado (1787–1792)," in *Actas del II Symposium de Historia de la Administración* (Madrid, 1971), pp. 448–467; and Guimerá, A., "Teoría y práctica del imperio: el Secretario de Marina e Indias Antonio Valdés en la Junta de Estado (1787–1792)," in *Andalucía, España, Indias. Pasión por la historia. Homenaje al profesor Antonio-Miguel Bernal*, eds. Martínez Shaw, C., Pedro Tedde de Lorca, P., and Tinoco Rubiales, S. (Seville: Universidad de Sevilla-Marcial Pons, 2015), pp. 513–543.

organize numerous and far-flung overseas territories. What was new about this body is that it persisted as an institution for more than four years. Thus, it was the first cabinet in the history of Spain.

The directives of the Junta de Estado were presented to the king by Floridablanca in July 1787. They constituted "the longest and most ambitious and comprehensive document ever received by a body of the Spanish central government."[12] It was the great political agenda of the reigns of Carlos III (1759–1788) and Carlos IV (1788–1808). Floridablanca could thus exercise more control, through the junta, over the work and the decisions of his fellow members of the cabinet and take an active role in the planning of new reform projects.

The document had 395 chapters, covering everything from foreign relations and the army to public works, the treasury, government councils, the Inquisition, education, learned academies, and so on. It included no fewer than 32 chapters, likely drafted by Valdés, on maritime matters, which likewise dealt with all imaginable subjects: ship construction, savings and cost-effectiveness in the navy, the officer corps and promotion, schools for midshipmen and pilots, rank and file sailors, science, maritime cartography and exploration, naval strategy, relations with other naval powers, support for trade, ports, fishing, and navigation, and so on. In general, the directives reflect a clear strategic vision, with insightful assessments of the resources of the Spanish monarchy and its empire, as well as the role played by the latter in Spanish geopolitics. Valdés was exceptional in the industriousness that he brought to his participation in the junta and made many contributions during those years.[13]

Coasts, seas, and oceans were key components of the Spanish Empire, serving both as channels of communication and natural borders between Spain and its colonies and other powers. For these reasons, the Real Armada played an essential role in Floridablanca's government. The success achieved in the American Revolutionary War in some naval operations convinced the Spanish monarchy to spare no effort to improve its navy.

In his directives to the junta, Floridablanca declared that a large part of the monarchy's military spending should be earmarked for the Real Armada, in order to safeguard Spanish trade and Spain's colonies:[14]

> Given that Spain is and must be a maritime power, due to its location, that of its overseas domains, the general interests of its inhabitants and its active and passive trade, there is nothing more appropriate, nothing to which it should give greater attention than to advance and improve the Navy.

---

[12] Escudero, J.A., *Los orígenes*, I, pp. 436–437.
[13] Escudero, J.A., *Administración y Estado*, pp. 113–124 and 135–203.
[14] Instrucción de Floridablanca a la Junta de Estado, 1787; Floridablanca, *Biblioteca de autores españoles*, pp. 214–272, article CLXIX.

The Real Armada played a leading role in this final push by the government to reorganize and preserve the Spanish Empire. It was the only institution, except for some parts of the army, that had the organizational structure, the experience in planning, and the logistical efficacy that were necessary to achieve these goals. In other words, it had the necessary money, know-how, technical staff, institutions – officer training academies, shipyards, college of surgery, astronomical observatory, courses of advanced study, royal factories – contractors, new technologies, scientific instruments, and so on.[15]

Valdés was highly respected in the navy. He was also much admired among his fellow members of the administration, among other political leaders, and among the intelligentsia of his time. He carried forward the efforts of his immediate predecessors in the secretary of the navy: the Marquis de la Ensenada, Julián de Arriaga, and Pedro González de Castejón. Under Valdés's management, the Real Armada became more effectively organized and reached its utmost potential.

Valdés chose his collaborators well and knew how to enlist their cooperation in his reform agenda, both at the secretariate of the navy in Madrid, and the navy's three maritime area commands – Ferrol, Cartagena, and Cadiz – and the naval station at Mahón, as well as at the naval bases and stations in the Americas and the Philippines. He also made use of his professional friendships, as in the case of his closest collaborator at the ministry, Vice Admiral José de Mazarredo (1745–1812), who was the leader of a distinguished group of naval

---

[15] Bustos Rodríguez, M., "La Politique des Bourbons et la marine espagnole (1740–1805)," in *Les Marines de la guerre d'Independance américaine (1763–1783). I. L'instrument naval*, eds. Chaline, O., Bonnichon, P., and de Vergennes, C. de (Paris, 2013), pp. 107–128; Casado Rabanal, D., *La marina ilustrada: sueño y ambición de la España del s. XVIII. Desarrollo y crisis (1702–1805)* (Madrid: Ministerio de Defensa, 2009); Cepeda Gómez, J., "La marina y el equilibrio de los océanos en el siglo XVIII," in eds. Guimerá Ravina, A. and Peralta Ruiz, V., *El equilibrio de los imperios: de Utrecht a Trafalgar* (Madrid: Fundación Española de Historia Moderna, 2005), pp. 447–482; *La armada española en el siglo XVIII. Ciencia, hombres y barcos*, ed. García Hurtado, M.R. (Madrid: Ed. Sílex, 2012); *Las innovaciones de la armada en la España del siglo de Jorge Juan*, ed. García Hurtado, M.R. (Madrid: CSIC, 2020); *La real armada. La marine des Bourbons espagnoles dans le XVIIIe siécle*, eds. Guimerá, A. and Chaline, O. (Paris: Presses de l'université Paris Paris-Sorbonne, 2018); *Vientos de guerra. Apogeo y crisis de la Real Armada, 1750–1823*, eds. Marchena, J. and Caño, J. (Madrid: Ediciones Doce Calles, 2015), 3 vols; Merino Navarro, J. P., *La armada española en el siglo XVIII* (Madrid: Fundación Universitaria Española, 1981); *Actitudes y medios en la real armada del siglo XVIII*, eds. Sánchez Baena, J.J., Chaín Navarro, C., and Martínez-Solís, L. (Madrid-Murcia: Ministerio de Defensa-Universidad de Murcia, 2011); and dossier "Política imperial y administración de industrias estratégicas: la armada española en el largo Siglo XVIII," *Espacio Tiempo y Forma*, 32 (2019).

officers, many of whom later became heroes at the Battle of Trafalgar.[16] Valdés likewise took advantage of connections he had as a member of the military Order of San Juan and relied on the support of some of his fellow members. Several of his subordinates were prominent in scientific and humanistic circles and took part in the great expeditionary age of the late eighteenth century.

Under Valdés's management, the navy was modernized: new regulations, published in 1793, after Floridablanca's downfall; unceasing technological innovation; the pursuit of national self-sufficiency in strategic raw materials or their direct importation from abroad; development of shipyards using an integrated system of state-run factories serving the Real Armada; an increase in the number of units in the war fleet; complete provisioning and equipping of all vessels; an increase in the number of officers, as well as an emphasis on their technical training; measures to grow the rank and file; and the culmination of the age of scientific expeditions and maritime cartography.

With respect to the war fleet, at the beginning of Valdés's term as secretary of the navy, in 1783, the Real Armada had 62 ships of the line and 40 frigates. Valdés calculated at that time that the fleet required at a minimum the construction of three ships and three frigates a year, which meant retaining dockyard workers at all costs.[17] When his resignation was accepted in November 1795, the fleet was larger than it would ever be again: 75 ships of the line – 14 of which were three-deckers, the kind of ship needed for the now common naval tactic of decisive battle – 51 frigates, and 182 smaller ships. By 1790, the combined tonnage of the bigger ships in the Spanish-French alliance exceeded that of Great Britain by 21%.[18] However, the number of ships-of-the-lines and frigates that France and Spain were capable of outfitting and maintaining on the open seas was much lower than their war fleets. The British navy outstripped them in this regard. Nonetheless, the fact that Spain and France possessed this fleet-in-being was a perpetual thorn in London's side.

---

[16] See British traveller Joseph Towsend's praise for Valdés' 1788 naval reforms in Towsend, J., *Viaje por España en la época de Carlos III, 1786–1787* (Madrid: Turner, 1988), pp. 250–251 and 304.

[17] Valdés' reforms on naval finances in Guimerá, A., "Naval leadership and Naval Expenditure in Spain, 1783–1795," in *The Spending of the States. Military Expenditure during the Long Eighteenth Century: Patterns, Organization and Consequences, 1650–1815*, eds. Conway. S. and Torres, R. (Saarbrücken: VDM Verlag Dr. Muller, 2011), pp. 201–211.

[18] Duffy, M., "World-Wide War and British Expansion, 1793–1815", in *The Oxford History of the British Empire. Volume II. The Eighteenth Century*, ed. Marshall, P. (Oxford-New York: Oxford University Press, 1998), p. 184, table 9.1. See British traveller Joseph Towsend's praise for Valdés' naval reforms in 1788; Towsend, J., *Viaje por España en la época de Carlos III, 1786–1787* (Madrid: Turner, 1988), pp. 250–251 and 304.

Valdés himself described how this fleet was handled a few years later:[19]

> Your Grace is aware that, since the navy was destroyed as a result of that war [1779–1783] and had the misfortune in that war to confirm the inferiority of our ships compared to those of the enemy, my foremost concern was to reestablish [our fleet] and improve the [ships'] construction; and this has been fully achieved, since not only have all the shipyards been fully stocked with the stuffs and supplies needed to outfit the ships but they have been built in all sizes.

By 1795, the year that Valdés left the Ministry of the Navy, the Real Armada had become a giant. But this had not been an easy task. For a naval power to fulfill its mission it needs ships, men, and money.[20] Valdés had to surmount two big obstacles of a structural nature: the Spanish monarchy's financial difficulties and the shortage of sailors.

The Floridablanca government's allocations to the Real Armada made for a real challenge. Fortunately, secretary of the treasury Pedro López de Llerena (1787–1792) was receptive to the needs of the navy. Thus, during the period 1788–1792 allocations to the navy came to account for 41% of the state's military spending, which included both the army and the navy, a proportion that would never again be so high.[21] Changes in naval spending over the course of the eighteenth century show that, during Valdés's term, the Real Armada was provided with more resources than ever before: taking the average of the five-year period 1770–1774 as a baseline, we see that there was

---

[19] Report of Valdés to Carlos IV, 06.08.1800; Escudero, *Los orígenes*, I, pp. 565–567. See also Fernández González, F., "La construcción naval en la armada entre 1750 y 1820," en *Vientos de guerra. Apogeo y crisis de la real armada, 1750–1823. Vol. I. Una armada en tiempos de la Ilustración. Política, ciencia, ingeniería y hacienda*, eds. Marchena, J. and Caño, J. (Madrid: Ediciones Doce Calles, 2015), pp. 520–660; and Marchena Fernández, J., *Vientos de guerra. Apogeo y crisis de la Real Armada, 1750–1823. Vol. II. Los buques de la real armada, 1700–1823* (Madrid: Ediciones Doce Calles, 2018).

[20] Baugh, D.B., "Naval Power: What Give the British Navy Superiority," in *Exceptionalism and Industrialism: Britain and Its European Rivals, 1688–1815*, Prados de la Escosura, L. ed. (Cambridge: Cambridge University Press, 2004), pp. 235–257.

[21] Merino Navarro, J.P., "La Hacienda de Carlos IV," in *Historia de España fundada por Ramón Menéndez Pidal y dirigida por José María Jover Zamora. Tomo XXXI. La época de la Ilustración. Volumen I. El Estado y la cultura (1759–1808)* (Madrid: Espasa Calpe, 1987), p. 868; and Tedde, P., "Una economía en transformación: de la Ilustración al Liberalismo," in *Historia de España fundada por Ramón Menéndez Pidal y dirigida por José María Jover Zamora. Tomo XXX. Las bases políticas, económicas y sociales de un régimen en transformación (1759–1834)* (Madrid: Espasa Calpe, 1998), pp. 327–425.

an increase of 79.6% in 1783–1787 and of 90.4% in 1788–1792 .[22] Valdés also proposed numerous improvements to the financing, contracting, and spending management systems.[23]

Nonetheless, the financial reality was dire. Spain's budgetary policy did not help matters, since in principle it avoided taking on public debt to finance spending. Moreover, Spain's military spending during the eighteenth century had been on a much smaller scale than that of Great Britain. The British monarchy had been able to mobilize all kinds of resources, incurring public debt as its principal means to finance war, especially naval warfare – the key to its booming maritime economy – which in turn stimulated economic growth. Spain, which was both a naval power and a continental one, had to divide its military spending between the army – to defend its many miles of land borders and to maintain domestic order – and the Real Armada, which was vital to its overseas shipping and trade.[24]

The Real Armada had another Achilles heel: the shortage of sailors, especially those who managed the rigging – topmen. The number of sailors

---

[22] Merino Navarro, *La Armada española en el siglo XVIII*, pp. 162–163.

[23] See "Plan de economía para la armada," 10.09.1785; Archivo Museo Naval-Madrid (AHNM), Estado, 3210, 1; and "Instrucción para el mejor régimen de los establecimientos fijos de Marina en Cartagena de Indias, Montevideo y San Blas de California," 20.03.1793, AMNM, 834.

[24] There is an important historiography on European military finances in the long 18th century, including Spanish case: *Mobilising Resources for War: Britain and Spain at Work During the Early Modern Period*, eds. Bowen, H.V. and González Ensico, A. (Pamplona: EUNSA, 2006); *The Spending of the States. Military Expenditure during the Long Eighteenth Century: Patterns, Organisation and Consequences, 1650–1815*, Conway, S. and Torres, R. eds. (Saarbrücken: VDM Verlag Dr. Muller, 2011); *Un estado militar: España, 1650–1820*, ed. González Ensico, A. (San Sebastián de los Reyes: Actas, 2012); *The Fiscal-Military State in Eighteenth-Century Europe*, Storrs, C. ed. (Farnham, Ashgate, 2009); *War, State and Development. Fiscal-Military States in the Eighteenth Century*, Torres Sánchez, R. ed. (Pamplona, EUNSA, 2007); Torres Sánchez, R., "Las prioridades de un monarca ilustrado o las limitaciones del estado fiscal-militar de Carlos III," *Hispania*, 229 (2008): 375–406; Torres Sánchez, R., *El precio de la guerra. El estado fiscal-militar de Carlos III (1779–1783)* (Madrid: Marcial Pons, 2013); Torres Sánchez, R., *Constructing a Fiscal Military State in Eighteenth Century Spain* (London: Palgrave Macmillan, 2015); Torres Sánchez, R., *Military Entrepeneurs. The Spanish Contractor State in the Eighteenth Century* (Oxford: Oxford University Press, 2016); Torres Sánchez, R., "El estado fiscal-naval de Carlos III. Los dineros de la armada en el contexto de las financias de la monarquía," and Serrano Álvarez, J.M., "La gestión económica de la armada española, 1750–1820," in *Vientos de guerra. Apogeo y crisis de la Real Armada, 1750–1823. Vol. I. Una armada en tiempos de la Ilustración. Política, ciencia, ingeniería y hacienda*, eds. Marchena, J. and Caño, J. (Madrid: Ediciones Doce Calles, 2015) pp. 325–432 and pp. 433–522.

needed for Spain's huge fleet is a hotly debated topic in Spanish naval historiography, one that remains to be studied in detail.[25]

Great Britain surpassed Spain in the size of its force of enlisted sailors. During the American Revolutionary War, the number of sailors and soldiers serving in the British Royal Navy rose from an average of 20,000 enlisted in peace times to some 100,000 individuals.[26] These figures are a clear indication of the spectacular growth of Britain's merchant marine, the reserve source of sailors for any naval power. Great Britain increased the volume of its merchant fleet between 1776 and 1800 by a factor of four, to more than 2 million tons. At that time, Spain's merchant fleet, including both coastal and transoceanic trade, totaled only 176,000 tons, ten times less than Britain's, five times less than France's or Holland's, and half of that of either the Italian States or Denmark.[27]

Valdés strove to create incentives for sailors. As we know, the Spanish monarchy had created the Matrícula de Mar (Navy Register) in the first half of the eighteenth century, just as France had done. But if we look specifically at skilled sailors, there were only 32,086 in the 1789 register, according to a report from the same year. They were too few to meet the needs of the war fleet. And these numbers do not take into account the depletion of forces due to desertion or casualties during the service period. Moreover, if all skilled sailors were engaged when there was a diplomatic crisis or a declaration of war, none would be available for fishing or trade, and these activities would have to be carried out by sailors who were not in the register. In addition,

---

[25] Guimerá Ravina, A.,"Trafalgar y la marinería española," in *El equilibrio de los imperios. De Utrecht a Trafalgar,* Guimerá Ravina, A. and Peralta Ruiz, V. eds. (Madrid: Fundación Española de Historia Moderna, 2005), II, 821–838; Martínez Martínez, M., *Los forzados de marina en la España del siglo XVIII (1700–1775)* (Almería: Universidad de Almería, 2011); and Vázquez Lijó, J.M., *La matrícula de mar en la España del siglo XVIII. Registro, inspección y evolución de las clases de marinería y maestranza* (Madrid: Ministerio de Defensa, 2007).

[26] Acerra, M. and Zysberg, A., *L'Essor des marines de guerre européennes, 1680–1790* (Condé-sur-Noireau, 1997), pp. 135–150 ; and Merino Navarro, J.P., *La armada española en el siglo XVIII* (Madrid: Fundación Universitaria Española, 1981), p. 109. We have also bigger numbers in British navy during the American War of Independence: 230.000 seamen and royal marines; Rodger, N.A.M., "A Little Navy of Your Own Making'. Admiral Boscawen and the Cornish connection in the Royal Navy," in Duffy, M., ed. *Parameters of British Naval Power, 1650–1850* (Exeter. University of Exeter, 1992), pp. 82–92.

[27] Tonnage of capacity of a ship: two casks, nearly a metric ton. See Alcalá-Zamora y Queipo de Llano, J., "Evolución del tonelaje de la flota de vela española durante los siglos modernos," *Estudios del Departamento de Historia Moderna* (1975): p. 193 and pp. 199–203.

replacement personnel for the following year would not be available.[28] This severely hindered Spain's ability to effectively supply its squadrons in the event of an international conflict.

Spain's maritime economy simply had no more to give, in the opinion of Mazarredo himself, who stated, correctly, many years later:

> ... and the nation's entire shipping business beyond its coasts during the years of its greatest flourishing, from 1781 to 1792, employed only 5,800 sailors; the remaining registered sailors were reduced to the poor work of fishing for the fresh fish market, except for a bit of dry salting of sardines in Galicia and some barely profitable coastal shipping. This [the level of non-military maritime activity] is the true measure of a nation's ability to outfit its war fleet.

Restoring the seafaring line of work needed to be prioritized by the monarchy, but this was dependent on an expansion of the shipping industry, fishing, trade, and manufacturing or agriculture for export.[29] These reforms required a great deal of time, money, and political will. Floridablanca's government had attempted to improve the situation through legislative means, and Valdés had supported him in his capacity as secretary of the navy and of the West Indies, but their efforts were not enough.

With the outbreak of the French Revolution, the political outlook in Europe became dire. After 1789 there was a spectacular breakdown in the traditional balance of powers, which affected the international legal order and the practice of diplomacy itself. As we will see below in our analysis of the Nootka Crisis, for the first time in the eighteenth century, the Spanish monarchy could no longer rely on French support in its naval and colonial rivalry with Great Britain. This fact directly affected Floridablanca's strategic approach, which had been based, among other things, on a new multilateral diplomacy, support for the Real Armada, and the alliance with the French monarchy, with the naval forces of the two powers banding together to thwart Great Britain's maritime ambitions.

The vast size of Spain's possessions in the Americas in 1783 posed a strategic challenge for the Spanish monarchy. The work of reinforcing a continent-wide system of defense, with the objective of protecting central areas of its empire – specifically, the viceroyalties of New Spain and Peru – was complicated

---

[28] Joaquín Gutiérrez de Rubalcava to Antonio Valdés, Isla de León, 23.06.1789 (AMNM) 2381, 300–310. The number of skilled seamen in the Matrícula de mar of 1792–1796 was similar: around 38.000 people (Estados Generales de la Real Armada, 1792–1796, Biblioteca del Palacio Real – Madrid, 2698).

[29] Mazarredo to Mariano L. de Urquijo, Aranjuez, 10.05.1801; Fernández Duro, C., *Armada española desde la unión de los reinos de Castilla y de Aragón* (Madrid: Museo Naval, 1973, facsimile edition of 1900), VIII, pp. 233–234.

and costly. At the periphery of these possessions there were enormous swaths of land unoccupied by the Crown – specifically the northwest coast of North America, southern parts of the Pacific coast and nearby islands, Patagonia, the Strait of Magellan, and Tierra de Fuego.

In effect, during the second half of the century frontier areas in the Americas started to play a more important part in the Bourbon Reforms: the Crown had sponsored expeditions to define borders with Portuguese-controlled territories; the creation of new jurisdictions; cartography and hydrography in the Caribbean, the northwest coast, and the Southern Cone; scientific expeditions; populating new frontier areas with colonists and missionaries; the creation of a new viceroyalty – Río de la Plata – and treaties with indigenous communities living in these borderland areas. Floridablanca's government followed this same strategic approach.[30]

The Junta de Estado also sought to control the immense maritime perimeter around its American colonies, by pushing for a three-part defensive apparatus in the main ports: fortification, military garrisons, and the deployment of navy units to their shipyards, bases, and stations. Spanish American ports needed to be cleared of any foreign elements, equipped, and fortified. The islands in the Caribbean, including Trinidad, needed to be colonized and secured. Trinidad was considered to be of great strategic importance: due to its location, its natural harbors, and the prevailing winds in the Caribbean, controlling it was essential to defending the Caribbean and the Gulf of Mexico.

The coast guard needed to continue to be on the lookout for fraud, contraband, and unauthorized direct trade with other European powers or their dependencies. In peace time, warships were to carry out cartographic or hydrographic missions, reconnoiter the coast and create nautical charts, coastal maps, surveys, and harbor maps.

The junta went even further in its intentions and, with an optimism out of all proportion to the circumstances, sought to close American coasts to all foreign ships:

---

[30] Instrucción de Floridablanca a la Junta de Estado, 1787, articles XCVIII–CXIV, CXXX, CXXXIX–CXLIII; Floridablanca, *Biblioteca de Autores Españoles*, pp. 214–272. There is a huge bibliography on Spanish American defense. See the recents studies of Chauca, J. "La defensa de la América meridional durante la segunda mitad del siglo XVIII," in *El equilibrio de los imperios: de Utrecht a Trafalgar*, Guimerá Ravina, A. y Peralta Ruiz, V., eds. (Madrid: Fundación Española de Historia Moderna, 2005), pp. 631–645; and Guimerá, A., "La stratégie navale et la navigation espagnole vers les Antilles et le Golfe de Mexique, 1759–1783," in *Les Marines de la guerre d'Indépendance américaine. II. L'opérationelle naval*, Chaline, O., Philippe Bonnichon, P., and Vergennes, C.P. de, eds. (Paris: Presses de l'université Paris-Sorbonne, 2018), pp. 67–90.

It is important not to leave any island near the mainland, any port or inlet that is capable of being used by war ships, particularly if there is a source of fresh water, lest an establishment be created there that could choke off and overpower the country.[31]

The Nootka Crisis was the baptism by fire of this strategy. In this international incident, the Real Armada played a key role.[32] What I present here is strictly the Spanish perspective on this conflict, based on Spanish sources.

A dispute over Nootka sound, on Vancouver Island in what is now the Canadian province of British Columbia, almost escalated into a war between Great Britain and Spain. Nootka was strategically valuable since there were no other known natural harbors in the area and because it provided a convenient base for fur trading and possibly for accessing the Chinese market. In accordance with the new frontier strategy outlined above, Nootka was discovered by Spain in 1774 and thereafter was visited by Spanish ships, until a settlement was finally founded in 1789. In the spring of that year, a packet boat and a sloop, both British, were seized by the Spanish, leading to a dispute between the two powers.

The Junta de Estado actively intervened in the matter. There are documents pertaining to the dispute from between mid-March 1790, when the junta was informed that the British government intended to mobilize a fleet, and mid-September of the same year, when Carlos IV presented a settlement proposal to the British ambassador, which would eventually be accepted by London the following month.

During those six months, the junta acted decisively. Floridablanca, in a meeting on March 15, called on his ministers to give their recommendations

---

[31] Instrucción de Floridablanca a la Junta de Estado, 1787, article CX; Floridablanca, conde de, *Biblioteca de Autores Españoles*, pp. 214–272.

[32] Proceedings of the Junta de Estado, 1790, in Escudero, *Los orígenes*, II, pp. 159–882. See the Spanish sources in Fuster Ruiz, F., *Final del descubrimiento de América. California, Canadá y Alaska (1765–1822). Aportación documental del Archivo General de Marina* (Murcia: Universidad de Murcia, 1997). See also Calvo Maturana, A., "Génesis del II imperio Británico y el ocaso del universalismo español: la doble vertiente del conflicto de Nootka (1790)," *Hispania*, 228 (2008): 151–192; Fernández Duro, C., *Armada española*, VIII, pp. 9–16; Guillamón Álvarez, F.J., "Floridablanca y la crisis de guerra de Nootka (1789–1790)," *Res publica* 22 (2009): 153–178; Olivares-Iribarren, I., "L'affaire de Nootka-Sound (1789–1790)," *Mélanges de la Casa de Velázquez*, 28, 2 (1992): 123–148; Sánchez Montañéz, E., "Vivir en el fin del mundo. El asentamiento español en Nootka a finales del siglo XVIII," in *La Constitución gaditana de 1812 y sus repercusiones en América*, Gullón Abao, A.J. y Gutiérrez Escudero, A., eds. (Cadiz: Universidad de Cádiz, 2012), 17–38; and Soler Pascual, E., "Floridablanca and the Nootka Crisis," *International Journal of Canadian Studies*, 19 (1999): 167–180.

regarding the diplomatic strategy to pursue with Great Britain and the defensive measures to be taken, not only in Nootka but also elsewhere in the Americas.

Valdés issued an initial opinion a few days later. From a political standpoint, he defended Spain's rights of conquest and possession of the lands in question. He interpreted Britain's exaggerated response as a calculated attack that exploited France's temporary weakness because of its domestic problems. According to Valdés, Great Britain not only sought to recoup its losses to Spain during the war in 1779–1783 but also had the South Pacific in its sights.

Valdés argued that it was necessary to strengthen the defenses of Spain's American possessions, without arousing suspicions, or else there could be a surprise attack on Puerto Rico, Trinidad, Cuba, or Santo Domingo. He recommended that the three maritime area commands – Ferrol, Cartagena, and Cadiz – begin preparations for assembling a fleet that would serve as a deterrent: it would signal to the government in London that Spain was prepared for an eventual rupture between the two countries and would not blindly entrust its fate to negotiations. For reasons of prestige, this fleet needed to be ready within four months. Valdés also included a status update on the country's naval forces, which possessed a total of 69 ships of the line and 39 frigates, most of which were ready to be deployed.[33]

But in his recommendations, Valdés also warns the junta that it would be necessary to make extraordinary expenditures, and without hesitation, in order not to show signs of weakness to the British and to bolster the Spanish monarchy's legal position in the dispute. Floridablanca's government will assume these extraordinary costs.

The junta agreed to assemble a fleet in Cadiz that would be ready to set sail in Valdés's recommended time frame.[34] In the months that followed, Floridablanca mobilized the three maritime area commands and ordered measures to defend the Balearic and Canary islands and the most important ports in the Caribbean and the Philippines, measures that involved both naval intelligence and the deployment of regular troops.[35] His main concern was that the British Royal Navy might stage a surprise attack against the strategic enclaves of Trinidad and Puerto Rico, prior to any formal declaration of war, which was one of Britain's common tactics. Time would prove the junta right in this regard: in 1797 the British captured Trinidad in a surprise attack and also struck Puerto Rico.

---

[33] Report of Valdés, 21.03.1790; Fuster Ruiz, F., *Final del descubrimiento*. Proceedings of the Junta de Estado, 22.03.1790, in Escudero, *Los orígenes*, II, pp. 159–882.

[34] Proceedings of the Junta de Estado, 22.03.1790, in Escudero, II, 159–882. The Junta de Estado had the information that the Royal Navy was planning to send a fleet to the Mediterranean (ibid., 15.03 and 29.03.1790).

[35] Floridablanca's plan, 1790; in Fernández Duro, C., *Armada española*, VIII, pp. 22–24.

The junta likewise believed that the British might seize the opportunity to expand the territories they controlled in Honduras. A decision was made to put these colonial sites on alert.[36] Orders were immediately given for several military officers to deploy for assignments in Cuba and Santo Domingo. Warnings were dispatched to all Spanish possessions in the Americas and the Philippines using a highly effective delivery system that went through a series of maritime strongholds.[37] Plans were made to send an expedition with regular troops to reinforce Puerto Rico and Cuba.[38] The government also planned to send frigates to Nicaragua to monitor the mouth of the San Juan River, which was, as we mentioned above, a prime objective for the British. Orders were given to dispatch troops to the northwest coast of North America in order to maintain control of the region. Likewise, it was agreed to dispatch two ships of the line and two frigates to the Pacific coast.[39]

From a diplomatic standpoint, Floridablanca did not want war, and he proposed a series of concessions and compensations to the British government. However, at the same time, he called for an alliance with the maritime powers of northern Europe – Russia, Denmark, and Sweden – as well as with Spain's neighbor, Portugal.

The chess game of deterrence continued. Replicating an operation that had been successful in the previous war with Great Britain, the Spanish government planned to array troops along the southern coast of Cuba, to threaten Jamaica, and was studying the possibility of an expedition to the latter if a squadron could be found to support the transport ships.[40]

As for the fleet, reinforcement units from other maritime area commands were sent to Cadiz, and after only a few months a fleet made up of 30 ships of the line, 12 frigates, and three smaller ships had been mobilized.[41] The speed with which Spain was able to accomplish this surprised the British.[42] Appointed to command the fleet was Vice Admiral José de Solano (1726–1806), the marquis of Socorro, who had distinguished himself in the campaigns

---

[36] Proceedings of the Junta de Estado, 15.03/ y 22.03.1790; Escudero, *Los orígenes*, II, pp. 159–882.

[37] Ibid., 24.05.1790.

[38] Ibid., 31.05.1790.

[39] Ibid., 24.05.1790.

[40] Floridablanca's plan, 1790; in Fernández Duro, *Armada española*, VIII, 22–24.

[41] Completed list of Cadiz fleet, with 30 ships of the line and names of their commanders (www.todoababor.es). Another source is giving a number of 25 ships-of-the-line: Fernández Duro, *Armada*, VIII, 9–17.

[42] British consul Anthony Merry, Madrid, 29.04.1790, quoted by J. Black (1992), "Naval power, strategy and foreign policy, 1775–1791," in Duffy, M. (ed.), *Parametres of British Naval Power, 1650–1850* (Exeter: University of Exeter, 1992), p. 108. Memorial of Valdés to the king Carlos IV, 06.08.1800; in Escudero, *Los orígenes*, I, pp. 565–567.

Spain participated in during the American Revolutionary War. His second-in-command was Mazarredo.

In the meantime, Spain called for support from revolutionary France, invoking the traditional alliance between the two monarchies. However, France's National Assembly, which arrogated to itself the power of declaring war and peace without the approval of the king, demanded that the two sides begin talks to resolve the conflict peacefully. In Floridablanca's opinion, "legal and dynastic obligations [were being substituted] for moral constraints that are more relative in nature."[43]

Without France's support or an alliance with the maritime powers of northern Europe, the Spanish monarchy's international isolation was clear. In the end, the Spanish government, unwilling to shoulder the entire weight of a ruinous war, capitulated. On July 24, Carlos IV signed an initial convention on Nootka, in which he was forced to concede to Great Britain's demands. According to Floridablanca, the objective was two-fold:[44]

> ... to get out of the predicament and to leave the door open so that [Spain] might improve its prospects at a more opportune moment ... or to make sure of England through a treaty that would free us from the greatest and the only enemy we have, or to make new friends with an alliance of the three maritime powers of the north.

However, diplomatic tensions persisted. On July 20, 1790, the Marquis de Socorro's fleet departed Cadiz, on Valdés's orders, in order to position itself off Cape Finisterre and follow the movements of the British fleet. Its cruising mission ended on September 8, when it returned to Cadiz. Floridablanca was also being pressured on a second front: Ceuta was besieged that year by the sultan of Morocco, a situation that would continue into 1791. This combination of circumstances led the king to make the final decision to reach an agreement with the British government. Floridablanca communicated this decision to the Junta de Estado on September 8 in a meeting where he specified the main points to be included in the draft of the accord.[45]

---

[43] López-Cordón Cerezo, M.V., "Tomar el timón, navegar por el mundo: Floridablanca, ministro de Estado," en *Floridablanca, 1728–1808. La utopía reformadora* (Murcia: Comunidad Autónoma de La Región de Murcia – Sociedad Estatal de Conmemoraciones Culturales – Ayuntamiento de Murcia-Fundación Cajamurcia, 2008), p. 151; and Floridablanca's letters to the new secretary of state, February–April 1792; Rumeu de Armas, A., *El testamento político del conde de Floridablanca* (Madrid: CSIC, 1962), pp. 71–78.

[44] Floridablanca's letters to the new secretary of state, February–April 1792; Rumeu de Armas, *El testamento político*, pp. 80–81.

[45] Proceedings of the Junta de Estado, 08.09. 1790; Escudero, *Los orígenes*, II, 159–882.

The dilemma that the Junta de Estado had debated during the months leading up to this can be seen clearly in the important session that took place on September 16.[46] During that session, Floridablanca informed the junta that Carlos IV had given his approval to a new agreement, which would eventually be accepted by London. In spite of this, both Valdés and Antonio Porlier, secretary of Grace and Justice of the Indies (1787–1792), read the statements that they had prepared ahead of this announcement.

In his second statement, Valdés reiterated that Britain was acting opportunistically by capitalizing on France's difficult circumstances in order to gain an advantage in its dispute with Spain.[47] However, he is realistic in his assessment:

> ... we are not in a position to make war, it is true; because, though we have a Navy, we lack an Army, and even if we had both, we do not have the money ... to finish the war with honor.

In any case, Valdés argued, it was in the interests of the Spanish monarchy to conceal its weaknesses in order not to handicap itself in the negotiations.

Porlier elaborated on the rights enjoyed by the Spanish Crown to possess, control, and wield authority in the lands already discovered and yet to be discovered in America, the lands already conquered and still to be conquered, and that these rights dated back to the fifteenth century.[48] He based this claim on various legal arguments as well as various treaties signed by Great Britain. He pointed out that the British proposal was not only detrimental to Spanish interests, but was "unseemly and a perverse example for other nations, which are all trying, to their utmost ability, to tear the two Americas away from us." As a graceful way out of the quandary, he suggested the following:[49]

> ... to voluntarily cede [the use of] that part of North America that is proposed by the British ministry, as an act of sheer generosity and benevolence toward the British nation, as a token of the harmonious cooperation that we, for our part, wish to maintain...

In the meanwhile, they could continue to debate an agreement on all the proposed points, as indeed they did. One of the stickiest points involved a

---

[46] Ibid., 16.09.1790.

[47] "Borrador del dictamen dado por el Sr. D. Antonio Valdés en Junta de Estado sobre desavenencias con la Corte de Londres por el apresamiento de un buque de esta nación ejecutado en el puerto de Nootka," 16.09.179; Fuster Ruiz, *Final del descubrimiento*.

[48] Proceedings of the Junta de Estado, 16.09.1790; Escudero, *Los orígenes*, II, 159–882.

[49] Ibid., 12.07.1790.

radical change to international law, which would now accept that the first nation to truly occupy a territory would automatically gain the right of possession and control, even if that territory belonged to another state that had discovered it, explored it, and formally claimed possession.[50] According to Porlier, Great Britain raised the principle of the freedom of the seas, like a flag, to counter the doctrine of *mare clausum* that Spain and Portugal had supported since the fifteenth century, which held that the Indian and Pacific oceans, as well as the Caribbean and the Gulf of Mexico, were under these two nations' jurisdictions and closed to all others and which had been sanctioned by two papal bulls and the Treaty of Tordesillas.[51]

If the ceding of the use of North American territories was not accepted by Great Britain, Porlier argued that Spain would have to declare war, in spite of the monarchy's unfavorable circumstances, in order to defend a centuries-old right:

> [such a course of action] would be a minor inconvenience compared to the prospect of allowing ourselves, without offering any resistance, to be robbed of the most sacred of our rights and possessions in both Americas. To do so would be to exhibit to the entire world a weakness that is altogether incompatible with the honor and reputation of the Spanish nation.

In order to avoid war, the Spanish government, after having been paid damages, signed with Great Britain the Nootka Convention of 28 October 1790.

The agreement authorized permanent British settlements in the Pacific northwest, beyond Spain's occupied territories in California, starting 200 leagues north of San Francisco. The buildings and lands in Nootka that had been confiscated the year before were returned to the British. Their status as private property was recognized, but not British sovereignty over them, as the area continued to be considered a Spanish possession. Spain accepted the payment of damages for its losses in land, buildings, ships, and merchandise.

The agreement ensured freedom of shipping and fishing in the Pacific to both Spanish and British subjects. King Carlos IV allowed the British to build provisional barracks for fishermen on coasts and islands north of San Francisco in North America or south of the territories that were already occupied by the Spanish in South America. The agreement includes a declaration of intent on the part of both monarchies to prevent shipping and fishing activities in the Pacific from being used as a pretext for contraband. To achieve this, the agreement stipulates that there can be no fishing within 10 leagues of the coast.

---

[50] Floridablanca's letters to the new secretary of state, 1792; Rumeu de Armas, *El testamento político*, 85.

[51] Ibid., 80.

In short, although the Spanish monarchy was forced to accept certain economic and legal concessions, it maintained its sovereignty over almost all of its American possessions, from Nootka to Tierra de Fuego, allowing it to safeguard, most importantly, the large viceroyalties of New Spain and Peru.

The Nootka Crisis imposed a large economic burden on the Spanish navy: the ordinary and extraordinary expenses of the three maritime area commands soared, and the debt incurred upset the balanced finances that Valdés had achieved.[52] But I believe that the agreement reached with Great Britain was not altogether unfavorable to the Spanish monarchy, and this was due to the strong showing of one of Spain's strategic assets, the Real Armada, which succeeded in putting to sea a formidable fleet in record time and taking emergency steps to defend Spain's American possessions. This act of deterrence must have influenced the negotiations with the British government. Secretary Valdés had done his job well.

After Floridablanca's downfall in February 1792, the Junta de Estado was immediately dissolved by the new secretary of state, the count of Aranda. Thus ended this period of "renewed reform," although some measures were taken on the economic and naval fronts afterward. In any case, Valdés lost his main advocate at court.

Generally speaking, Valdés exercised good naval leadership during the Spanish intervention in the War of the French Revolution (1793–1795). Spain's Real Armada achieved its strategic international mission despite great difficulties, especially the shortage of sailors. However, the disappearance of his patron, Floridablanca, together with court intrigues and the monarchy's financial crisis – factors that became more obvious toward the end of the conflict, with the Peace of Basel in July 1795 – led Valdés to petition the king for his dismissal as secretary of the navy. The king finally accepted his resignation in November of that year.

Valdés's great legacy persisted up to the Napoleonic invasion of the Iberian Peninsula in 1808, during the rapid decline of the Bourbon navy, but this is a subject that goes beyond the purview of this study. Mazarredo and his team continued the work begun by Valdés under difficult circumstances. Seen in this light, the collaboration between Floridablanca and Valdés should be considered a golden age of the Real Armada in Spain's long eighteenth century.

---

[52] Guimerá, A., "Naval Leadership and Naval Expenditure in Spain, 1783–1795," in *The Spending of the States. Military Expenditure during the Long Eighteenth century: Patterns, Organization and Consequences, 1650–1815*, Conway. S. and Torres, R. eds. (Saarbrücken: VDM Verlag Dr. Muller, 2011), pp. 201–211.

5

Defining French Eighteenth-Century Naval Strategy

OLIVIER CHALINE

If the word 'strategy' is now essential for us, it was however absent from French vocabulary of the eighteenth century. At that time no theorist of naval war considered anything than 'tactics', that is to say 'the art to arrange the Navies in the order which is appropriate for the object that one proposes & to regulate their movements'.[1] It meant a science of naval evolutions, or, in other words, operations, which a squadron could carry out. This science is the general officer's one, but, reading the French theorists, from the P. Hoste to the vicomte de Grenier via Bigot de Morogues, it is clear that its subject was not yet a 'universal science of the war' including the art of preparing a plan of campaign. That was the task, not of the seaman, but was the monopoly of the king and some of his ministers. On the other hand, the vocabulary then of use in France strained to catch a reality of this. Although the neologism 'la stratégique' appears in 1771 from the quill of the Lieutenant-Colonel Joly de Maizeroy, the erudite translator of Byzantine military writings, and it was useful to name such a science which forms and prepares the projects before directing them, the word, nonetheless, remained rare and was not yet applied to the sea.[2]

To this first linguistic difficulty is added a second, related to the frequent absence of sources in archives on the discussions and the methods of decision making by the king in his council. Generally, the design of a plan of operation remains opaque to us. Only the orders given as a result are directly known; all the former stages remaining a state secret. At most we can guess that the development of a plan of campaign was conditioned by political objectives of the Bourbon monarch, by the theoretical structure of the naval forces, fixed

---

[1] *Journal de Marine ou bibliothèque raisonnée de la science du navigateur*, Premier cahier (Brest: Malassis, sd [1778 ?]) 3.

[2] Joly de Maizeroy, *Institutions militaires de l'empereur Léon le philosophe* (Paris: Claude-Antoine Jombert, 1771) see 5–6 his 'Observations du traducteur sur l'Institution première'.

on different occasions during the century, and by the concrete constraints amongst units available or likely to be so a few months later.[3] Everyone always expected a short war, such as only one campaign at sea, of a few months, would be enough to confirm the decision. The clear inferiority of the French Navy under Louis XV and Louis XVI led to hopes of quick and resolute offensive actions against the British Royal Navy, but also to requests for the naval support of Spain.

The way in which the naval strategy in France under Louis XV then Louis XVI was defined thus remains largely *terra incognita* and requires us to dig deep to understand the gaps and open new research. This chapter will explore the actors in the decision-making process, then how they took into account the sea, with which they were not very familiar, and finally, what allowance they made in their plans for their Spanish, and particularly, their American allies.

The king was logically the central personality because he alone decided as a last resort. But if he was very well informed on the relations between the States, his geographical and maritime knowledge was often quite deficient. It is impossible to claim that he was at the origin of the plans of naval or colonial operations nor that he intervened significantly in their design. His intervention took other forms. He stated or pointed out the political objectives of the war. At least during the years 1740–1750, he supported the implementation of the programme of naval construction conceived by Maurepas, then continued by the successors, Rouillé and Machault d'Arnouville. It was the same from 1762 with Choiseul, albeit in a different context. These construction schedules were defined according to the maritime needs and the expected type of war to be waged against the Royal Navy.

Concerning the operations, without any naval competence, Louis XV could only approve what his ministers prepared, after discussing with them, either during the meetings of the council, or in conversation with some of them in what was called then the 'King's work'.[4] The monarch approved the strength (ships and men) and the name of the future commander. Even in the case of Louis XVI, who was passionate about geography, travel and the navy, the

---

[3] The size of forces was defined several times: 55 vessels in 1732, theoretical size continued until the end of the Seven Years' War, then 70 vessels and 30 frigates in 1762, according Choiseul, who shortly afterwards raised it to 80 vessels and 35 frigates in 1763, later 40 in 1765. See Estienne R., *La Marine royale sous le ministère du duc de Choiseul (1761–1766)* (Paris: thèse École des Chartes, 1979), pp. 313 and 411, from Archives Nationales [now AN] Marine G 127, f°113 v.; 'Mémoire remis au Roi en 1765', in *Journal des savants* (mars 1881): 171–184 (avril 1881) pp. 250–257, quoted here p. 252. In 1787, Louis XVI increased his naval forces order for following year to 81 ships of the line, 63 to be immediately available, and the remaining 18 to be constructed rapidly.

[4] Antoine, M., *Le Conseil du Roi sous Louis XV* (Paris-Geneva: Droz 1970).

sources do not make it possible to highlight incontrovertibly his role in the final decisions.

Then the most important role was left to ministers. The secretary of state of the navy was not always the most influential among them. All depended here, not on the naval competence he displayed, but on the political weight he enjoyed and on the challenge which the projected operations presented. It was a matter of authority and influence in the King's Council and much depended on whether there was or not a minister whose influence was dominating the council and if the secretary of state of the navy was able to make his voice heard because of an acknowledged competence with the subject. When Maurepas conceived the French plans of campaign in 1738–1739, he had been a long time in office and had headed the patient material reconstruction of the Navy. But his political weight largely exceeded the sole department of the Navy (including the Colonies) since he also held a post in the king's household and had become minister of state in 1738. He was unquestionably the originator of the plans of attack of Jamaica and St Lucia adopted in the Council of Compiègne in August 1740[5] and the French attempt to recapture Louisbourg in 1746.[6]

Conversely, when in 1759 landings in England and Scotland were planned and prepared, Berryer, the secretary of state for the navy was admitted for the first discussions, when the plans were still very vague, but he was not invited to the Council of 14 July when the true decisions were taken. This administrator without maritime experience did not seem to be considered as more than a rather marginal executant.[7] The position of the marquis de Castries at the beginning of 1781 was very different. This officer general from the army was a new secretary of state for the navy, but enjoyed the support of the Queen Marie-Antoinette.[8] With the Secretary of State for the Foreign Affairs, Vergennes, he succeeded making the Spanish give up a new attempt in the

---

[5] Le Bot, P. "'Ce maudit pays des îles': L'expédition du marquis d'Antin (1740–1)" in *Navigations militaires aux Antilles (1620–1820)*, J.-S. Guilbert and B. Lesueur eds. (Paris: L'Harmattan, 2019), pp. 133–151.

[6] Pritchard, J., *Anatomy of a Naval Disaster. The 1746 French Expedition to North America* (Montreal and Kingston: McGill-Queen's University Press, 1995), pp. 36–37.

[7] Binet, H., 'Le Conseil du Roi du 14 juillet 1759 et le plan de descente en Angleterre du duc de Choiseul', *Académie de Marine* XVIII (1939): 181–210.

[8] We still need a biography of that prominent Navy minister. See Dull, J.R., *The French Navy and American Independence. A Study of Arms and Diplomacy 1774–1787* (Princeton: Princeton University Press, 1975), pp. 216–224 about Castries's preparations for the 1781 campaign at sea, especially the memorandum he ordered in February 1781 and sent to Vergennes.

English Channel and then prepared the operational planning in the Caribbean and in North America as well as the instructions given to the admiral de Grasse.

Two other ministers could play a considerable part, sometimes much more decisive than that of the secretary of state for the navy: they were his colleagues in charge of the departments of war and foreign affairs. Their intervention in the strategic development is easy to understand because landing in the British Isles, the army would have to be ferried by the navy, before gaining a foothold on the enemy's shores and if it was necessary to operate with allies, it was a matter of high diplomacy. Moreover, because all the main maritime wars of France, from Louis XIV to Napoleon, except the American War of Independence, were only part of mainly terrestrial conflicts, the secretary of state for war (i.e. the army) necessarily participated in the discussion of all the plans of operations envisaging the landing of the army in England or in Scotland. In 1759, the old marshal of Belle-Isle, supported and probably inspired by Madame de Pompadour, played a decisive role. Thanks to him the young duke of Aiguillon, soon to be commander in chief in Brittany, was appointed to lead the Scottish expedition. Thus it was this high-ranking army officer who consequently became the ministers' real advisor, and not the marshal de Conflans, the commander of the Brest squadron.

The secretary of state for the foreign affairs, if he was powerful at court, also enjoyed a very important influence on the design of the plans of operation. In 1759, the duke of Choiseul was associated with the whole process. The intended landings had to be carried out partly from the Austrian Flemish coast, and implied, for the attack of Scotland, the participation of Swedish troops. Then, when Choiseul, after the death of Belle-Isle, took control of the departments of the foreign affairs, the war, and the navy, all that we could call the agencies of French 'strategy' depended on him. During the War of American Independence when alliances were so essential, the count de Vergennes, secretary of state for the foreign affairs, was a key minister because nothing could be done without him, not with the Americans, the Spanish, nor with the Dutch. The decision to send a squadron of Admiral d'Estaing in North America in 1778, is attributable to him as much as to the secretary of the navy, Sartine, and he had to lead the difficult negotiations which preceded the Spanish entry in the war.

Among the various meetings of the King's Council, the Council of State was the most important for such decisions. Only the few ministers to whom the monarch granted a patent of 'minister of state' could attend it. The recipients were not necessarily heads of government departments. Conversely, not all the secretaries of state for the navy were ministers of state. Each secretary of state for the navy had different political weight: in 1759 Berryer's weight was obviously limited, unlike that of Maurepas before 1738, or Sartine under Louis XVI.

Thus, the making of 'strategy' with all the decisions it entailed did not emerge from a consistent-and durable process. The political circumstances weighed heavily, like the extent of influence of a minister at that time and the role of factions at court. The political objectives and the development of the resulting plans of operations were linked to the work of the King's Council, which could be reduced to indecision, because of lack of allies in Europe, divisions inside the country, or the intrigues at court, as well as the potentially changing favour of the monarch. This explains why at certain times, the king and his ministers hesitated as to which 'strategy' to adopt. A good example of this indecision occurred in 1755 in confronting the increasingly hostile actions of the British Royal Navy in the Atlantic. Except for protests, no concrete response was given.[9] If these essentially political factors could weigh heavily on the definition, or the absence of definition, of a strategy, it should be noted that the decision-makers were also hindered sometimes by a lack of understanding of the maritime realities.

To answer this question initially requires us to determine to what extent the navy department took part in the operational preparations.[10] In the 1740s when Maurepas was still in office, a project or plan of campaign was first elaborated in the offices of the navy. It was then discussed between the secretary of state and the king. What was debated when the council met was to undertake or not an operation, whose details were already more or less formed. If it was approved, discussions still happened downstream to regulate details and the exact importance of the forces which would be committed. It is not an exaggeration to note that the less the secretary of state for the navy participated in the construction of the plans of operations, the less the sea was taken into account.

It was obvious in 1759 that neither Belle-Isle, nor Choiseul had any idea of the maritime conditions specific to the English Channel, of the characteristics of these waters surrounding British Isles, and of the terrible constraints due to the winds. Nobody seems to have had a clear understanding of the time the preparation of the ships would take. It was as if it was only a matter of sending troops towards such or such point of landing. Nobody saw the extreme difficulty not only of gathering the squadrons with the transports they had to protect, but still more, to coordinate forces sailing from shores very distant

---

[9] Dull, J.R., *The French Navy and the Seven Years' War* (Lincoln: University of Nebraska Press, 2005), pp. 20–24; Baugh, D., *The Global Seven Years War 1754–1763. Britain and France in a Great Power Contest* (London: Longman, 2011), pp. 141–146 and 162–168.

[10] These offices are still not very well known, see Ulbert, J. and Llinares, S. (eds.) *La Liasse et la plume. Les Bureaux du secretariat d'État de la Marine (1669–1792)* (Rennes: Presses universitaires de Rennes, 2017).

from each other, with different weather conditions. No source allows us to suppose that the two ministers chaired the council of well-qualified people.

Twenty years later, when Vergennes and Floridablanca tried to settle, via the ambassadors, the common sea campaign they had to carry out against Great Britain with the Franco-Spanish combined armada, their understanding of the hydrographic and climatic data proved to be minimal. They agreed on a calendar of operations and the Spanish admirals arranged to meet with the French at the Sisargas Islands close of La Coruña, in order to be at the entrance of the English Channel during July.[11]

Obviously, everyone understood that in September the bad weather starts in the English Channel, but nobody imagined the French sailors, waiting for their ally and being obliged to consume their stores of food and water. The failure of these supplies, which because of the rapid departure of the fleet had not been possible to build up to the quantities envisaged, was the reason for the tragedy that followed.

The fact that the secretary of state for the navy played a significant role, did not mean that true seamen were consulted by him or had been associated with this work. This gap is all the more notable as the naval operations were, with the resumption of the Franco-English confrontation, to be carried out far from Europe, even if nobody gave up the plans for the invasion of England. In 1740, when Maurepas sent the duke of Antin to the Caribbean, so much was expected, but it failed completely despite deployment of forces. The limits of the consultations and intelligence were obvious.[12] When in 1738, Maurepas had ordered the governors of Martinique and of Santo Domingo to indicate to him which attacks could be attempted against the British islands. The answer of the latter took more than one year to arrive and remained unclear.

The unforeseeable duration of the crossings and the outward journeys and returns of mail between France and the islands was not sufficiently taken into account and it was detrimental for the operational planning as well as its implementation. The same applies to the climatic and medical data. In the navy's offices, the clerks who surrounded the secretary of state had in general had neither the knowledge of the zones of operation, nor experience of the sea.

However, France was in advance of its rivals in terms of maritime cartography, thanks to the Dépôt des Cartes et Plans established in 1720, but nothing enables us to know exactly how these maps were used when preparing a future campaign.[13] The naval commanders of the ports were consulted too, less on

---

[11] Del Perugia, P., *La Tentative d'invasion de l'Angleterre de 1779* (Paris: Presses universitaires de France, 1939), p. 83.

[12] Le Bot, P., 'Ce maudit pays des Iles...', art. cit., forthcoming.

[13] Le Guisquet, B., 'Le Dépôt des cartes, plans et journaux de la marine sous l'ancien régime', *Annales Hydrographiques*, 5e série 18 (1992): 5–31.

the operation considered, than on the ships available or on those likely to be prepared for the campaign to come.

Real seamen were for a long time far from these naval offices which had to turn instead to administrators and managers for advice. When their opinions were requested, it was initially about shipbuilding and which types of ships to produce. Choiseul, when secretary of state for the navy (a subject completely unknown to him), turned to some officers, including the Capitaine de vaisseau Bigot de Morogues, to prepare some reforms at the end of the Seven Years War. However, there is no evidence to confirm that he ever discussed objectives and operations with them. The question arises again at the time of the American War of Independence, but without much clarity owing to the lack of studies and sources. In September 1776, Sartine obtained from Louis XVI the appointment of Charles-Pierre Claret de Fleurieu, a major general in the navy, as director of the ports and arsenals, who was previously the head of the Dépôt des Cartes et Plans. The function was now in the hands of a real seaman. Sartine wanted 'a man who led the operations of the others', but while Fleurieu certainly carried out the plans, the lack of archival sources makes it far it is more difficult to say with precision what role he had played in their design'.[14]

Sartine also had other naval personnel serving as advisors to him: the two brothers Louis-Charles and Charles-Augustin Latouche who were both admirals.[15] Castries, secretary of state for the navy from October 1780, did not dismiss Fleurieu but turned especially to the count d'Hector, naval commander in Brest, to prepare the principal naval forces. Although it is difficult to know the exact part these naval officers played in the development of a strategy, it will be noted at least that seamen were by then close to the minister.

Which maritime information was available the to the decision-makers? First statistical data on the enemy squadrons in a specific zone at a given time, would be necessary to plan an effective operation. Sometimes more detailed and qualitative information was available on the state of preparation of a force or the possible intentions of the enemy (present or future) from preparations going on in enemy naval bases. Despite the use of spies, it was obviously extremely rare to enjoy first-hand information directly from the adversary.

---

[14] Even if Prosper Levot, in Hoefer, *Nouvelle biographie générale* (Paris: Didot, 1873), p. 17, claimed that Fleurieu had designed all the naval plans from 1778 to 1783. Bonnel, U., 'Fleurieu et les États-Unis. Guerre et diplomatie, in Bonnel, U. (ed.), *Fleurieu et la marine de son temps* (Paris: Economica, 1992), pp. 275–279 and Bonnichon, P., *Charles-Pierre Claret, Comte de Fleurieu (1738–1810)* (Paris: Société des Cincinnati de France, 2010), pp. 27–28.

[15] Monaque R., *Les Aventures de Louis-René de Latouche-Tréville, compagnon de La Fayette et commandant de L'Hermione dans la guerre d'Indépendance américaine* (Paris: SPM, 2000), pp. 78–79.

Throughout the eighteenth century, it was usual to ignore the enemy's shores. Maps existed but often proved to be dubious. The data on coastal piloting were also not very reliable. The gap is thus striking between the recurrence of projected landings in the British Isles and the very slight familiarity with English waters. It produced a lot of unrealistic plans. Another consequence, not always fortunate for strategic design, is, the lack of knowledge of British waters and shores. The recourse was to experts (true or supposed) whose competence was sometimes heavily controversial. Foreigners who were sometimes defectors claimed a thorough knowledge of the ports and shores of their country, and sometimes promised to provide intelligence. It was not uncommon for such people of uncertain origins to arrive in the anterooms of a minister, and then enjoy for a rather long time indisputable credit. It seemed obvious to consult them, more frequently than the king's seamen.[16] In 1779, Admiral d'Orvilliers had to support, with difficulty, on his ship such an expert sent by the minister who trusted him as an authority on the British coasts: the so-called marquis of Paradès. Paradès was simultaneously an impostor (from a non-aristocratic birth) and a very skilful spy.[17] Sartine also employed the count de Wall, a Jacobite, brigadier in the French army who had provided a report for Maurepas on the advantages of a landing in Ireland. A Scottish defector from the Royal Navy, Lieutenant Mitchell Hamilton, who had written reports on the coasts of the British Isles was in French service too. Only very late in a plan was it possible to go further with the operational intelligence (How many enemy forces and where?) and to order real secret reconnaissance in the operational zone in order to obtain the exact topographic information in the event of a future landings or raids. It was the case for Jamaica shortly after the war of American Independence, when the French and Spanish had learnt to work together.[18]

What was the place for the allies in operational planning?

To define objectives and to anticipate military forces reaching them did not concern only the king of France and some of his ministers. To fight successfully against Great Britain, needed allies but, consequently, the plans became more complicated because they had to be discussed with them. The

---

[16] Del Perugia, P., *La Tentative*, pp. 66–67; Michel J., *Du Paris de Louis XV à la marine de Louis XVI. L'Œuvre de Monsieur de Sartine*. II, *La Reconquête de la liberté des mers* (Paris: Les Éditions de l'Érudit, 1984), p. 152.

[17] His true family name was Richard and he was the son of a butcher of Phalsbourg, Alsace. But he could keep his composure as well at court, gaining a somewhat high-ranking position in the army, during intelligence missions in Britain.

[18] The chevalier de l'Espine, young navy officer who became famous during the war for accomplishing special and secret operations which he was commissioned to do. Prudhomme, F., and Th. Moné. *Un dragon au service du Roi. Les destinées maritimes du chevalier de l'Espine de 1778 à 1793* (Paris: CNRS Editions, 2022).

consequences were unavoidable, not only because of the distance and the time it took to communicate with them, but also the interests of all concerned were not always convergent.

The diplomatic environment sometimes made it necessary to consider naval operations with allies. This was the case, after the first Family Compact (1733), when, at the end of the 1730s, Spain had to wage war against Britain, in the so-called The War of the Jenkins' Ear. Maurepas intended to send a powerful French naval force to the Caribbean to help the Spanish to overthrow the offensive British were planning in the West Indies. But the alliance was set aside in 1756 by King Ferdinand VI of Spain. When Ferdinand died in 1761 an active alliance became possible again, but Louis XV's navy was no longer in a position to support the new king, Carlos III. Shortly after the peace of 1763 Choiseul and the Spanish minister Grimaldi tried to bring together the two Bourbon navies. But this remained something less than truly strategic. The third Family Compact, was purely defensive, and provided that if one of the two branches of the House of Bourbon was attacked it would receive from the other a naval reinforcement of 20 vessels.

The history of the Franco-Spanish diplomatic and military relations throughout the eighteenth century was a long succession of meetings, not always fortuitous, divergent priorities, and uncoordinated calendars, but also of hopes born of necessity, and at the time of the War of American Independence the possibility of real naval co-operation. The plans of campaign were more the business of the diplomats than seamen. If the dream of an 'union of the maritime forces of the two Crowns' – as Maurepas called it – crossed the century from the first Family Compact in 1733, its effective realization occurred really only later with the War of American Independence.[19] The French strategy sometimes could be strongly modified by allies. Because the court of Versailles, already at war with Great Britain, so badly needed Spanish assistance, it had to accept a complete reorientation of its own strategy.

In 1778, France had chosen to attack Great Britain in North America and much was expected from the squadron of Admiral d' Estaing sailing from Toulon. Simultaneously, the Brest fleet led by Admiral d' Orvilliers had to retain large British forces in the English Channel and the western approaches.[20] While the second part of the plan succeeded the first did not, so the war continued. It was obvious that the Royal Navy would be able to increase its initial numerical advantage compared with the French navy. For

---

[19] Le Bot, P., 'Nouvelle marine d'Espagne', pp. 279–300, especially p. 281, letter from Maurepas to M. de Court, 26 July 1734 with this expression.

[20] Villiers P., 'La Stratégie de la marine française de l'arrivée de Sartine à la victoire de la Chesapeake', in Acerra M., Merino J., and Meyer J. ed., *Les Marines de guerre européennes* xviie–xviiie *siècles* (Paris: Presses Universitaires de Paris-Sorbonne, 1998 [1985]), pp. 211–247.

that reason, the contribution of the Real Armada was vital. But to obtain it, France had to accept Spanish conditions. The design of the strategy to be carried out jointly was thus the result of robust discussion and in the end the triumph of the Spanish conception of a direct strategy against England. Carlos III and his ministers thought it was the most effective way to protect the sea routes and the colonies from Spain. For them it was necessary, like the Romans, to attack Carthage directly, therefore undertaking a landing to obtain a quick decision quickly and to prevent a long and expensive war.[21]

How and where was the allied strategy agreed? It was largely in Madrid, during the arduous discussions between Louis XVI's ambassador, Monsieur de Montmorin, and Carlos III's minister for foreign affairs, the count of Floridablanca. From the French Embassy, the count de Montmorin, observed the Spanish fleet. But Floridablanca required and absolute silence from Vergennes, prohibiting him from consequently consulting both his colleagues in the navy and the war departments as well as the admirals. Consequently, Vergennes had to improvise as a strategist while Louis XVI could confer only with Maurepas and Vergennes. In August 1778 Floridablanca proposed as a matter of discussion a joint attack on the British Isle by a fleet of 60 ships of the line with a landing of troops to oblige London to come on terms. Supporting French operations in North America was not the Spanish aim, but instead another naval campaign opened in Europe in the following year.

When the autumn came, Madrid put pressure on Versailles by demanding from Vergennes a campaign plan.[22] If they did not get it, Spain would content herself with sending 20 vessels, as required by the Family Compact. In September Vergennes proposed two options: an operation against the South coast of England to disorganize enemy trade or a landing in Ireland, which he preferred. But Floridablanca did not give up his own project of an attack on Britain, reminding Vergennes, as late as March 1779, that Spain remained uncommitted to war or peace.

However in March 1779, Vergennes held a committee to which were invited the secretaries of state for the navy and for war, both of whom were astonished to learn that not only was Spain was on the verge of war against Britain but also that they were expected to organize an attack on the Isle of Wight. Vergennes explained to them that it was a diversion to reduce the task in

---

[21] Del Perugia, P., *La Tentative*, pp. 52–65; Dull, J.R., *The French Navy and American Independence*, pp. 136–158; Murphy O.T., *Charles Gravier, Comte de Vergennes. French Diplomacy in the Age of Revolution 1719–1787* (Albany: State University of New York Press, 1982), pp. 252–279 ; Bernard de Montferrand, *Vergennes. La gloire de Louis XVI* (Paris: Tallandier, 2016), pp. 223–257.

[22] Archives du Ministère des Affaires Etrangères, Correspondance politique Espagne, t. 592, f°70, 14 January 1779, quoted by Del Perugia, P., *La Tentative*, pp. 23–24.

America occupying at least part of the island and to hold the trade to and from Bristol, Cork, and Liverpool to ransom. The shift is obvious from the great Spanish plan with French troops landing and marching against London to cut Great Britain down to size, to Vergennes' more modest ambitions to affect British trade, but without destroying the European balance of power. The members of the committee wrote Floridablanca an explanatory note on arrangements to attack the Isle of Wight in which they restricted themselves to only military and technical aspects. A secret convention was signed on 12 April at Aranjuez.

The failure of the combined Armada of 1779 resulted in returning to an indirect strategy, in the Caribbean and America. Let us now see how the French plan of operation for 1781 was developed with Spain and the United States. After a period of uncertainty in 1780, successes were absolutely required to finish the war as quickly as possible. In an apparent paradox, France sent the most powerful naval force it had ever gathered on other side of the Atlantic, under Admiral de Grasse, without a real strategy. The instructions given to the admiral at the time of its departure made it very clear that he had to act as an auxiliary of the Spanish.[23]

This strategy, in effect, demanded that France forget its own objectives in order to strengthen the alliance with Spain and meet the Spanish objectives which were to drive the British out of the Gulf of Mexico and attack Jamaica. The main purpose was to establish allied superiority in the Caribbean. However, within this framework, the instructions suggested to Admiral de Grasse some possible operations, if the Spanish ally had judged them timely. For example, he should send his whole force, or at least part of them, to North America during the Caribbean hurricane season, in order to establish French naval superiority over the Royal Navy and effectively to help the continental army of George Washington.

It is worth noting the double abnegation by Versailles of French strategy and operations. First, they accepted the priorities of their Spanish ally and then deferred to the understanding of the commander of the naval forces on the spot, who was best able to appreciate what was possible. It was a complete innovation, but one that was repeated in the instructions to the Baillie de Suffren when he was sent to operate in the Indian Ocean, out of the control of the French court.

To conclude, what we would today define as the naval strategy of France includes several elements for which there was not an appropriate word in French language at that time. First, the foremost purpose of the eighteenth-century French navy was protect the Atlantic trade and colonies, a mission

---

[23] The original instructions are lost but two letters from Castries, the first to Vergennes, 16 March, and the second to De Grasse, 17 March, allow us to know their content, Archives nationales, Marine B4 216, f°201 r.–205 v. and 199 r.–200 v.

very different from the time of Louis XIV. To face a more numerous enemy in battle was not the raison d'être of the navy before the American War of Independence when a somewhat effective protection of the trade was organized. This explains why France usually accepted a numerical inferiority of between half and the two thirds of British forces. This was the sort of navy that it had been planned and then to be maintained. A consequence of this was the importance of seeking a Spanish alliance in order to match the strength of the British. Ultimately, it was with this theoretical – but available – strength that campaigns were planned, with or without the allies. These plans could be divided into two categories: those aiming to maintain maritime communications, in particular by convoys, and those, often more ambitious and often unrealistic, aiming at a decisive success, including the quick defeat of the enemy.

There were several times when these two plans or strategies were combined over a period of 50 years. This fed into the medium-term shipbuilding programmes of the navy as well as the short-term arming and fitting out of ships necessary for the few months of the next sea campaign. But in the end, whatever the strategy, it was always the very short-term factors of the winds and the currents which determined the success of failure of an operation.

6

Casto Méndez Núñez: The Admiral who could have been Regent, 1861–1868

AGUSTÍN RAMÓN RODRÍGUEZ GONZÁLEZ

One of the greatest exemplars of personal leadership in the history of modern Spain was a naval officer, the son of a humble postal worker from Vigo, whose brilliant career would be acclaimed by contemporary literary figures such as Benito Pérez Galdós and Gustavo Adolfo Bécquer. His name and accomplishments would be commemorated in streets all over Spain, and he would even be proposed as Regent of the Kingdom after the 1868 revolution that deposed Isabel II (who, even so, remained steadfast in her affection for him). Méndez Núñez would never get a chance to play this role, however, because he succumbed to illness only a year later and died at just 45 years of age.

The Spanish navy has memorialized Méndez Núñez several times by naming ships after him: an armoured frigate (up to 1886), a light cruiser (1922–1963), a destroyer (1973–1992), and a new class F-100 frigate (2007–). Among the other ships in this last class, some are named after such illustrious seafarers as Christopher Columbus, Álvaro de Bazán, and Blas de Lezo. Thus, despite ever-shifting political winds, Méndez Núñez's name has continued to be celebrated almost without interruption from the time of his death until the present, a period of almost 150 years.

It is true that Méndez Núñez did not discover a new world or win any decisive battles like Lepanto, Ponta Delgada, or Cartagena de Indias, but his prominence transcends his naval accomplishments, and he has come to be considered a paragon of good character, personifying what it means to be a Spanish patriot.

Born in Vigo on 1June 1824, Méndez Núñez joined the navy as a midshipman before the age of sixteen and was promoted to sub-lieutenant on 11 June 1846, thus rising to an officer's rank more quickly than he ought to have.[1] This was

---

[1] García Martínez, José Ramón, *Méndez Núñez (1824–1869) y la campaña del Pacífico (1862–1869)* (Santiago de Compostela: Xunta de Galicia, 2000), 2 vols.

due to his outstanding service in the reconnaissance expedition to Equatorial Guinea aboard the brigantine *Nervión,* which earned him his first decoration: the Fernando Poo Cross. Later, serving in Spain's expedition in support of Pope Pius IX, he earned the Pontifical Cross and the Pontifical Medal.[2]

He served both at sea and on land, excelling in particular on account of his technical training. He was part of the planning commission for the railway between Tarragona and Reus (1856), and he translated from English – a language that he learned after having entered the navy – a treatise on artillery written by the British general Howard Douglas.

Promoted to lieutenant in 1850, he went on to serve in the Philippines, which in the nineteenth century was tantamount to attending the naval academy and almost *de rigeur* for naval officers. The same cannot be said for army officers, who were rarely deployed in the Philippines. The remoteness of the islands – still scarcely known and mapped – their vulnerability to hurricanes and typhoons, the fact that Spain had little presence there and resources of all kinds were hard to come by, as well as the danger posed by Muslim pirates from Jolo and Mindanao, the threat from European contraband runners – especially the ones who supplied weapons to the pirates – and the imperial ambitions of other powers in the Philippines, all contributed to a remarkably challenging situation for the young Spanish naval officers deployed there. The ships' crews were made up mostly of indigenous sailors, and the ships operated far from their bases, which meant that it was impossible to receive orders, information, or support of any kind within a reasonable timeframe, or before the local circumstances would have changed. And it should be noted that these were the years when navies the world over were adopting steam power, which revolutionized seafaring and naval warfare throughout this period, Méndez Núñez's ratings by his superiors improved continuously, until eventually he was rated as excellent.

At this point it is worthwhile pausing to consider the battle that would catapult Méndez Núñez to glory, even at the risk of seeming to go into unnecessary detail, because of the significance of this battle for later developments and because these events are generally little known.

One of the centres of Muslim piracy was on the large island of Mindanao. Their base was well into the interior, with access to the sea via Río Grande de Mindanao. This meant that an attacking force had to make a dangerous and difficult incursion upriver. Anticipating this, the pirates built their *cotta* or fortification in Pagalugán. It was a square fort, with walls 7 metres high and 6 metres thick. These walls were more than sufficient to repel any attempt to storm the fortress, as they could easily absorb fire from the small and medium pieces that the Spanish light boats would use to attempt to create a breach.

---

[2] Méndez Núñez's naval expedient in Archivo General de Marina Don Álvaro de Bazán, Cuerpo General, pp. 620–735.

To make things even more difficult, the pirates dug a wide moat around the fort, making access nearly impossible. Moreover, the *cotta* was built on the riverbanks, in order to accommodate the pirates' own boats, and was surrounded by a mangrove or marshy forest, making it extremely difficult for an attacker to approach, to build siege-works, or even to set up camp. The humidity, the heat, and tropical disease conspired to make even a short siege impracticable if not impossible.

In addition to these numerous obstacles to taking the fort, its defenders had armed it with four medium-calibre pieces and many *lantakas* (light canons) and garrisoned it with no fewer than 500 men in the fortress itself and 1,000 more in the surrounding area, whence they could attack a disembarking force. Lastly, to prevent or seriously hinder any naval force from reaching the fort (a land offensive would have been virtually impossible), the pirates blocked off the river with a barricade made of tree trunks bound together with ropes and vegetation.

Attempting to take this enclave would be a difficult mission that could very well end in disaster, with all the consequences that would ensue from such a failure. However, the decision was made to make such an attempt in 1861, using a joint expedition of the army, which would provide the bulk of the landing force, and the navy, which would provide the ships for this amphibious operation.

The army was made up of elite companies, the *cazadores* (light infantry) and grenadiers, belonging to the Príncipe and Infante regiments of the Philippines garrison, along with a battery of four field guns and a contingent of workmen. Except for the officers and many sub-officers, the land forces were made up indigenous soldiers who were accustomed to the terrain, in addition to being highly motivated to take on the pirates. The commanding officer was José Ferrater. The naval forces included two schooners, the *Constancia* and the *Valiente*, steam gunboats numbers 5, 12, 13, and 18 – the *Luzón, Arayat, Pampanga*, and *Taal*, respectively – and tenders numbers 1, 11, 13, 14, 36, and 37, with European officers and indigenous crewmen. To transport the land troops, three small merchant vessels were mobilized – the *Scipión*, the *Soledad*, and the *Vicente*. The naval force was led by Méndez Núñez, who had recently been promoted from lieutenant commander to commander of the corvette *Narváez,* and named head of a division of gunboats and other minor vessels in Mindanao, called the *División de Fuerzas Sutiles del Sur de las Visayas*. Lieutenants José Malcampo and Zoilo Sánchez Ocaña commanded the *Constancia* and the *Valiente*, respectively.

In order to have an accurate idea of these ships, it should be noted that the schooners were simply large gunboats, weighing only 500 tons apiece, with steam engines and propellers and armed with two 32-millimetre cannons each. The gunboats were only 50-ton vessels and also had propellers; the tenders were simple large sailing and rowing boats, some of which were armed with a small cannon on the bow.[3]

The expedition thus had a total of some 850 men, between the four companies mentioned above, a battery, and a contingent of workmen, as well as the vessels mentioned above: two schooners, four gunboats, and six tenders, in addition to the three merchant vessels. Supreme command was vested in Colonel Ferrater, since he outranked Méndez Núñez, whose rank was equivalent to that of a recently promoted lieutenant colonel in the army.

The expedition rendezvoused on 16 November and made the difficult trip up the river. As it approached its objective, just before a bend in the river, Ferrater ordered two companies to disembark to carry out a reconnaissance.

After ordering the fort to surrender – and following much to-ing and fro-ing in an attempt to reach an agreement with the pirates – at 4:30 a.m. on 17 November 1861, the ships' cannons opened fire on the fort, while the boats landed two companies of rangers and one company of grenadiers supported by two field guns. Fire proliferated from both sides. Shortly before, the ships had succeeded in breaking through the barrier, allowing the expedition to pass through.

But the terrain surrounding the fort made it difficult to manoeuvre. The soldiers met a barrage of fire from the enemy hidden among the mangroves, and the thick, high walls made it impossible to storm the fort. The pieces that had been brought ashore could barely move in the swampy terrain, and neither they nor the ships' cannons were able to create a breach in the fort's thick walls. Moreover, the engine of the gunboat *Luzón* was disabled after being hit twice by enemy cannons, and by 7:30 a.m., large numbers of wounded were being transported downstream.

Faced with the prospect of a complete debacle, Colonel Ferrater opted for a hasty retreat, before things could deteriorate even further. The intelligence that had been gathered about the terrain, the fortifications, and the size of the enemy force had obviously been inaccurate. But Méndez Núñez, who had gone ashore on a reconnaissance mission, decided to disobey his disheartened superior, declaring, 'The Navy will not retreat!' – a phrase that would soon become legendary, and as a result, the situation was completely turned around. Here it is best to quote Méndez Núñez's own words describing what happened next [4]:

> ... having come to an agreement with Colonel of EM [Ferrater], I ordered him and the commander of the infantry, Don Francisco Moscoso, who led

---

[3] García Martínez, José Ramón, *Buques de la real armada de SMC Isabel II (1830–1868)* (Madrid: DVD, 2005).

[4] García Martínez, José Ramón, 'Pagalugán', *Revista Española de Historia Militar* 4 (2000): 202–209.

the land force after Commander García Carrillo was wounded, to be ready to scale the walls, and returning to the *Constancia*, I ordered all available riflemen onto the crosstrees, the yards, and bowsprit. To the schooner's commander I gave the order to raise anchor and charge the *cotta* with the prow, at full steam, the order was carried out with the utmost skill, and at 8:15, with great zeal and shouts of 'Long Live the Queen!,' the schooner collided with the enemy fort, and the sailors and soldiers on board the *Constancia* and those who were on land simultaneously went over the walls. Then began the hand-to-hand fighting, which lasted for quarter of an hour, during which time the lieutenant leading the storming party [Malcampo] took a bullet above his left breast, and Sub-Lieutenant Pascual Cervera y Topete took command of the ship's crew. At 8:30, the enemy began to flee from the far side of the *cotta*, but since this area was within sight of the swivel gun on the bow of the *Constancia*, they were sprayed with grapeshot and rifle fire, resulting in a large number of casualties. In short order, we were in complete control of the fort, and the Spanish flag was flying victoriously above its walls and being saluted with great zeal by land and sea troops alike.

Both bold and dashing, this astonishing feat is believed to be unique in naval history: a fort taken by boarding. The deed demonstrates Méndez Núñez's levelheadedness and determination. His decisiveness made it possible to turn an operation that was on the verge of disaster into a great and unanticipated victory, with the myriad consequences that follow from victory, not least of which was the effect on the enemy's morale and the morale of Spain's own troops.

The next day, Méndez Núñez set out in the gunboat *Pampanga* and together with two of the rowing boats belonging to the schooners went a distance upriver on reconnaissance, but the enemy had disappeared.

The casualties on the side of the victors were appreciable: 18 dead and 106 wounded. Among them were officers, such as Malcampo and Commander Moscoso. Almost all the casualties were inflicted by bladed weapons, or by grapeshot from enemy cannons and *lantakas*, and few were the result of individual firearms. The total number of casualties represented about 14.7% of the expedition's force, an indication of how fierce the fighting was. Among the navy, the *Constancia* was hit six times by enemy cannon fire and had one dead and six wounded; the *Valiente*, eight wounded, and the *Luzón*, which took several hits and whose engine failed, four wounded; the *Arayat*, one dead and five wounded; the *Pampanga*, one dead and six wounded; the *Taal*, one dead and four wounded; plus three more wounded on tenders 14, 36, and 37. Some 110 corpses of pirates were found in the *cotta* and another 26 in the surrounding area. However, given the Muslim custom of recovering the bodies of the dead at any cost, it was estimated that there must have been many more, possibly as many as 200. Among them were the *datto*, or supreme leader, Maghuda, and another leader's firstborn son.

It was deemed inexpedient, in every respect, to garrison the fort. So, explosives were set and it was demolished to its foundations. Then, the expeditionary force boarded the ships and returned with news of the sensational victory.

Another interesting detail is that the men who boarded the *cotta* from the *Constancia* did so both from the bowsprit, the nearly horizontal spar extending out from the prow, and from boards that served as ramps between the ship and the fortress's walls. The schooner was positioned at a 60-degree angle to the wall, which recalls Cervantes's famous 'Discourse on Arms and Letters' in *Don Quijote*, in which he reminisces about the Battle of Lepanto and the difficulty and danger involved in naval boarding.

These events, which had a huge effect on public opinion both in Spain and in the Philippines, garnered Méndez Núñez a new, well-deserved promotion. He had been promoted to commander in May 1861 and was promoted again to captain in January of the following year; a space of only nine months.

Méndez Núñez was later deployed in the Caribbean as commander of the veteran and poorly maintained paddle steamer *Isabel II*, where he served with distinction, despite his ship's shortcomings. His first mission took place in the middle of a civil war in Venezuela. The city of Puerto Cabello was under siege and the neutral parties trapped there were in need of supplies. Méndez Núñez, combining firmness with diplomacy, was able to deliver the needed aid, without firing a single shot.

Shortly thereafter, he came to the aid of the besieged garrison in Puerto Plata, on the island of Santo Domingo. This garrison found itself in an awkward position when, after Santo Domingo requested and was granted reincorporation into the Spanish Empire, a revolution broke out in opposition to the voluntary annexation. In his old steamship, Méndez Núñez took a landing force of 650 men, horses, and cannons, and on a moonless night, among treacherous shoals, he succeeded in delivering these decisive reinforcements without mishap and without casualties.

After being given command of the screw frigate *Princesa de Asturias*, he continued his active service in the Caribbean. In recognition of his abilities, he was named chief of staff in the Ministry of the Navy. However, he lasted only one year in this capacity. Despite many clear advantages that accompanied the position, he was not comfortable being privy to and caught up in the partisan clashes of the day and the constant struggle of each individual and faction to advance its own interests.

In 1864, Méndez Núñez's ability and integrity earned him the command of a new armoured frigate, the *Numancia*. With its ironclad hull and armour, this ship was revolutionary for its time, as were its precursors, the French frigate *Gloire* and the British *Warrior*. In a clear sign of the esteem and respect with which he was regarded, he was allowed to select all of the ship's officers, as well as the subalterns and crewmen.

Méndez Núñez's leadership was not confined to effective and efficient command. He had also earned a fine reputation as a leader concerned for the welfare of those that served under him. Everyone knew that he made great efforts to stay abreast of the personal lives of even the lowest of his subordinates. At a time when photography was still in its infancy he kept albums of photographs of members of his crew, including rank-and-file sailors, which are still preserved in the Pontevedra Museum.

It was a formidable challenge to be the commander of a ship as new as the *Numancia*. In addition to the serious problem of navigation itself, since ironclads were very heavy and thus vulnerable in stormy seas, it was understood that such ships would present hygiene and health problems on long, oceanic voyages. As it turned out these were the least of the challenges that Méndez Núñez would have to overcome.

Off the west coast of South America, an expedition was made up of two frigates and two screw schooners was cruising between ports. It was under the command of Luis Hernández Pinzón, a descendent of one of Columbus's collaborators. It was essentially a public relations mission, to 'fly the flag' in Spain's former American possessions. At the same time a high-profile scientific expedition was dispatched, as if to remind the world of the achievements of the Spanish navy in the Age of Enlightenment. It had been planned back in 1860, but its departure was delayed until the summer of 1862.

Everything went as planned in the Atlantic ports, but as soon as the expedition reached the Pacific, problems arose one after another: Spain still did not have normal diplomatic relations with Chile or Peru, and many people in these countries feared that the expedition was merely a cover for Spanish designs on its former colonies. This was not an unreasonable fear, given that there was a full-scale French invasion of Mexico happening at that very moment.

These suspicions were exacerbated particularly in Peru, where some emigrants from Spain were assaulted, one of whom died while four others were injured. Following complaints by Pinzón and Spain's plenipotentiary – Eusebio Salazar y Mazarredo, a devious and inept high-ranking official in Spain's ministry of foreign affairs, tensions mounted and Pinzón finally ordered the occupation of the Chinchas Islands as a guarantee of Spanish immigrants' rights. The Spanish were able to occupy the islands without any violence. During this period, this archipelago had great economic importance for Peru because it was a source of guano – a valuable natural fertilizer that was exported to countries all around the world. On top of all of this, in order to further his own personal interests, Salazar had concealed from Pinzón Madrid's entirely peaceful and conciliatory instructions. This episode led to Pinzón's resignation and Salazar's removal. In addition, one of the Spanish frigates, *Triunfo*, was lost in an accidental fire, though there were no casualties.

José Manuel Pareja took command of the squadron. He was the son of a Trafalgar hero and had, oddly enough, been born in Lima and served as a royalist leader in Peru and especially Chile during the wars of Spanish-American independence. Foreseeing further problems, Spain sent three more frigates to reinforce the squadron. However, Pareja clearly favoured the diplomatic route and decided to sign an accord with the Peruvian minister Vivanco and to order the withdrawal from the Chinchas, after which tensions seemed to ease.

However, many in Peru saw the episode as an affront to their country's dignity, and enraged mobs attacked off-duty crewmen from the squadron in the port of Callao, killing a corporal, Esteban Fradera. Although there were no immediate confrontations between the Spanish squadron and the Peruvians, it is true that a civil war erupted across the country between those who favoured peace with Spain and those who wanted war, and the latter, led by General Prado, eventually had their way.

In the meantime, Pareja had sailed south with the squadron hoping to reach an agreement with the Chilean authorities, who were supporting their northern neighbour in the crisis. But this time Pareja was not able to come to an understanding, and in response to riots that broke out against Spanish citizens and Spanish interests, he ordered the squadron to blockade the Chilean coast.

Formal hostilities had still not been declared, but given the clear damage being done to their economy, the Chileans decided to challenge the blockaders. Without any declaration of war and flying a neutral flag, the corvette *Esmeralda* staged a surprise attack and, following a hard-fought battle, captured a schooner *Covadonga*, which was very much its inferior. When the news reached Pareja, including a false report that the other schooner, the *Vencedora*, had also been taken, it left him completely shattered and he committed suicide.[5]

Meanwhile, Méndez Núñez, along with the *Numancia*, had just joined the squadron involved in these events. He had been promoted to brigadier – equivalent to the rank of commodore today – and thus became the squadron's supreme commander. We can imagine the situation: diplomacy had failed to resolve a minor dispute that had become increasingly complicated, and Méndez Núñez's predecessors as commander of the squadron had either resigned (Pinzón) or committed suicide (Pareja). What is more, Méndez Núñez also had to take on the role of plenipotentiary in the negotiations with the American republics, which now included – in addition to Chile and Peru – Ecuador and Bolivia, which had joined the fray.

No less of a challenge was the task of leading a squadron that had no safe havens between the Strait of Magellan and the coast of Colombia and that

---

[5] Rodríguez González, Agustín Ramón, *La campaña del Pacífico: España frente a Chile y Perú (1862–1871)* (Madrid: Agualarga, 1999). There is a second edition (Madrid: Real del Catorce, 2017).

was further hampered by slow and unreliable communications with Madrid, making an already volatile and complicated situation even more challenging. To make matters still worse, Méndez Núñez was considerably younger and had less seniority than his subordinates The commanders of the squadron's ships each had their personality, experience, and ideology, but were obliged to accept as their leader not only the youngest officer but also the one who had most recently arrived on the scene.

But Méndez Núñez succeeded in overcoming all of this with real leadership: he dispatched two frigates to engage the Chilean-Peruvian combined fleet sheltering on Chiloe Island, in an archipelago surrounded by extremely dangerous waters, in the hope that this would force an agreement and that the *Covadonga* and the prisoners would be returned. However, in the Battle of Abtao, which ended with no clear victor, the allies decided to take refuge in an inaccessible cove, and nothing was resolved. Proof of the treachery of those waters is the fact that a frigate and an armed steamship were lost in an accident.

Méndez Núñez approached the allies again, this time with the *Numancia* and a different frigate, but they had sheltered in an even more inaccessible place. However, the second expedition did dissuade the allies from attempting any offensive moves and they remained sheltering there passively throughout the entire war. Moreover, the steamship *Paquete del Maule* was taken, along with its more than one hundred Chilean officers, sailors, and soldiers, whom the Spaniards offered in exchange for the prisoners from the *Covadonga*, an offer that the Chilean government inexplicably rejected.

Left with no other choice than to punish the capture of the schooner, the government in Madrid ordered Méndez Núñez to bomb the port of Valparaíso. Méndez Núñez was dismayed by this course of action but he had to accept the decision, of the command authorities, and because he could see no other option. However, a British squadron under the command of Rear Admiral Joseph Denman and a US squadron commanded by Commodore John Rodgers were in the theatre to fiercely resist the bombardment, following instructions from their governments. This seemed to be an insurmountable obstacle, especially because the US force began to prepare for battle, with the goal of dissuading the Spanish from their planned course of action.

But Méndez Núñez's resolve and diplomatic skill – in addition to the Chilean government's indefensible position – cleared the way, persuading even Denman and Rodgers that bombarding Valparaíso was the only possible option. However, it is also true that Méndez Núñez was loath to bombard a defenceless city (the Chileans had withdrawn their cannons from the port's battery). He warned the city four days ahead of the attack, so that the people could be evacuated, and he directed fire only at government buildings and warehouses. Because of this, the bombardment which took place on 31 March

1866 resulted in very few casualties – two deaths and a few wounded, at most – which were the result of the failure to heed Méndez Núñez's warnings.

More than the bombardment itself, the thing that made the biggest impression in Spain and in other countries, where these events were being watched closely, was that Méndez Núñez succeeded in prevailing upon the British and the Americans and gaining their agreement for his actions and even their admiration.

As far as the government in Madrid was concerned, that would have been the end of the campaign, but Méndez Núñez and his subordinates were of a very different mind. Madrid had told him, as he faced Valparaíso and the British and American squadrons, that it was better for him to 'succumb gloriously in enemy waters than to return to Spain without honour or shame', and now he took the government at its word and decided that 'honour without the navy comes before the navy without honour'. He thus prepared to attack the formidable defences of the Peruvian port of Callao, so that it could never be said that his squadron only bombarded unprotected cities and captured harmless merchant vessels.

The challenge was formidable, given that the port's artillery included more than 90 large-calibre pieces, among them Armstrong guns and Blakely rifles, which fired 300- and 500-pound shells, while the Spanish squadron's largest cannon only fired 68-pound projectiles. Moreover, the Peruvians had installed underwater mines that were operated through electric cables from land, and they had at their disposal a flotilla of two small ironclads and three steam vessels, all armed with torpedoes.

On top of all of that, only 12 years earlier, in the Crimean War, a French-British allied squadron had bombarded the Russian port of Sevastopol, proving once again that batteries arrayed on coasts were superior to the ships that attacked them. And the Russians did not have cannons as large as the Peruvians' or torpedoes, mines, and ironclads. Nelson himself said that a cannon positioned on land defences was worth five ships with the same calibre guns.

Thus, ignoring the orders of his government (he responded famously to the messenger who brought him the order to retreat, 'Let us agree that you arrived tomorrow'), Méndez Núñez decided to attack this redoubtable foe, and he did so significantly on 2 May, a date cherished by Spanish patriots.[6] The fighting was fierce. Two Spanish frigates were forced to withdraw from battle when a single hit by enemy mortars seriously damaged their wooden hulls; and on another, a spectacular fire threatened to blow the entire ship sky high. Despite all of this, Méndez Núñez kept up the fight and in the end claimed victory.

---

[6] The famous 1808 uprising in Madrid against French forces, immortalized by Goya, took place on May 2.

The only vessel whose armour made it nearly invulnerable was the *Numancia* itself, Méndez Núñez's flagship. However, he disliked availing himself of its protection when his crewmen could not. So, he led the battle from the *Numancia*'s unprotected bridge, and was seriously wounded by enemy grapeshot.

A noteworthy example of his leadership is that, when the enemy's resistance had begun to flag and when munitions were almost spent, his second-in-command came to his cabin for orders, and Méndez Núñez's reply was: 'Have the boys had enough?'; and only after receiving an affirmative did he give the order for the fighting to stop. And he did so by sending the crews up the rigging, before the eyes of the defeated enemy, and giving the required salute to Isabel II, in a clear challenge to the enemy.

Afterwards, he ordered the retreat. He sent the *Numancia*, a second frigate, and some transport vessels back to Spain via the Pacific, a voyage that would turn out to be the first circumnavigation of the globe in a battleship and a reprise of Juan Sebastián Elcano's heroic completion of Magellan's voyage. Despite his wounds, Méndez Núñez set sail for the Atlantic with four frigates. He sailed past the enemy fleet in Chiloe (which had grown larger with ships bought by Spain's enemies in Europe). He was on his guard in Uruguay's and Brazil's ports, expecting an allied counterattack that never materialized. All of this was accomplished following a long and exhausting campaign, through cold and stormy seas, with crews suffering from scurvy due to the lack of fresh food and who had not set foot on land for years. He kept up his vigilance until December 1868, when he finally reached Cadiz.

When word of the victory reached Spain, excitement spread among the general public. The campaign was hailed in the popular and literary presses alike (a topic we address below), streets all across Spain began to be named 'Méndez Núñez', 'Pacífico', 'Callao', and so on, and the same plaza that today faces the Senate was called at that time 'La Marina española' in honour of the campaign and all that it represented. Even the government, whose indecisiveness and ineptitude were revealed in the mismanagement of the whole affair, was forced to recognize Méndez Núñez's great merit, and on 10 July 1866, not long after news about Callao reached Spain, he was promoted to squadron leader – rear admiral – his fourth promotion in just over four years. And since even this reward seemed inadequate, before the month was out, he was awarded the status of National Hero and the Great Cross of Carlos III. The government went on to award him the Navy Cross – 'Cruz de la Marina de la Diadema Real' – on 10 January the following year, in a crowning acknowledgement of his accomplishments.

In addition to these honours, Méndez Núñez earned the respect of those the world over who knew anything of naval affairs, who appreciated the sound judgement he had exercised and the significance of his achievements. In the Battle of Lissa, between the Austrian Empire and an Italian fleet, which took place on 19 July 1866, soon after the bombardment of Callao, the Austrian fleet commander, Admiral Tegethoff, could think of no better way to rally his sailors than to put before them the example of the Spanish in their offensive against the Peruvian port. Many of the veterans of the shelling of Sevastopol were of the same opinion.

It is often forgotten that the great Spanish Romanticist poet, Gustavo Adolfo Bécquer (1836–1870), chronicled these events as a contributor to the weekly *El Museo Universal*, an illustrated magazine of the kind that was typical at the time. It published meticulous engravings and included pieces on cultural criticism, developments in the arts, and scientific and geographical discoveries, as well as serial novels, and much more. But the most serious and influential section was the 'Revista Semanal', an editorial-like feature occupying the front page that was penned by Bécquer between June 1865 and September 1866, a period coinciding with the final, most eventful phase of what came to be known as the Campaign of the Pacific. For a while, Bécquer was a simple though astute commentator on the events, as the news trickled in from the far-away scene of the hostilities. But when the time came to make an overall assessment of the significance of the episode, Bécquer, again echoing a widely shared opinion, noted enthusiastically that the resurgence of the Spanish navy was now a reality (see Appendix).

After describing the decadence into which the navy had fallen during the reign of Fernando VII, Bécquer pointed out that it recovered during the reign of his daughter, Isabel II, when Spain once again commanded one of the best navies in the world, ranking it in a respectable fourth place. But it was not just about having the ships; Spain had everything it needed to be able to boast of an effective fleet. The Campaign of the Pacific made this clear, and under some of the most difficult conditions that one can imagine, and that was what prompted the feelings of satisfaction and pride.

In my opinion, these declarations by Bécquer are not merely those of a journalist discussing current events. They are deeply felt pronouncements by a man whose desire for national regeneration has been fulfilled. At the time, the most reliable barometer for this regeneration was the status of the naval forces since they were a reflection of a country's prestige abroad. Still, in this matter, as in so many others, Bécquer was giving voice to a common sentiment among Spaniards at the time, from the staunchest *Carlistas* to most forward-thinking progressives. It should be pointed out here that the role assigned to the army, which was enmeshed in national politics and charged with maintaining domestic order, was very different from the role of the navy, which acted on the world stage, away from the political infighting, and was keenly attentive to the revolution in science and technology.

For his part, the great novelist Benito Pérez Galdós (1843–1920) immortalized Méndez Núñez's heroic feats in his 'Episodios Nacionales' series, in a novel titled *La Vuelta al mundo de la Numancia*. However, the novel was written and published in 1906, after the fateful events of 1898, when Spain lost most of its overseas colonies. And thus, the author's tone is understandably nostalgic, as he recalls the enthusiasm he felt during his youth.

Méndez Núñez did not want to have any part in the popular revolution that broke out in September 1868, which deposed Isabel II. In fact, at the time he was still at sea, patrolling American ports. But it should be noted that the navy did participate actively in the revolution. Indeed, the leader of the revolution was Admiral Juan Bauptista Topete, who until recently had been a subordinate of Méndez Núñez's. However, the navy acted *en bloc*, unlike the army, which was divided into factions for and against.

Although Méndez Núñez was decidedly apolitical, his conduct in the Pacific was a clear counterpoint to the government's ineptitude, and his famous 'honour without the navy comes before the navy without honour' was immediately adopted by the revolutionaries, who changed it to 'long live Spain with honour'. But it was not just that. True to his principles, he turned down a promotion to vice admiral of the navy that the provisional government offered him in October 1868, citing his reasons in the following words:

> I beg Your Excellency and the Administration to take into consideration that only seven years ago I was honoured with the modest epaulettes of a lieutenant. For me to be useful to my fatherland and the Navy Corps, it is not necessary for me to be granted a position that I would only hope to deserve when further services on my part to my country should render me worthy of it, not only in the opinion of the Administration but also in the people's opinion and my own.

This was a wake-up call, as well as a demonstration of his leadership status in the navy, since it set a precedent and afterwards other members of the navy refused to accept any promotions, honours, or rewards for their participation in the revolution, claiming that they had merely fulfilled a grim duty for the good of the country. This was in marked contrast to their counterparts in the army.

Isabel II herself appealed to Méndez Núñez at this point. The queen had congratulated and enthusiastically praised him in a private letter she sent him on 9 July 1866. However, she had ignored his request to be relieved of his command two years later, when he was still patrolling off the coast of Rio de Janeiro. After being deposed, she appealed to his sense of patriotism and his concern for Spain and its navy, addressing several letters to him from her exile in Pau and Paris in November and December 1868. Méndez Núñez refused to be manipulated, however, and never sent a response.[7] Still, the letters make clear that he was a key player in Spanish affairs at the time. This

---

[7] González, José Antonio, 'Méndez Núñez y la revolución de 1868: tres cartas inéditas de Isabel II', *Revista de Historia Naval* 6 (1984): 89–97.

is why, despite his rejection of promotion, he became a member of the navy's ruling body, the Navy Board, and in March 1869 was named vice president of the admiralty.

Méndez Núñez was in line for an even greater destiny. The revolutionaries soon began their search for a new occupant for the throne who was not a member of the previous dynasty, which posed serious problems. As negotiations dragged on over the different candidates from other countries, the idea began to take hold that Méndez Núñez, whose patriotism, honour, and leadership were universally admired, should assume the regency of the kingdom while a suitable successor to the throne could be found. It is indicative of the respect he commanded in Spain at the time that he was not proposed as president or minister of the government but, despite his modest background, as nothing less than head of state, even if only for an interim period.

To everyone's surprise, Méndez Núñez developed a sudden and mysterious illness. He died on 21 August 1869, after a long and painful confinement, in his house in Pontevedra, having only recently turned 45 years of age. Given the primitive state of medicine at the time, it makes sense to assume that he died of natural causes, as a result of the wounds he received at Callao and the hardships suffered during the prolonged campaign. However, the theory has also been expressed that he was poisoned. This possibility cannot be totally ruled out, if only because, a little more than a year later, General Juan Prim (1814–1870), Spain's other leading military figure at the time, was assassinated (though his politics were completely different from those of Méndez Núñez). The consequences of Prim's death for the history of Spain have been the subject of much conjecture, and so it is not unreasonable to speculate about what might have been if Méndez Núñez had not died prematurely.

Méndez Núñez continued to receive honours even after his death. The new king, Amadeo I of Savoy, created the title Marquis of Méndez Núñez for his successors, which still exists today. In 1883, during the reign of Alfonso XII, Méndez Núñez's remains were moved to the San Fernando Pantheon of Illustrious Naval Officers in Cadiz, and the coffin was transported in the frigate *Lealtad*, which seems to have been deliberately chosen for its name, meaning 'Loyalty'. The ceremony that was held in Vigo's port was impressive, but even more so was the fact that a British squadron commanded by the illustrious vice admiral Sir William Montagu Dowell (1831–1912) – who not coincidentally had served in the Crimean War and the shelling of Shimonoseki – was also there to pay tribute. This homage by the world's premier navy, and by such a decorated fellow officer, would surely have gratified Méndez Núñez, the great naval officer and leader, more than any other.

Appendix

Gustavo Adolfo Bécquer's editorial commentary on Méndez Núñez's successful Pacific campaign ('Revista Semanal', in the weekly *El Museo Universal,* June 1865–September 1866).

Having ships is not the same as having a navy; this is often said, and for good reason. If land armies are not thrown together hastily, then much less so the personnel required for battle at sea.

As the glorious traditions of our navy were temporarily broken, due to the miserable state into which it had fallen not so long ago – and not only in the far-away regions where we wage war but also in the countries that are capable of knowing the exact state of our affairs – it was still doubtful whether the navy could truly be rehabilitated.

Little by little, the seas have filled with ships – some built in our own arsenals and others in France and England – whose highest masts fly the Spanish flag. Year by year, the numbers have registered a significant increase in the country's naval forces, which, before falling into an inconceivably shameful state, had once been counted among the powers known as masters of the seas. But having ships is not the same as having a navy, as has often been said by those who are displeased to see Spain gradually regaining the status to which it is entitled by virtue of its circumstances, its position, and its history. The zealous champions of our national honour, commanded by their brave and expert leader, Mr. Méndez Núñez, are at this very moment washing away the insult to our flag in the blood of the enemy and are providing by their conduct and their heroic deeds an appropriate response to those who still harbour such doubts.

The long suffering and the constancy needed to bear with glad heart and zeal the sheer exhaustion of such a rough and arduous activity, the expertise and the knowledge given by the terrible element in which he lives, the quiet valour that makes it possible for him to risk his life in the most dangerous of undertakings. These are the great qualities that define a good sailor…

Our brothers have displayed each and every one of these qualities before the eyes of the world. The *Numancia* resolved the nautical problem posed by the difficulty of taking an armoured ship to far-away regions, and the *Blanca* and the *Villa de Madrid*, under enemy cannon fire with the sole aid of a maritime chart, manoeuvred among the treacherous shallows and shoals surrounding the port of Abtao, on Chiloe. All have provided irrefutable proof of being well-seasoned and highly skilled.

Throughout four straight years of being on a war footing, four years of suffering and privation, during which time they sometimes lacked the most basic of necessities and had to rely on their wits, on backbreaking labour, and on their prodigious capacity to repair all the deficiencies and the malfunctions that are typical of such a long and dangerous voyage – during all this time they also demonstrated the signs of their character, their admirable discipline, and the pleasure and readiness they bring to the most arduous of tasks in service to their country, a country that founds its hopes and its pride on them.

The justice that the most noteworthy men and publications abroad could not help but to do them will duly rectify the mistaken idea about our real significance that the enemies of the glories of Spain wish to assert.

Therefore, we have ships and we have a navy, because our shores are amply peopled with those long seasoned to the challenges of life at sea, and we can claim brave and knowledgeable officers to lead them. This is what needed to be proven and this is what we proved at the first opportunity that our fleet was given to do so.

7

Teaching by Example: Julian Corbett's *The Campaign of Trafalgar* of 1910

ANDREW LAMBERT

This essay examines the recovery and development of strategic leadership as an educational aid for senior officers and statesmen. Between 1902 and 1914 Julian Stafford Corbett (1854–1922) provided history and strategy lectures for the Royal Navy's senior level war course, an educational programme designed to prepare the navy's leadership for future conflicts through in depth study of strategy, technology, intentional law, historical and contemporary experience, and national policy.[1] Corbett, a lawyer by training, was wealthy and politically engaged. In the less than a decade he developed his limited initial brief, providing historical content, into a programme to capture and define national strategy, and disseminate it as doctrine. He worked closely with service leaders, including First Sea Lord Admiral Sir John Fisher (1904–1910) and successive directors of naval intelligence, the navy's chief war planner, and the officer responsible for the war course. Not only did he teach almost all the middle and senior level naval officers who served in the First World War, but his extensive publications ensured national strategic doctrine was widely understood, by service leaders and civilians.

Corbett's work was shaped by service agendas, but the navy left him to deliver the programme. This intellectual partnership between the navy's strategic leadership and a sophisticated Clausewitzian intellectual proved to highly effective. In 1907 Corbett published *England in the Seven Years' War: A Study in Combined Strategy*, which demonstrated the impact of limited maritime strategy in a global war with extensive continental military operations.[2] It was a template for a future conflict, written for admirals and

---

[1] Lambert, A.D. ed. *21st Century Corbett* (Annapolis: United States Naval Institute Press, 2017).

[2] Corbett, J.S. *England in the Seven Year's War: A Study in Combined Strategy* (London: Longman, 1907).

statesmen, not academics. The book stressed that British maritime/amphibious strategy had triumphed over French-continental methods, and remained the basis of national strategy in 1907. He highlighted the critical role of civilian strategic leadership, working in partnership with sophisticated service leaders, in this case Pitt the Elder and Admiral Lord Anson. His argument shaped contemporary strategic choice, ensuring Britain did not create a mass conscript army before 1916.

The leadership he studied was national, not individual, rational rather than heroic, and his focus was on the evolution of contemporary strategic doctrine. In his study of the Trafalgar campaign Corbett emphasised strategic continuity, not tactical innovation. Nelson was not the centre of his study: instead he focused on the critical relationship between civilian and naval leaderships in the development and execution of national policy, and developed a strategic doctrine in response to the existential threat posed by Napoleon's total war methods. The Trafalgar study argued that British limited maritime strategy had triumphed in a total war.

In early January 1909 Corbett completed editing a volume of old tactical instructions, designed to stimulate fresh thinking among contemporary officers. *Signals and Instructions* also focused his attention on a noisy, but ill-informed debate about Nelson's tactics at Trafalgar.[3] He began work on a series of Trafalgar lectures for the war course on 20 January, and advised his friend Sidney Colvin, keeper of prints and drawings at the British Museum, on a recently discovered plan of Trafalgar.[4] The following day he went to the Public Record Office, to read the reports of two controversial British admirals from the 1805 campaign; Sir John Orde and Sir Robert Calder. Both would receive sympathetic, insightful treatment in Corbett's lectures and his final text.[5] The lectures were delivered in Devonport the same week. Further research, aided by a permit to see restricted Foreign Office files concerning Lisbon in 1805, was followed by a second series of lectures at Sheerness, His host, Admiral Sir Francis Bridgeman, lately appointed second sea lord, discussed his intentions for the office without reserve. Bridgeman would be responsible for naval education, so Corbett sent copies of his books; which had long been shaped for the professional military educational needs of the Royal Navy. Other attendees at the lectures included Rear Admiral Alexander

---

[3] Corbett, J.S. ed. *Signals and Instructions 1778–1794* (London: Navy Records Society, 1909).

[4] In contrast to his earlier writings the presence of a full diary makes it possible to connect the compilation of Corbett's *The Campaign of Trafalgar* with his War Course lectures and other, related activity.

[5] Sir Julian Stafford Corbett Papers, Royal Museums, Greenwich (hereafter CBT). Diary 27.1.1909: CBT 43/10.

Bethell, the new director of naval intelligence (DNI), to whom Corbett offered his services.[6]

Corbett continued working on the lectures until late February, when the word 'lectures' was dropped.

> Began writing Trafalgar campaign, with many doubts as to wisdom thereof – in spite of being urged to by Slade, Bridgeman and many other naval officers. But I have found so much that is unknown about it that all recent criticisms go on a misconception of what its object was, thus I think I will go on with it, tho' against my feeling to crib history in scraps.[7]

Plans to continue his projected sequence of case studies by addressing the American War of Independence were abandoned because the service demanded he address the crowning glory of the naval art, one where the strategic, political, and tactical issues remained unsettled. His work on tactics and the preparation of these lectures had uncovered a familiar historiographical problem, the poverty of existing scholarship. There was no study of the campaign in English, and relatively little published work dealing with the battle that could assist naval students. Once he had expounded these ideas to his naval audience, including the incoming second sea lord, the sea officers pressed him to act. Such pressure was more than Corbett could resist, not least because the material was so attractive, and, as his tactical studies had emphasised, this was the capstone of the experience of the age of sail. It may not be accidental that on the previous day he had been discussing a possible translation of Colonel Edouard Desbrière's text.[8]

With his lecture notes and printed sources already in hand, Corbett launched into the book the very next day, 'made a real start' on the diplomatic preliminaries, and was soon engaged in the diplomatic correspondence relating to the formation of the *Third Coalition*.[9] Outside it was snowing hard, and the 'We Want Eight' Dreadnought crisis was threatening to split the Liberal Cabinet.

Among the first issues to be addressed was the relative value given to the first, second, and third rate ships of the line in 1805. Alfred T. Mahan, Admiral Sir Reginald Custance, and naval architect Sir William White had all argued that the third rate 74 was the ideal type, in order to criticise Admiral Fisher's revolutionary HMS *Dreadnought* of 1906. Corbett quickly established that Nelson, and most other naval men, reckoned a three decked first rate like

---

[6] Diary 8–12.2.1909: CBT 43/10.

[7] Diary 23.2.1909: CBT 43/10. The diary was written as an aide-mémoir.

[8] Desbrière, E. *La Campagne maritime de Trafalgar.* Service Historique Paris 1909. See Corbett *Trafalgar*

[9] Rose, J.H. *Select Dispatches Relating to the Third Coalition against France, 1804–5* (London: Camden Society, 1904).

HMS *Victory* equal to two double decked 74 gun third rates, a calculation he would use throughout the book when balancing off the fleets and squadrons that surged across his pages. These finding were worked into the Trafalgar lectures he delivered at Portsmouth between the 9 and 12 March. It appears the controversy that ensued was too much for the highly strung author. A recurrence of erysipelas confined him to bed and delayed the delivery of Trafalgar lectures at Chatham.[10] Heavily bandaged he stayed at home and continued writing. Working chronologically Corbett had reached the end of Chapter 4 within a month. The printed edition of Napoleon's correspondence, read while he was lecturing at Portsmouth, enabled him to demonstrate that Napoleon agreed with Nelson on the superior value of three decked ships.

By 4 April Corbett, taking his usual spring family holiday at his country house in Stopham, was engaged on Chapter 8, Nelson's decision to go to the West Indies. Three weeks later, having wrapped up Chapter 9, he returned to London, and was invited to join the Naval War Staff by DNI Admiral Bethell. He refused, but remained on stand-by to attend a CID invasion enquiry. After delivering the postponed lectures at Chatham he pressed on with research at the Public Record Office and the British Library, writing any new findings into the drafts as he went. His French colleague Colonel Edouard Desbrière provided critical information on the target of Villeneuve's West Indian Campaign, an issue which had been troubling Corbett, the difference between the direction north (Barbude in French) and Barbade. Desbrière had a copy of his book despatched, and apologised that as a colonel of the 27th Dragoons he was no naval expert.[11]

On 11 May Corbett persuaded his old mentor Professor John Laughton to allow him access to the papers of Admiral Lord Barham, which he was editing for the Records Society. A week later he began writing up Sir Robert Calder's action, only to be pole-axed by the birth of his son Richard on the 27th. Too ill to work he retreated to Woodgate, 'with nervous breakdown and lumbago' on doctor's orders. After a week's rest he returned home to find the family were doing well, and resumed work on Calder's action the next day.[12] A visit to Laughton's home in Wimbledon uncovered a wealth of strategical material the old professor had overlooked.[13] Former student Captain Hudleston RN provided notes on Lord Keith's operations in the North Sea, and later 'some good cruiser stuff'. He would be thanked in the preface.[14] Corbett became transfixed by the evolution of British cruiser work in this campaign, demonstrating how sound doctrine enabled cruiser commanders

---

[10] Diary 17.3.1909: CBT 43/10.
[11] Desbrière to Corbett Versailles 17.5.1909: CBT 14/2/23.
[12] Diary 25-5.–8.6.1909: CBT 43/10.
[13] Diary 12.6.1909: CBT 43/10. *Trafalgar* p. x.
[14] Diary 30.6. and 13.7.1909: CBT 43/10.

operating alone to reach sound, consistent decisions about the movement of intelligence and the priorities that drove national strategy. Research in warship log books highlighted the importance of this theme, as did the co-operation between Barham and Nelson that established a more effective system to cover the Western Approaches. Throughout the book Corbett employed a variety of phrases to encapsulate the modern concept of doctrine, a word he began to use in 1913.[15]

In early July Corbett observed: 'Having got Villeneuve to Cadiz feel the back of the book is broken'.[16] The combination of concentrated intellectual effort, public debate, domestic events and illness left Corbett exhausted, so he and Edith spent a week at Rye. He spent the time sketching Camber Castle, and dining with old friends, including novelist Henry James, Francis Darwin, and other members of Charles Darwin's family. Chapter 19 was wrapped up soon after the family returned to London.[17]

A summer holiday at the family retreat of Woodgate was spoiled by lumbago, and the heat, restricting work to revising. New discoveries made by Lieutenant Keate RN at the Public Record Office, notably the long overlooked signal logs of *Temeraire* and *Defence*, forced him to revise the battle chapter The final draft was complete at Stopham on 9 October, after a mere seven months' work. That period included three weeks lecturing, and two laid up ill. A week later he was back at Portsmouth, lecturing on Trafalgar. He dedicated the book to his wife Edith, whose birthday was on 21 October.

In November the chapters were sent to his friend Miss Keate for typing, and he began work revising his Russo-Japanese War lectures.[18] The corrected typescript was delivered to his usual publisher, Messrs Longmans, on 4 February 1910. Charles Longman 'seemed glad to have it & inclined to be generous about maps etc'. The number and sophistication of charts used at Trafalgar far exceeded anything that had been provided before, including contemporary drawings, and a number of large folding sheets in three colours. Corbett had evolved from a literary man who used pictures to illustrate his text into a strategic analyst who exploited charts, a tool only too familiar to his target audience of naval officers, to demonstrate and sustain his arguments. The chart work in his last two books, both official histories, followed this model. The maps and the preface had been settled by mid- February before

---

[15] See: Lambert, A.D. '"Doctrine, the Soul of Warfare": Sir Julian Corbett and the Teaching of Strategy in the Royal Navy before 1914', in Delaney, D.E. Engen, R.C., and Fitzpatrick, M. eds. *Military Education and the British Empire, 1815–1949.* UBC Press, Toronto 2018, pp. 48–68 for the last stage of this work before the First World War broke out.

[16] Diary 6.7.1909: CBT 43/10.

[17] Diary 21–28-7.1909: CBT 43/10.

[18] Diary 5 and 17.11.1909: CBT 43/10.

the contract had been signed. A bad cold followed the proofs, sending sent him to recuperate at Bournemouth. The proofs and the index were despatched to Longmans on All Fool's Day; the maps, which required more work, were finally settled on 13 April, 'so completed my Trafalgar campaign'. Good luck go with it I fear it is full imperfections.[19] Corbett and Edith set off for Florence the next day. The death of King Edward VII led Longman to suggest delaying publication and it was agreed the book would appear a week after the state funeral. Copies arrived on 6 June 1910. The first edition was limited to 1,500 copies, and by August almost 600 had been sold,

By the time he wrote *Trafalgar* Corbett had settled his methodology, following the same approach that had been successful in *The Seven Years' War*. He began by exploiting printed correspondence to provide the diplomatic and political background, with Desbrière's great book, John Leyland's Navy Records Society volume on the *The Blockade of Brest, 1803–1805,* along with the printed correspondence of Napoleon, Nelson, and William Cornwallis to address the civil-military interface and development of strategy. This secondary source base was refined and refracted by extensive archival work at the British Library, the Public Record Office, and in the manuscript Barham correspondence at Professor Laughton's house. Material Corbett had gathered for the 1907 Committee of Imperial Defence invasion enquiry was re-used to establish how control of the Western Approaches and the Channel Islands linked to the North Sea, rendering Napoleon's projects futile.[20] In contrast to his previous book, *Trafalgar* concerned the greatest conflict in which Britain had ever been engaged, a total war lasting 12 years in which the very existence of Britain was at stake. Even so, limited maritime strategy, directed by skilled leaders, had been successful against French total war methods, without a mass army.

In the preface, Corbett reminded his audience that the campaign could only be fully understood by starting with the Cabinet, in order to recognise 'the inward springs at work by which the fleets at sea were really controlled and mark the flow of intelligence ... that set them in motion, or stayed their action'.[21] He used the preface to deliver a startling challenge to the complacent attitudes of nation and navy to the development and application of doctrine, a word nowhere written, but everywhere inferred. The attraction of Trafalgar was that he could hang all his strategy and policy arguments on a misunderstood masterpiece, the ultimate symbol of British imperial might. To ensure he was taken seriously Corbett combined rigorous research in British sources with French and Spanish perspectives, demonstrating a mastery of

[19] Diary 13.4.1910: CBT 43/10.
[20] Morgan-Owen, D. *The Fear of Invasion: Strategy, Politics and British War Planning, 1880–1914* (Oxford: Oxford University Press, 2017).
[21] Corbett 1910, p. viii.

his brief. This book saw Corbett, the national strategist, at the height of his intellectual powers, challenging complacent assumptions, and flawed speculation. He demolished the myth that Trafalgar had prevented an invasion, along with half a decade of flawed tactical speculation, while eviscerating the inadequate and incompetent in a series of devastating footnotes. He praised those among his friends who had supported and encouraged the work as he sought a higher truth.

Alongside the obvious focus on fleet battle and grand strategy he laid special stress on the doctrine of cruiser work, which William James had had arbitrarily detached from fleet operations 90 years earlier. He combined this with a clear statement of purpose:

> To naval officers, and indeed all serious students of naval warfare, history so written must have a flavour of unreality … What they require is a co-ordinated account of the movements of all classes of ships engaged in each operation, and a clear knowledge of the instructions and intelligence under which it was carried out. In short, if Naval History is to establish itself as a matter of real instructional interest, students must be able to find in accounts of the old campaigns at least an indication of what they would look for in a report on manoeuvres today.

Dismissing the book as 'tentative and imperfect' he called for the establishment of a historical section at the admiralty to rewrite virtually the whole of British naval history 'on Staff lines', 'a laboratory where civilian and naval experts can work side by side to supply each other's defects and ripen each other's ideas'.[22] He did not favour a university professorship because it would not meet the practical needs of the service. Instead the navy must take the job in house, like any other scientific establishment, on a scale commensurate with Fisher's *Dreadnought* fleet. The model was French. He detested the German model of official military history, packed with excessive detail. Desbrière's work had been conducted within the war ministry, only in such conditions would 'the soul of the matter', by which he meant doctrine, be recovered. A decade later he would be less impressed with the admiralty as a host for history, but the mission to recover doctrine from past practice remained unchanged.

The opening chapter situated British limited maritime strategy in the national context. He stressed long-term strategic continuities: keeping a hegemonic power like Napoleonic France out of the Low Countries with Portugal and Sicily providing the core of British policy in Europe, the necessary corollary to a diplomatic balance of power. That said it is hard to avoid the conclusion that the prominence he accorded to the Baltic reflected the strategic situation in 1907–1909 more than that of 1803–1805. The prominence accorded to Pitt

---

[22] Corbett 1910, pp. xi–xii.

the Younger, along with the link to his father, to the Duke of Marlborough and William III was consciously crafted to stress doctrinal continuity, and the critical role of educated statesmen.

The book followed Pitt's attempt to recover the strategic initiative from Napoleon, build a European coalition, and restore the balance of power.[23] It began with the recapture of St Lucia, a very small, distant action, one that had to be defended against German continentalist arguments that called for 'concentration' on the 'decisive theatre'. By clearing the West Indies of both Dutch and French privateers' bases, Britain reduced 'the chief danger to our sea-borne commerce'. This mattered because: 'the retention of our financial position eventually enabled us to beat Napoleon down.' Corbett wrapped up his masterly exposition of the maritime nature of British strategy by citing G.F.R. Henderson's famous quip about the proper role of the British army: 'the great maxim that the naval strength of the enemy should be the first objective of the forces of a maritime power, both by land and sea', and condemning the unthinking application of the principle of concentration of force to global maritime strategy.[24] The first four pages expounded everything he had learned about strategy and policy in two decades, enabling him to stress that Pitt was working for a counterattack against France, and not, as had been assumed, holding a strict defensive.[25] Not only did Europe need British help to restore a balance of power, but Britain's role was a 'fundamental law' of international politics, one that coincided with the continental interests of other great powers. Such insights flowed from his long-term project to master the strategic history of the state since the sixteenth century; they were among the 'principles of maritime strategy' he would publish in 1911.[26]

When Russia sought military support in Southern Italy, the offensive project could begin, and from that point Corbett traced the campaign that ended at Trafalgar. Russian aims coincided with Pitt's anxiety to secure Sicily, which was vital to supplying Malta, which in turn enabled the Royal Navy to command the Mediterranean. Despite the threat of a French invasion Pitt refused to sacrifice Britain's strategic interests to Russia. He would not hand Malta back to the Knights of St John or sacrifice British maritime belligerent rights. He knew Russia was no more to be trusted than France. If Russia refused to co-operate Britain would, as Pitt told their ambassador, 'continue

---

[23] Corbett 1910, p. 25 cited the sound advice of Charles Dumouriez, although Holland Rose J. and Broadley A.M., *Dumouriez and the Defence of England against Napoleon* (London: Bodley Head, 1909), pp. 240–246, was published too late to shape his wider approach.

[24] Henderson, G.F.R. *The Science of War: A Collection of Essays and Lectures 1891–1903* ed. Col. N. Malcolm (London: Longman, 1906), p. 28.

[25] Corbett 1910, pp. 1–4.

[26] Corbett, J.S. *Some Principles of Maritime Strategy* (London: Longman, 1911).

the war alone: it will be maritime'.[27] Russian procrastination delayed the application of British strategy; until St. Petersburg was committed Pitt could not decide where to use his limited strike force. Once the alliance had been settled the navy would be the key enabler for a continental coalition.

Military manpower for British offensives would be provided by recruitment, and released from defensive roles by improved local defences on the south coast. The latter raised the size of the necessary invasion force, thereby reducing the prospect of a surprise. The naval side of this issue was well understood. Senior offices afloat knew their duty, and the need to use their initiative. Lord Barham's instructions to Admiral Sir William Cornwallis encapsulated everything that had been learned in the eighteenth century.[28] Corbett did not believe Napoleon's invasion threat was real, pointing out that the transports and troops were never in place. That said Napoleon knew that he must persist, because *Delenda est Carthago!* remained the war cry of the new France.[29] When Napoleon tried to pressurise Britain into peace Pitt bluntly rejected his terms, and ignored his imperial pretensions. He trusted the 'rising spirit of the nation', a clear reference to ideas that Clausewitz elaborated when discussing total war.

In a powerful critique of Mahan, and other historians who accepted Napoleon's version of events, Corbett declared the whole British campaign had been offensive. The aggressive demolition of comfortable old concepts was critical to his contemporary argument that Britain could contribute effectively to a future major war in Europe without raising a mass conscript army. Nor was Mahan the only naval 'expert' to come in for criticism, Admiral Sir Reginald Custance's obsession with battle was ridiculed. Speaking of Nelson Corbett observed: 'No great Captain ever grasped more fully the strategical importance of dealing with the enemy's main force; yet no one ever less suffered it to become an obsession, no one saw more clearly when it ceased to be the key of a situation, and fell to a position of secondary moment'. He also demolished Custance's advocacy of small battleships.[30] In the latter case Corbett observed that Napoleon, and Nelson agreed a three decked ship was worth two 74 gun two deckers. Size did matter.

Once the action moved from the Cabinet Council to the open ocean Corbett expanded on the fluid, uncertain nature of command of the sea in an age when communications were slow and uncertain, and intelligence flows random and irregular. This reality placed a premium on strategic leadership, explained how Nelson had missed Villeneuve off Sardinia, and how another apparently skilful combination had resulted in nothing. Throughout the book

[27] Corbett 1910, p. 21.
[28] He cited Desbrière to sustain his version, in a brilliant footnote at p. 34.
[29] Corbett 1910, p. 19.
[30] Ibid., pp.26, 32, 94, and 43–47.

he picked out examples of excellent work by detached cruisers, captains who understood their mission, and used the initiative. This was key lesson for his contemporaries, and a major reason for developing sound doctrine.[31] He also commended the decision-making of Admirals Sir John Orde and Sir Robert Calder, long dismissed as inadequate and short-sighted by those who did not recognise the limits of the art. Nelson's judgments on both men had been made without all the facts, in Orde's case it was also coloured by personal factors.

Ultimately the doctrinal cohesion of the Royal Navy, based on long experience, triumphed over Napoleon's complex schemes. This cohesion was more important than 'genius' in the wider picture because it could be relied upon. At the admiralty Barham grappled with a rapidly changing situation and uncertain intelligence: he had to plan on the assumption that his senior officers were using the same ideas. In Barham Corbett found an ideal replacement for the master strategists of the Seven Years' War, Pitt the Elder and Lord Anson.[32] By contrast he condemned Napoleon's 'interminable modification' which ignored the reality of war at sea and the experience of his admirals. This masterly turn of phrase elevated British decision-making to a higher plane, and demolished Napoleon's credibility as a strategist of maritime war. Myths of omnipotence, based on his own claims to have outwitted the dull British, trumpeted in Adolphe Thiers' massive text, evaporated under Corbett's careful scrutiny.[33] Napoleon 'entirely failed to fathom either the subtlety or the strength of British strategy'.[34] The irony that the critical evidence came from France was not over-played.

When Napoleon condemned the opening stage of Pitt's counterattack as 'the movement of pygmies', his words reflected the bitter realisation that his invasion threat had failed to pin the British on the strategic defensive. By the middle of June 1805 the British blockades had been re-established. Nelson was in hot pursuit of Villeneuve and Britain was secure against anything the emperor might attempt. Furthermore the ease with which General Craig sacrificed his escort to ensure British superiority off Ushant demonstrated the

---

[31] See, for example, pp. 74 and 111.

[32] Ibid., pp.113–126.

[33] Thiers, the most industrious historian of the era, used his 22-volume account of the years between the Revolution and Waterloo to regenerate Napoleonic glory. That he had been prime minister, and was dismissed by a king anxious to avoid a war with Britain in 1840 gave Thiers' work on the Consulate and Empire a powerful anti-British bias. The success of his works, and translation into many languages made it a standard reference. In *Histoire du Consulate et de l'Empire* (21 vols; Paris: Paulin, 1840–1862), Thiers claimed that Nelson had been 'decoyed' to the West Indies, outsmarted by Bonaparte. This nonsense appeared in English in 1845, helping to generate an invasion scare. Gildea, R. *The Past in French History* Yale, London 1994, p. 98.

[34] Ibid., pp. 127–129.

synergy between the two services, 'and how complete was their mutual understanding of the principles of combined warfare'.[35] Corbett's inference, made active by the using the past tense, was that such synergy no longer pertained, and that its restoration was both long overdue, and essential to the effective development of national strategy. Craig, like G.F.R. Henderson, understood that command of the sea was the primary concern of British strategy, and when it was necessary act on that principle he 'did not flinch'.[36] With the Strait of Gibraltar securely held, British strategy began to unfold, without let or hindrance from France and Spain.

Ultimately British doctrine triumphed over Napoleon's complex plans because 'a living instinct for naval war' was shared by every officer, not just men of Nelson and Barham's stamp. Even Sir Alexander Cochrane 'one of the least of Drake's heirs' knew what to do in an emergency.[37] Collingwood saw through all of Napoleon's schemes, and identified his ultimate purpose, while Barham countered them with a consummate ease only equalled by the synergy between his directions and the anticipation of them by the admirals at sea.[38] The French admirals, unsettled by the emperor's complete disregard for their opinions, and unsure of their strength, had no such guide.

Amidt the dissection of Napoleon's strategy Corbett provided a striking contemporary lesson. When discussing the British response to Napoleon's use of an army based in Texel as a diversion for his real intentions he observed.

> The disturbing power of an army by the sea with transports and escort alongside – a specially English device – is often questioned. Here at least is evidence of Napoleon's faith in it.[39]

His target was obvious, continental strategists at the contemporary British war office, army officers who had ignored the effect of British naval power in the Baltic on the outcome of the Crimean War. He held up Napoleon's use of this device in the hope they would understand that the mere threat of amphibious power would affect military operations, as deterrent and strategy. He was careful to leave the issue moot for another 50 pages, before revealing how easily Lord Keith penetrated Napoleon's invasion sham: he used half a dozen small, weak third rates to contain a Dutch demonstration that was meant to unlock the British system.[40]

---

[35] Corbett 1910, p. 149.
[36] Ibid.
[37] Ibid., p. 171. Alexander Cochrane was a better officer than Corbett realised.
[38] Ibid., p. 179.
[39] Ibid., p. 174.
[40] Ibid., pp. 227–229, 243.

Ultimately Napoleon's complex schemes collapsed in the face of a well-established principle of British strategy, which Corbett encapsulated as: 'When in doubt make sure of the mouth of the Channel.' As Barham observed the Western Squadron was 'the mainspring from which all offensive operations must proceed', and having secured the channel he was happy to detach Calder to intercept Villeneuve.[41] The French admirals recognised that any sailing battlefleet entering the channel would be destroyed, leaving the Boulogne flotilla to attempt an invasion without support. Furthermore Napoleon's invasion force, both land and sea was not ready at the critical time, or indeed at any time. After a thorough review of the evidence Desbrière's French staff history dismissed invasion as a real issue: 'we must surely ask ourselves if he ever seriously intended to make a sudden departure'.[42] Little wonder Corbett considered Desbrière the ultimate authority, not only was he a serving French soldier, but his testimony crushed the absurdities penned by Napoleon, Thiers, and a generation of British soldiers. French admirals saved their master from the inevitable consequences of launching such an effort.

Having administered a lesson to the soldiers Corbett shifted focus, employing Calder's engagement with Villeneuve on 22 July to demonstrate the limits of simple tactics, the impact of chance, and the overriding importance of three decked ships. Calder's three deckers were the heart of his battleline, shattering the enemy formation, despite taking heavy punishment. The shadow of Fisher's *Dreadnought* hung heavy over this controversial action, and the rest of Corbett's book.[43]

Having established that Napoleon's invasion scheme was never going to work Corbett shifted his focus to British counterstrokes. Anticipating Napoleon would shift his line of attack to India, British strategists did not rest content with a simple concentration of power off Ushant. General Sir David Baird's expedition was despatched to seize the Cape of Good Hope from the Dutch, to secure the Indian Ocean. This apparent digression from the core narrative emphasised the larger purpose of the text. Corbett objected to 'crude' ideas of concentration, and widened his focus because 'the whole question will serve as a warning that the broad combined problems of imperial defence are not to be solved off-hand by the facile application of maxims which are the outcome of narrower and less complex continental conditions'.[44] To emphasise the

---

[41] Ibid., pp. 183, 231.

[42] Ibid., p.191 from Desbrière *Projets et débarquements* vol. V, p. 406.

[43] Ibid., pp. 201–202. Corbett criticized Calder for being too concerned to secure his prizes, sacrificing any opportunity to renew the action, of this failing 'he was assuredly guilty', p. 206. It was a mistake; one he hoped his readers would recognize. Evidently Ernest Troubridge did not read the passage with attention.

[44] Corbett 1910, p. 237.

profundity of his point Corbett once again resorted to challenging, provocative language, dismissing alternative views as facile and crude.

When Villeneuve finally departed from Corunna in mid-August, Cornwallis's fleet off Ushant was at full strength, enabling him to detach Calder south to secure the Mediterranean, his decision perfectly anticipated the orders he would receive from Barham. Cornwallis carried the fate of the nation in his hands, and acted with absolute confidence in the soundness of his appreciation.[45] This synergy of mind between Whitehall and the flagship was the ultimate expression of Corbett's concern to establish and promulgate clear strategic and operation doctrine.

Napoleon called the division of Cornwallis's fleet 'stupid', a judgment that Mahan echoed. Yet as Corbett observed in a telling footnote, the American was the only naval officer, either contemporary or modern, to do so. The put-down was necessary because Mahan's French-continental perceptions were unsuited to British imperial interests. He added that Mahan had written that text before he had any experience of the higher direction of war, which he gained in 1898. Corbett secured his point by quoting Mahan's discussion of the subject in *The War of 1812* of 1905, which was 'incompatible with his censure of Cornwallis'. Ultimately Cornwallis's critics failed the most basic test: the admiralty had pointedly approved Cornwallis's decision. Nor were these moves at all defensive; they spread British power to counterattack at the Cape and Sicily. In the text he attacked less competent foes 'It is curious that the critics who most severely condemn the movement are just those who are the most fanatical prophets of the offensive.' Naval strategy should never be judged by 'the elementary maxims derived from warfare on land'. The discussion of concentration served two purposes, reducing Mahan's credibility with British policymakers, while destroying the more extreme position taken by his less subtle British followers, and other 'purists trained in the continental schools'.[46]

No amount of concentration off Ushant could secure the Mediterranean, where a fleet and an army were absolutely essential to the emerging alliance with Russia and Austria.[47] This was a classic example of the deflection of strategy by politics, and on the largest scale. This was why Cornwallis acted.

Furthermore commerce protection occupied a prominent place in British decision-making during this season. Corbett traced the great oceanic convoys as they entered the Western Approaches, an overriding issue that had no

---

[45] Ibid., p. 247.

[46] Mahan, A.T. *The Influence of Sea Power Upon the War of 1812* (London: Sampson Low, 1905). Corbett 1910 pp. 248–252, esp. fns. The final quote may have been aimed at Spenser Wilkinson and Repington. For another example of Corbett's incisive historiographical analysis see p. 294 fn 1.

[47] Ibid., p. 251.

parallel in land warfare. The inbound East India convoy was so rich that its capture would be 'a disastrous blow to the national finance, and commercial ... influence demanded that it must be saved at any cost'.[48]

Even if Villeneuve had linked up with Allemand and Ganteaume and the combined fleet of 50 sail had entered the channel it would have been annihilated before it could have achieved anything off Boulogne. To make sure this did not happen Cornwallis, at the critical point of the entire campaign, drove Ganteaume back into Brest on 22 August 1805. Two days earlier Villeneuve and his shattered fleet had limped into Cadiz, and submitted to being blockaded by Collingwood's tiny force. The moral ascendancy of the British was absolute. Ten days later Calder arrived off Cadiz with 18 sail, locking up the combined fleet.[49] Only Allemand's five ship squadron remained unaccounted for. The invasion threat, if it had ever been serious, passed at the end of August. Napoleon gave up the idea before he knew where Villeneuve was heading, under the pressure exerted by Craig's tiny expedition, and that of Baird, which he believed was a follow on Mediterranean force.[50] On 31 August the emperor ordered the flotilla to be demobilised and secured, and the battlefleet split into raiding squadrons.

Throughout his book Corbett consistently highlighted smart and effective British cruiser work, praising the judgment of young officers, and emphasising the striking consistency of their conduct. Again his purpose was doctrinal. These men understood their duty because they had learned it in war, on the quarter deck, from experienced officers. British doctrine had been studied on the job, not in a French text book.[51] When Barham and Nelson re-organised and improved the cruiser patrol lines they exploited additional cruisers released by Keith to close the distance between ships, increasing the ability to intercept the enemy and maintain links between the main fleets along lines modern officers would recognise. He deployed a newly discovered Nelson letter to reinforce the point. It highlighted 'a distinct advance towards more scientific systems of intelligence and commerce protection'.[52] Corbett reinforced the point by including a classic example of a convoy escort sacrificing itself to enable the merchant ships to scatter. It was a model his students might have to emulate.[53] Wrapping up the trade section Corbett stressed the limits of cruiser warfare: the only area where such attacks might have a serious effect was the Western Approaches, where the presence of a large fleet made sustained operations impossible. Holding the terminal points was the key. Allemand's

[48] Ibid., p. 279.
[49] Ibid., pp. 260–270.
[50] Ibid., p. 278.
[51] Ibid., pp. 265–266.
[52] Ibid, pp. 297–301.
[53] Ibid, p. 309.

long and lucky cruise did not shake British strategy, or weaken the grip it exercised over the enemy fleets: instead it served 'to demonstrate the futility of seeking to entice our fleets away, so long as a sound strategical tradition remains green in the service'.[54] By 'sound strategical tradition' he meant doctrine. He had written the book to teach the importance of recovering and teaching that doctrine.

The impact of the British offensives was obvious. Napoleon, startled by Craig's expedition, ordered Villeneuve to carry his troops to Naples, delaying the launch of an imperial oceanic raiding strategy to serve terrestrial ends. As Corbett concluded: 'Pitt's strategy was working, by sheer force of strategical law.'[55] Nelson, a minor presence in the text until the very end, had been determined to destroy the combined fleet because he knew, from hard-won experience, that it would be difficult to blockade Cadiz effectively in winter. To that end the government prepared bomb vessels, and re-deployed Congreve's new rockets, developed to attack Boulogne, to the south. Although the rockets were new the idea of attacking an enemy fleet skulking begins fortifications was one of the oldest in naval warfare. An English amphibious force had captured and destroyed Cadiz in 1596. Nelson hoped coastal attacks and bombardments might help drive the enemy to sea, in combination with a close blockade that cut food supplies.[56]

At the end of a book about grand strategy and leadership Corbett rewarded his readers with a 10-page examination of the operational and tactical handling of the battle, before moving to the larger issue of what had been achieved. His conclusion was a masterpiece of advocacy, setting up the straw man of the battle's irrelevance, 'so barren of immediate result' as to inspire the legend that it had prevented an invasion of England. This legend has remained in place into the twenty-first century because no one reads Corbett's brilliant book. Then he began to construct a different position, one that took a far grander view of the war, and the ultimate outcome. Sicily, the central point of the entire campaign, would be secured by Craig with 8,000 British troops. Pitt acted alone, because after Austerlitz Russia withdrew, Austrian power disappeared like 'like the baseless fabric of a dream', while Prussia crouched before Napoleon. Although another continental coalition had failed, Britain would fight on alone; Trafalgar ensured she would do so with absolute command of the sea. Holding Sicily ensured Malta could be held, and with that Britain's command of the Mediterranean was secure. Control of the Cape went a long way to securing India. Britain, the empire and the wider world had been

---

[54] Ibid., pp. 313–314.
[55] Ibid., pp. 296 and 303.
[56] Ibid., pp. 320–321.

placed beyond Napoleon's grasp, but Pitt had failed to liberate Europe: 'The sea had done all that the sea could do, and for Europe the end was failure.'[57]

Those final lines consciously stressed the limits of sea power unaided: it could not settle the destiny of Europe without land forces. This was a lesson for all his readers, soldiers who needed to understand their vital, but limited role in British strategy, and for Jacky Fisher, who fancied he could do it all himself. The future, as Corbett would demonstrate in subsequent lectures, lay in the extension of that maritime strategy to Iberia.

Trafalgar would be Corbett's last history book, the long series he had projected had been overtaken by the demand for contemporary official texts, ever more closely aligned with the intellectual needs of the modern service. Books on the American Revolution, the Napoleonic conflict after Trafalgar, and perhaps the Crimean War, proceeded no further than aspirations and lecture notes. Yet it would be a mistake to regret the end of the historical phase of his work, Corbett had little left to say, moving seamlessly from *Trafalgar* to *Some Principles of Maritime Strategy* of 1911, emphasised his emergence as a mature strategist, able to order his ideas into a conceptual framework, free from the restraints of narrative and period. The *Trafalgar* footnotes contain evidence of this process in action, Mahan and other strategic authorities were found wanting, and corrected without hesitation. Yet the historical narrative format was ill-suited to the message he needed it to carry, in the next book he reversed the model: ideas and argument took centre stage, backed by historical evidence.

Trafalgar was a great success with public and professional audiences. Desbrière noted both high praise and subtle correction with equal pleasure, delighting in the synergy of their ideas.[58] Sir Francis Bridgeman, second sea lord, shared Desbrière's delight with the gift, but had made less progress with the text.[59] Henry Newbolt's copy came with fulsome praise for the poet's 1905 book, contrasting it with his own 'cold blooded dissection'.[60] Newbolt was delighted by the commendations, and ended his letter with a line that must have touched Corbett to the very core, 'My dear Julian you know how proud I am of you and your work. I hope this will put the coping stone on your reputation and be recognised as a national service'.[61] Admitting he liked 'pleasant things from those who know', he acknowledged the mistake Newbolt had noted on page 344 where Corbett mistakenly gave Israel Pellew command of the *Colossus* and not the *Conqueror*.[62]

---

[57] Ibid., pp. 416–424.
[58] Desbrière to Corbett Versailles 8.6.1910. CBT 14/2/24.
[59] Bridgeman to Corbett Admiralty 8.6.1910: CBT 13/3/15.
[60] Corbett to Newbolt 9.6.1910: CBT 3/7/70.
[61] Newbolt to Corbett 12.6.1910: CBT 3/64.
[62] Corbett to Newbolt 16.6.1910: CBT 3/69.

Charles Firth. Regius Professor of History at Oxford, took a little longer to finish the book, and accepted the big point about Nelson's memorandum, a point that would become significant two years later.

> The explanation of the reasons for the different orders issued by the admiralty and the process of reasoning which led Nelson or Cornwallis or Barham to come to the conclusions they did is extremely interesting, and excessively instructive. I felt that I understood not only that bit of the naval war but the whole war much better than I did before. No other book I know of throws the same sort of light on the principles of naval defence as they were worked out during that period. In particular I feel that the whole working of the blockade and the system of concentrating the fleet wherever it was necessary explains a great deal to me.'[63]

A day later Admiral Sir Wilmot Fawkes, commander in chief at Devonport, joined the chorus of praise. Fawkes had read the book twice, picked up three small errors, and demonstrated why he was held in such high regard by Lord Selbourne, Fisher, and other naval intellectuals.

> I think you have made the whole campaign for the first time clear, given us the meaning of it all and told its story so clearly, by giving in detail what the Admiralty & the Admirals knew, the facts on which their decisions were based. How splendidly they worked together, anticipating orders & taking responsibility whenever necessary. I also like your battles so much. You have made Trafalgar, Calder's action and Strachan's very clear & I congratulate you most heartily & hope the book will be well studied by the rising generation of naval officers.[64]

Fawkes, (1840–1926) was an unusual officer; he had matriculated at Cambridge after receiving his commission. He had been Fisher's commander on HMS *Northampton* in 1880, and remained a key ally thereafter.[65] Admiral Lord Fisher was so impressed that he sent the book, complete with reading directions, to Arthur Balfour, the former prime minister, leader of the Conservative opposition, and a member of the Committee of Imperial Defence.

---

[63] Firth to Corbett 28.6.1910 Oxford: CBT 14/3/3.
[64] Wilmot Fawkes to Corbett 29.6.1910: CBT 13/3/28.
[65] Mackay *Fisher* pp. 149, 245–246, and 275. He had also commanded a royal yacht, been naval advisor to the Inspector General of Fortifications, and Naval Secretary to First Naval Lords Goschen and Selborne, ADC to Queen Victoria, and Commander in Chief on the Australia Station. He retired in 1911. A sophisticated and well connected officer with a serious interest in history Fawkes remained close to Corbett.

I will certainly read the passage in Corbett's book to which you call my attention, indeed, I have already ordered the book; and propose reading the whole of it. Corbett is an admirable writer.

This exchange neatly disposes of the myth that no one who mattered read Corbett: 'Delighted to find a brilliant epitome of Corbett's text book in the *Times Literary Supplement*: "about as admirable a bit of war Bovril that was ever boiled down from a great book such as yours Do read it!"'[66] When he returned to office in late 1914 Fisher would follow Corbett's strategic model. Balfour, who held high office between 1915 and 1922, was equally cognisant of the nature of British strategy.

Herbert Richmond, then a Staff Captain on board HMS *Dreadnought*, picked out Corbett's overriding concerns:

> It is a great work, and really will do something, I feel sure, to open people's eyes to the fact that the old wars were not a mere heedless jumble of ships running about like mad dogs looking for someone to bite, but were organised concerns, planned on definite lines, & governed always by some particular objects. If it should do something towards the formation of an Historical Section it will have done a great deal: but I hope it will do that & more besides.[67]

Royal Marine Colonel George Aston thanked Corbett for his copy from distant Pretoria. 'I can only hope that every officer in the Fleet and Army, and every Statesman will read the book and keep a copy by him. Your power of work must be wonderful.' He hoped Corbett might be able comment on his *Letters on Amphibious Wars*.[68] Finally he received the endorsement he really wanted. Former DNI Admiral Edmond Slade wrote from his distant East Indies command: 'I think it is just what we want and if men will only study it we shall not have so much loose talk going on.'[69] *The Campaign of Trafalgar* had passed the ultimate test, satisfying the Regius Professor at Oxford, strategic sailors, a clever Royal Marine, a statesman, and a master of English prose who just happened to be an expert on the battle.

Public reviews were fulsome, and favourable. *The Athenaeum* found much to praise, enjoyed the debate, and anticipated further discussions, even if it did not agree with everything Corbett said.[70] *The Spectator* recognised the higher educational function of the book, how it elucidated principles for a target audience of statesmen, soldiers, and sailors. Reckoning the book 'a

---

[66] Balfour to Fisher 9.7.1910 in Fisher to Corbett 16.7.1910: CBT 12/54–56.
[67] Richmond to Corbett 30.6.1910: CBT 13/1/10.
[68] Aston to Corbett Pretoria 9.9.1910: CBT 5/2/41.
[69] Slade to Corbett Calcutta 27.12.1910: CBT 13/2/51.
[70] *The Athenaeum* 2.7.1910, pp. 5–6.

very considerable success' the reviewer noted Corbett's innate modesty, but the suggestion that he would have done better by 'omitting everything in the nature of controversy' reflected a Tory political perspective, and a complete failure to understand the transformational nature of the text. The reviewer did not see how correcting other writers or analysing the material advanced Corbett's case. Nor did they agree with the central argument that Sicily was the centre of the campaign, preferring to focus on the battle. The review contained powerful, resonant echoes of Reginald Custance's opinions.[71] By contrast *The Saturday Review* considered it 'a book that would rank among our naval classics', 'for Mr Corbett understands how to make the most of any subject he takes in hand'. The critic emphasised the argument about the relative value of two and three decked ships, and accepted Corbett's case.[72] *The Westminster Gazette* offered fulsome praise of the book, and its author.

> Mr Corbett excels as an historian because his strategical understanding it as great as the profundity of his knowledge of the facts, and he never fails to write in such a manner as to command the interest of the general and well as the professional reader.[73]

The longest, and most scholarly of reviews, laced with footnotes, appeared in the *English Historical Review* of April 1911. The reviewer C.T. Atkinson, a councillor and editor of the Record Society knew Corbett well. He accepted the argument that Craig's expedition had brought on the battle, but questioned how far that justified describing the whole campaign as 'essentially offensive', concluding Corbett's arguments were more ingenious than convincing. He preferred Mahan's model, in which defeat at Trafalgar drove Napoleon to fall back on the Continental System. He reckoned Corbett's unusual approach 'the price one must pay for those very qualities of insight and ingenuity which make his volumes so vivid and suggestive'.

At that point Atkinson began to backtrack on his criticism, acknowledging the centrality of Sicily to Pitt's planning, the brilliance of the division of the Western Squadron, and the striking endorsement of British cruiser work. He ended with a delightfully barbed assessment of the 'tactics at Trafalgar' debate, suggesting Corbett was as guilty of 'fragile web spinning' as those he criticised, and his methods 'a rather double edged sword'.[74] Too wise to complain, one suspects Corbett rather enjoyed being taken seriously in the

---

[71] *The Spectator* 23.7.1910, p. 17.
[72] *The Saturday Review* 6.8.1910, pp. 173–174.
[73] *The Westminster Gazette* 28.7.1910.
[74] Atkinson, C.T. Review *English Historical Review* April 1911 vol. XXVI, pp. 398–402.

leading national academic history journal. It is unlikely many of his core audience looked to the *English Historical* for guidance.

Corbett could rest content with labours, the book sold well, ensuring his message would be widely consumed. That message re-stated the intellectual argument of the *Seven Year's War*, emphasising the distinctive character of British strategy: that a maritime-imperial power must not march to the tune of continental theorists. It must develop Clausewitz's analytical framework to address very different requirements. By January 1911 half the copies had been sold and Longman was anxious to prepare the reduced type.[75] No sooner had he completed the typescript of *Some Principles of Maritime Strategy* than he began revising the proofs of *Trafalgar* for the second, two volume edition.

Trafalgar prompted naval war course director Admiral Sir Lewis Bayly to demand lectures on the Great War at sea after Trafalgar.[76] Corbett delivered those lectures in June 1911, they were written in a week, following a short period of research at the Public Record Office.[77] While Corbett might have hoped to write them up as a book, there was never an opportunity. They finally appeared in print in 1922, as the text of his last public lecture, where they served a very different purpose.[78]

Corbett's biographer Professor Donald Schurman described *Trafalgar* as 'a careful description of cause and effect' demonstrating 'that sea power was the limited but effective arm of British state policy', a lesson aimed at naval officers who needed to understand the interplay of central and peripheral positions. 'It brought together his unrivalled knowledge of the strengths and weaknesses of sea power.'[79] Schurman argued Corbett's work had relatively limited impact, a view that is still widely shared. It stands in need of a comprehensive overhaul. Not only did Corbett write for the navy; he did so at the behest of senior officers focused on naval education and doctrine development. His war course lectures were refined by academic research, and a rich exchange of ideas and evidence across his broad range of contacts, from poets to first sea lords. *Trafalgar* hit the target – but the lesson would be imperfectly applied. Rather than responding to the emergency of August 1914 within the doctrinal strategic frame work of Corbett's limited maritime strategy the statesmen abandoned control of the process to a soldiers bent on waging mass continental warfare on German lines. The catastrophic consequence of that mistake was

---

[75] Diary 10.1.1911: CBT 43/12.

[76] Diary 10.10.1910: CBT 43/11.

[77] Diary 21.5–4.6.1911: CBT 43/12.

[78] Lambert, A.D. 'Writing the Battle: Jutland in Sir Julian Corbett's Naval Operations', *The Mariner's Mirror* 103 (2): 175–195, 2018.

[79] Schurman, D.M. *Julian S. Corbett, 1854–1922: Historian of British Maritime Policy from Drake to Jellicoe.* London 1981 is the only full length biography; see pp. 62–63.

not military defeat, but the shattering of Britain's economic, industrial, and global power base. It was a high price to pay for wilful ignorance, weakness and the failure of strategic leadership.

Trafalgar explained the eternal realities of British strategy, the dominance of maritime over continental concerns, the need for clear and consistent naval doctrine, and the critical role that it played in shaping the tactical appreciation of great commanders, including the greatest of them all. In 1910 there was no more compelling case study of naval strategy in a total war, of the place of naval power in national policy. Corbett's book had educated statesmen, admirals, and soldiers on the eve of a total war – that they failed to listen cannot be blamed on the author.

8

Spanish Naval Leadership during the Second Republic: José Giral Pereira

ADOLFO MORALES TRUEBA

An examination of strategic leadership in the navy during the Second Republic is of great interest for multiple reasons. These include our current lack of knowledge about the naval sphere and the actions aimed at steering naval policy during those years, the fact that this period coincided with a great upheaval in international politics, and that it was also a period of transformation at home.

Taking only a brief look at the several figures between 1931 and 1936 who were responsible for setting naval policy, we can conclude that, with few exceptions, the continuity, knowledge, and time necessary to develop a policy with any kind of long-range perspective by the Republican government were missing. As a consequence, there was a lack of strategic leadership at a time when the most serious threat to Spain's national security lay in the naval situation.

Going back to the beginning of the century, the Spanish navy had endured incomplete and ill-considered plans, multifarious and discontinued shipbuilding projects, and, in general, the lack of a balanced, viable agenda that was consistent with the country's economic reality. A profound change was therefore needed for the navy to become an efficient tool. The first requirement was to understand its structural problems, the second was to define exactly what was expected of it, and the third was to formulate a plan to invest resources, realistically, in a way that was consistent with the navy's needs and its mission.

One of the Second Republic's naval leaders stands out from the rest, José Giral Pereira (1879–1962), who served two separate terms as minister of the navy (10 October 1931–11 June 1933, and 19 February–18 July 1936). Giral, who was a pharmacist by profession, was the only navy minister to push for a plan aimed at dealing with the main challenges mentioned in the previous paragraph. His plans were ready to be approved in July 1936, but the process was interrupted by the war, and since then they have languished in the navy's archives.

However, because of their quality and sense of direction, they are among some of the best plans formulated in the first third of the twentieth century. Likewise, the way the plans were developed and their contents reflect a visionary political leadership that would have made Spain much more capable of defending itself from foreign naval threats during those years.

Together with these sound structural plans, Giral adopted a personnel policy that was intended to guarantee the navy's loyalty to the Republican regime, although it ended up having disastrous consequences. Because of the measures he adopted, the Second Republic was able to retain the most important ships, but it also led to a loss of control of the fleet for several months and a shortage of commanders capable of using the ships effectively against the initially small 'Nationalist' fleet.

Throughout the twentieth century, the strategic vision and actions of numerous figures in Spanish history have been studied whose influence on politics made them stand out, for better or for worse. Some of these figures come from the spheres of culture, science, economy, and so on, but it should be noted that most of these studies have traditionally focused on the sphere of politics in general, and where they have dealt with the military, they have focused on figures linked primarily to the army and the political and military activities in this sphere.

The sphere of naval politics has thus been mostly consigned to the margins and with few exceptions has received little attention. This is perhaps due to the fact that historiography on the Spanish military in the twentieth century has generally ignored the navy, particularly the period between the start of the century and 1936. However, an examination of strategic leadership in the navy, especially during the period of the Second Republic, is of great interest for multiple reasons.

The first is our lack of knowledge about the importance of the actions aimed at guiding naval policy during these years, whose evolution and demands were essential to national security. Though this policy was directed at a very specific sphere, it inevitably involved many others.

To speak of naval policy is to speak of national security, but also of foreign policy, economic policy, and industrial policy. Naval policy had to be framed necessarily within a mid- and long-term perspective; it thus had to be given a strategic vision beyond the others, since its effects would never be immediate.

The second reason has to do with its coinciding with a tremendously tumultuous period in world history. The steady deterioration of political stability worldwide and the growing belligerence of the Axis powers in theatres such as the Mediterranean convinced Spanish leaders to look at the crisis in terms of national maritime interests and to emphasize naval policies as particularly vital to national security.

The third was that the development of this policy was carried out during a period of transformation at home that sought to effect great change in all spheres of national life. This also coincided with a great clash between the country's different projects. This clash, however, seems not to have been transferred to the larger policies implemented in the navy. There are some exceptions that will be discussed below, such as the policy that was adopted to deal with the difficult internal situation that existed in the principal tool of Republican naval policy, navy personnel.

The short time that elapsed between the proclamation of the Republic in 1931 and its partial collapse in 1936 prevented the implementation and development of most of the key naval plans that were designed in those years. The failed coup in July 1936 tore the Second Republic's policies out by the root and together with all naval projects; the coup was followed by a period of war in which the leaders and their objectives changed radically. This makes it difficult to identify the figures whose thinking and actions might have been important enough for them to be classified as strategic leaders.

The historiography of the Republic's strategic leadership of maritime policy highlights three particularly important pillars:[1]

- The set of ideas that Republican politicians applied to the entire armed forces, which focused primarily on guaranteeing their loyalty to the new republic and, secondly, on the way in which naval and military capability should be defined.
- The political factor, which established the guidelines for security and defence and guided the Republic's objectives in order to sustain national sovereignty and national interests, and the role of naval power in that endeavour. Without going into this in too much detail, the goal was to achieve neutrality and to maintain national security on the basis of the system of collective security articulated by the League of Nations.
- The geo-strategic factor, which located and defined the existing value of risks for, and threats toward Spanish interests, and reconciled priorities and directed naval efforts especially towards the Balearic Islands and the Strait of Gibraltar.

If we focus on the naval sphere, we can see that the first major change to take place under the new regime had to do with the model selected for exercising strategic leadership. This led to the appointment of civilian figures with strong political profiles (especially during the leftist administrations), who were generally people with scant technical credentials. New models of action

---

[1] Morales Trueba, A., 'El marco del liderazgo naval español durante la Segunda República', in Guimerá Ravina, A., ed. *El liderazgo estratégico. Una aproximación interdisciplinar* (Madrid: Ministerio de Defensa, 2018), pp. 197–218.

appeared in the ministerial office that took the lead in promoting reforms and policies directly from the strategic level. This was a clear break from what had gone before, when military figures shouldered most of the development of these reforms and policies, either directing it themselves or designing it and pushing it from the uppermost technical echelons.

However, over a period of little more than five years (i.e. not including the Republican period coinciding with the Spanish Civil War), there were thirteen different ministers of the navy, some of whom held the position for less than a month: Santiago Casares Quiroga (April–October 1931), José Giral Pereira (October 1931–June 1933), Lluis Companys Jover (June–September 1933), Vicente Iranzo Enguita (September–October 1933), Leandro Pita Romero (October–December 1933), José Rocha García (December 1933–January 1935), Gerardo Abad Conde (January–April 1935), Javier de Salas y González (April–May 1935), Antonio Royo Villanova (May–September 1935), Pedro Rahola y Molinas (September–December 1935, Javier de Salas y González (14–30 December 1935), Nicolás Molero Lobo (interim minister up to 31 December 1935), Antonio Azarola y Gresillón (January–February 1936), and, for a second term, José Giral Pereira (19 February–22 August 1936).

A quick glance at the dates of these fourteen terms makes clear that, with few exceptions, it would have been difficult to address naval policy without the continuity, knowledge, and time necessary to develop agendas with long-range perspective. In general, we can say that the high rate of turn-over at the head of the ministry is a reflection of lack of interest on the part of the government, which was inevitably translated into a lack of strategic leadership at a time when far-sightedness and long-term policies were sorely needed. There were only two exceptions, José Rocha and, especially, José Giral, both with a longer track record.

Although it is not the subject of this study, there was another kind of leadership in the navy, which existed alongside strategic leadership and in some ways served to drive and bolster it. Technical leadership, which affects the operational and tactical realm, is an exclusively military form of leadership. During the period in question, there were numerous officers who did high-quality work in this regard, both in the field of naval theory and in naval practice, devising reliable wide-ranging projects. Out of their ideas emerged the main studies and programmes during those years, which could support the strategic leadership or give an impetus to action. One example is Francisco Moreno Fernández (1883–1945), who at the time held the rank of commander but would be the leader of the Nationalist fleet during the Spanish Civil War. His involvement in all important projects that were commissioned during those years is a sign of the professional prestige he enjoyed, despite his modern outlook. The respect for Francisco Moreno transcended the level of performance and went all the way up to the strategic level. Even José Giral, whose political sympathies during the war were opposed to those of Moreno

Fernández and who moreover paid little attention to the technical sphere during those years, recalled him in the draft of his memoir, written after the Spanish Civil War, as a 'studious and competent leader', whom he met often, bypassing the naval hierarchy, to study different questions, especially improvements to the ships and the fleet's formation.[2]

The importance of a technical figure like Francisco Moreno is made clear by his official collaboration on the critical naval commissions of the day, including the one formed in June 1931 by the then minister of the navy Santiago Casares to analyse and propose changes to the navy's personnel structure, the commission established by Giral in April 1932 to report on the state of the navy and its primary needs, on which the Republic's naval plans would be based, and the inter-ministry commission created in 1934 to study the defence of the Balearic Islands.

The technical expert Francisco Moreno would later go on to excel as an operational leader in the Spanish Civil War, as commander of the Nationalist fleet. Though this force began the conflict with clear operational disadvantages (most importantly ships, the destroyers, naval aviation, the submarines, and most of the crews in the fleet remained with the Republican government), Moreno succeeded in rebuilding the fleet, and under his command it came to control the seas.

That said, the purpose of this study is to analyse naval leadership at a higher level, at the level of strategy, where personal qualities and performance had to respond to other determinants and demands. Here, the main challenge resided in the fact that the regime was in power for such a short time, which prevented it from developing a naval policy that yielded results, and the fact that most of the projects that were developed were unfinished and ignored.

Thanks to the good fortune of having unearthed previously undiscovered documents, it has been possible to identify in the person of José Giral a leader with a clear strategic vision for the navy. As will be seen, he spearheaded the most comprehensive naval agenda of this period, one that was fully consistent with Republican priorities in politics and security.

José Giral has been studied up to now from the perspective of his political and even his scientific contributions, especially his work in academic pharmacology and chemistry, his activity in Republican movements in Spain before 1931, his early participation in the Spanish Civil War, and his leading role in the Second Republic's government in exile. This is the perspective taken in Francisco Javier Puerto Sarmiento's comprehensive *Ciencia y política: José*

---

[2] Archivo Histórico Nacional, Madrid (AHN). 'Notes for the book on José Giral'. Diversos, José Giral, leg. nº 8, N1. P. 14. Giral is making a mistake here, talking about Salvador Moreno Fernández (1886–1966), another naval officer, instead of his brother Francisco Moreno. The officer was then in one of the naval bases, either Vigo or Ferrol.

Giral Pereira, which provides a detailed and well-rounded portrait of Giral, and his memoirs, edited by Francisco Giral González, *Vida y obra de José Giral Pereira*.[3]

The importance of his political and scientific accomplishments has had the indirect consequence of overshadowing his work as head of the ministry of the navy. The fact that his naval projects were interrupted when war broke and thus were never implemented is another reason why this work has been forgotten. However, the recent chance rediscovery of these projects reveals not only the quality of Giral's work but also his strategic vision for Spain's maritime interests. They show that he was well aware of the need to have a solid naval policy in order to guarantee these interests in the context of international upheaval.

José Giral's background was decidedly political, with strong republican leanings. This, in addition to his idealism had, in fact, landed him in jail. He was one of the founders of Acción Republicana, along with several other intellectuals including Manuel Azaña, with whom he shared a close friendship, and this undoubtedly coloured his views on the military and how to reform it.

After the new regime came to power, Giral became an important member of the Izquierda Republicana party.[4] By nature he was somewhat shy, modest, and wary of the spotlight, though extraordinarily committed to his principles and ideas. His intellectual training had been in the sciences, and this undoubtedly made him more pragmatic in his approach to the navy's problems. He was a freemason, having joined the organization in 1926 as a member of the *Dantón* lodge. It should be noted that during this period, being a mason did not have the negative connotations that became common after the civil war. Nonetheless, this is an important fact about Giral since this activity gave him access to unofficial links and ways of thinking that were outside official channels and hidden from the State government.

Positioned at the political level within the ministry of the navy, he possessed some qualities that evidently were not the most suited to making him a charismatic leader in a sphere that was so markedly military. However, his far-sightedness – one of the most important qualities for a strategic leader – helped him to devise a naval agenda that was well suited to Spain's circumstances, security objectives, and real needs.

---

[3] Puerto Sarmiento, F., *Ciencia y política: José Giral Pereira (Santiago de Cuba, 1879–México D.F., 1962)* (Madrid: Real Academia de la Historia-Boletín Oficial del Estado, 2015); and Giral González, F., *Vida y obra de José Giral Pereira* (Mexico: Universidad Autónoma Nacional de México, 2004).

[4] This party resulted from the union of several political organizations in 1934: *Acción Republicana*, a sector of the Partido Radical Socialista Independiente, Organización Republicana Gallega Autónoma, and others.

His vision would clash with two proposals that in themselves were at odds. On the one hand, the different Republican governments all tried to balance the national accounts and to make budgetary adjustments, and this would require the navy to be realistic about their projects. On the other hand, there were those navy technicians who traditionally threw realism to the wind and devised and proposed grand plans that were inconsistent not only with what was possible for Spain but also, in many cases, with what was needed. This was true of many of the leaders of the navy during the Restoration (1874–1931) period in Spain, who were keen to undertake costly programmes centred on building large units that contributed little to national security, usually cruisers, which were the largest ships they could afford. These ministers were much less proactive in other aspects of naval operations that were less visible but equally necessary for an effective and balanced navy that was aligned with the fact that Spain's key maritime interests were near the coast, as for example, the Strait of Gibraltar and the Balearic Islands.

A fine example of this was the last agenda to be drawn up before the Republicans came to power. It was presented by the then minister of the navy Salvador Carvia (January 1930–February 1931) and proposed ordering several large units – among them battleships, aircraft carriers, and cruisers – for 2.638 billion pesetas, at a time when the total national budget was around 3.627 billion pesetas.[5] Even though the sum was to be paid over a fourteen-year period, Carvia was still proposing a venture that included building new units for the navy at a cost equal to 73% of all state spending. All this took place at a time when Spain was drowning in an economic crisis. This proposal was made when there were not even enough torpedoes for the launchers in the fleet, when there was a shortage of ammunition and fuel, and when navy personnel would have been insufficient for crewing the proposed ships.[6]

José Giral's First Term in the Ministry of the Navy (October 1931–June 1933)

Giral's first term in the ministry of the navy began during a campaign to discredit him that strongly criticized his ability to perform the duties of the position. His critics pointed out that his training in pharmacology hardly made him a suitable candidate – they referred to him pejoratively as 'the druggist' in articles questioning whether he had the making of a minister of the navy. For example, shortly after his appointment, Wenceslao Fernández Flórez published a column in the newspaper *ABC* in which he derisively

---

[5] Morales Trueba, A., *La marina de guerra de la Segunda República* (Madrid: Actas, 2018), pp. 168 and 197.
[6] Morales Trueba, *Marina de guerra*, p. 332.

contrasted Giral's profession as a pharmacist to his complete lack of familiarity with naval operations.[7]

Giral himself notes in his memoires that he was surprised by the appointment, and not exactly pleased by it: he compared it to a 'lead weight'.[8] On the other hand, if we look at his career up until that time we can see how he would have brought to the ministry of the navy an outlook that fitted perfectly with the mould of Republican thinking at the time – an outlook that was doubtlessly influenced by Manuel Azaña and his minimal respect for the military establishment. He shared the common prejudices that tended to equate the problems of the navy with those of the army, suggesting that Spain's navy was bloated and in need of serious reforms in order to reduce the number of its troops and that its officers were strongly anti-Republican and aristocratic in their views, none of which was actually true.

Armed with this mindset, shortly after his appointment at the ministry, Giral presented to the Cortes an austerity budget for the navy that included freezing new shipbuilding, in which Giral remarked on the need to 'adhere to the utmost restraint in spending'.[9]

However, his opinion soon changed, as had happened as well with his predecessor, Casares Quiroga. The latter, shortly after coming to the ministry, in May 1931, declared: 'I believe, in contrast to the minister of War, that the size of the Navy is insufficient to the nation's requirements.' Giral also quickly came to the conclusion that the reality of the situation was very different from what he had at first assumed.[10]

Soon afterwards, he scheduled a series of visits to almost all of the navy's units and facilities, in an attempt to gain a thorough understanding of the institutional culture. According to the descriptions in his memoires, he visited all of the naval bases, the different dependencies in Cadiz and San Fernando, Cartagena, and Ferrol, the arsenals, shipyards, and factories of the Spanish Society of Naval Shipbuilding, the naval academy, the firing ranges, the submarine base, the San Javier navy air station, and so on.

In Ferrol, for example, he stayed onboard the warships anchored there, where he interacted with officers, subalterns, and rank-and-file sailors.[11] In essence, he spent time getting to know the organization, which was completely new to him, and he disregarded the hierarchy in order to learn first-hand about the organization's problems. Giral very quickly began to develop his thinking about the navy, coming to the conclusion, as had Casares Quiroga before him, that the navy was insufficient for the nation's requirements, that

[7] Fernández Flórez, W., 'Acotaciones de un oyente', *ABC* (17 October 1931).
[8] AHN, Diversos, José Giral, leg. nº 8, N1. P. 13.
[9] *ABC* (16 March 1932), 19–20.
[10] *La Voz* (2 May 1931).
[11] AHN, Diversos, José Giral, leg. nº 8, N1. P. 14.

it lacked many things and was in dire need of investment if it was to be even minimally prepared to fulfil the mission assigned to it.

By April 1932, Giral was more than cognizant that, given Spain's geo-strategic position at the intersection of important maritime routes and its central location in the western Mediterranean, it was essential and urgent to carry out reforms of the navy, 'putting it in a position to be maximally effective'.[12] In the interesting document cited in the previous paragraph, Giral laid out his strategic vision. Keeping in mind Spain's posture of neutrality and its security policy, which was first and foremost a defensive policy, as well as its maritime interests, he concluded that the navy needed to redefine its means and its make-up in order to be able to effectively fulfil its purpose.

He demonstrated that he was firmly committed to fulfilling the task that had been assigned to him and, after his tour of the different facilities, he did a very simple thing: he made an attempt to familiarize himself completely with the true circumstances of the navy, its problems, and its needs, in order to be reasonably assured of fulfilling the mission that the Republican regime had entrusted to him.

To this end, he established a commission made up of officers, charging them with drafting a report analysing the true circumstances of the different components of the naval force and the naval bases and their most pressing needs.[13] But he did not do this carelessly; rather, he steered the commission to approach the issue in a particular way, making clear what the strategic vision was that the tool to be analysed needed to respond to. He provided the following objectives, the 'what' and the 'why', formalizing the Republic's naval strategy by indicating in the 'directives of the Ministry of the Navy for the commission charged with studying and proposing solutions for naval defence':[14]

> A) To oblige other nations to respect our neutrality in any and all conflicts:
> 1st, because the other nations will know that our naval forces are in a state of readiness to enter into hostilities at any time.
> 2nd, because these naval forces are powerful enough that the fear that ..., weighed together with our strategic location, they would tip [the] balance, would keep [other nations] from obliging us to intervene.
>
> B) That, if we are obliged to go to war in support of one of the sides, the one that we favour would be able – thanks to our position and the

---

[12] Giral Pereira, J., 'La república y el ministerio de marina', *Nuevo Mundo*, special issue, 14 April 1932 (1932), 20–22, quote in 20.

[13] Ministry Order of 25 April 1932. *Diario Oficial del Ministerio de Marina* (DOMM). n° 97/1932.

[14] Cerezo Martínez, R., *Armada española siglo XX* (Madrid: Poniente, 1983, 4 vols.), I, pp. 391–395, quote on p. 391.

reinforcements provided by our naval assets – to dominate at all times the Strait of Gibraltar, and that our communications between the ports in the Balearic Islands, Morocco, and the Iberian Peninsula remain secure, and also prevent the success of any attack on the Balearic Islands, mainly.

In this way, Giral formalized the Republic's intention to create a defensive navy that was subordinated to the policy of national neutrality that was powerful and sufficiently prepared to present a clear deterrent to potential aggressors, while at the same time being viewed as valuable to a potential alliance in order to be used on behalf of neutrality.

The studies undertaken by the commission came to unexpected conclusions. They showed that the navy had serious shortcomings and was, in short, inefficient. It was a hollowed-out organization, having a large number of ships that had seen too many years of service and lacking the most basic things: ammunition, mines, torpedoes, fuel, logistical capacity.

The report also showed disproportion in the navy's resources: it had serious shortages in the areas of auxiliary fleets, minelayers, submarines, destroyers, and support vessels in general. One data point is illustrative: the day the Second Republic was proclaimed, the navy possessed among its ships that were ready for action two battleships with a total displacement of 31,400 MT (metric tonnes) and seven cruisers with a total displacement of 46,000 MT, compared to nine destroyers with a total of 12,000 MT and fourteen submarines with around 12,400 MT.[15]

The naval fleet was thus extremely unbalanced in terms of the tonnage of its cruisers compared with other units. This was paradoxical, given that this kind of ship, which offered little protection and limited offensive power, was mainly deployed for naval operations far from home, to engage in offensive exploration and pursuit, to protect shipping, and to coordinate with battleships. All these activities were inconsistent with the mission of the Spanish navy, which served a nation without colonies or far-flung theatres of action and which had almost no battleships.

The situation was so dire that Giral took everything that he had learned and made a radically different proposal in the budget debates in the Cortes that December, compared to what he had presented only a couple of months earlier. Making clear reference to the navy's deficiencies and its overall unsatisfactory state, he expressed his new opinion in the following declaration:[16]

> [O]ur Navy is so lacking in resources that at any given moment, if it were necessary to defend our neutrality, it would be impossible to do so. This needs to be stated clearly. We need a thousand torpedoes, we need eight

---

[15] Morales Trueba, A., *Marina de guerra,* pp. 317–327.
[16] *ABC* (8 December 1932).

thousand mines to defend, at least, the Balearic Islands and ... fuel storage tanks on all our naval bases.

Therefore, the commission proposed a ten-year plan for the navy that abandoned the traditional fixation on building large ships and that would cost around 1.056 billion pesetas. Given that the proposal was made at a time when the new regime was absorbed in the redirection of spending and coming out of the necessary process of justifying assets, this expenditure was not approved.[17]

In the end, Giral only succeeded in getting much more modest plans approved during his first term: contracting for a survey vessel (the *Tofiño*), two tankers (the *A-1* and the *A-2*),[18] and a Sigma II-type submersible (the *D-1*), which was finally delivered in 1947. As he states in his memoirs, all his plans and programmes clashed head-on with the minister of the treasury, Jaime Carner (1931–1933), who blocked programmes that were more ambitious and decisive than the ones mentioned previously.[19]

Nonetheless, Giral's efforts helped to fill out his vision for the navy and his ideas about how to transform the Republic's ineffective, unbalanced, and ill-provisioned naval force into a useful tool for the country's defence. He would not abandon this line of thinking and it would give him a firmer jumping-off point and considerable momentum during his next term as minister of the navy.

Thus, from the very beginning, Giral demonstrated discernment and assiduity towards the institution, which did not go unnoticed. Earlier, we pointed out that Giral respected Francisco Moreno's qualities, and here we should mention that the respect was mutual. In 1935, when Moreno was on trial for a breach of discipline and Giral was out of power, Moreno sought to highlight the importance of Giral's management of the navy in 1932. He pointed out that one of Giral's first steps at the ministry was to order a study to be done and a full and complete report to be made of the navy's circumstances and its main deficiencies, and then adopted its conclusions. Francisco Moreno declared:[20]

---

[17] Cerezo Martínez, *Armada española siglo XX*, I, p. 342.
[18] Decree of 21 July 1932 and Law of 30 August 1932. *Gaceta de Madrid* (GDM) no. 245/1932 and no. 208/1932.
[19] AHN, Diversos, José Giral, leg. no. 8, N1. P. 14.
[20] Archivo del Museo Naval, Madrid. Fondo Moreno de Alborán. 'Defense of Francisco Moreno by his brother, lieutenant commander Salvador Moreno, in 1935, regarding the incident with the sub-secretary of the navy'. 30 July1935. Carpeta 58, documento 1. F.6 (a).

[that he] had never had even the slightest acquaintance with Mr. Giral, but the very fact that the latter had attempted to pursue, under the circumstances at the time, a project that looked at the logical development of our naval assets gave the minister a respectful place in his memory.

Giral finished his first term with an accurate and clear strategic vision for the navy that included an investment in resources in order to transform the navy into a useful, defensive organization, a tool that could be used in the service of Spain's maritime interests in a way that was feasible within the means of the State.

Giral's Second Term as Minister of the Navy and the Plan for 1936

Following the electoral victory of the Popular Front, in February 1936 Giral returned to the naval ministry. This time it was an institution that was already familiar to him, and he brought to it a clear vision and clear plans to transform the navy by providing it with the necessary means to become an effective tool for bolstering national security.

As we have seen, in his previous term he was unsuccessful. His proposals found no support in the government, and the treasury was not willing to invest in anything not considered a priority. However, the situation in 1936 was different. The previous year, Italy had begun to worry international observers, drawing attention directly to the Mediterranean, an area that involved Spain, of course, and where it had a large and sensitive part of its maritime interests. Italy's invasion of Ethiopia in October 1935 constituted a clear threat to Great Britain's naval interests, and the focal point of a confrontation between the two nations shifted to directly off the coast of Spain. Likewise, the obvious rearmament and aggressivity of the Axis powers and the failure of the League of Nations to prevent the escalation of the international crisis made the Republican government more sensitive to issues of national security.

This was the context in which Giral wrote up the findings of the work done during his previous term as a bill containing a plan to address the navy's existing shortcomings. On 22 June 1936, he sent the bill to prime minister Casares Quiroga (May–July 1936), before it was released to the entire government.[21] Unlike what happened in 1932–1933, this time Giral had the support

---

[21] Archivo General de la Marina 'Álvaro de Bazán', Ciudad Real (Archivo General de la Marina 'Álvaro de Bazán', Ciudad Real (hereafter AGMAB). 'Law project on constructions and habilitations of naval bases presented to the Cortes by the ministry of the navy'. June 1936. Leg. no. 8921. Letter of José Giral to Santiago Casares Quiroga. 22 June 1936. AGMAB. Leg. no. 9719.

of none other than the president of the Republic, Manuel Azaña, whom Giral recalls in his memoirs, saying how 'this time' he was 'fond of my plans'.[22]

Giral attached to his proposal a letter addressed to the Cortes (parliament) as well as a confidential report in which he indicated the current state and the needs of each one of the sectors of the navy. The letter detailed his thinking about the navy and the agenda's purpose, rationale, limits, and contributing factors. With great clarity and brevity, he highlighted the importance of naval power at that time for guaranteeing national sovereignty, which, in light of Spanish geography, was more important than the army. He also highlighted Spain's need and right to defend itself from any aggression, and the need to prepare for this.

He summarized the frightful state of the navy's operational capability: its ships without fire control systems; its antiquated battleships; its shortage of ammunition, torpedoes, and mines; its lack of storage tanks, dry docks, spare parts, and auxiliary vessels; as well as the multitude of supplies needed on the bases. He stated clearly, 'What we have is not at all functional.'[23]

The report was based on him having studied the state of all assets either currently in service, under construction, or what were considered necessary: battleships, cruisers, destroyers, submarines, minelayers, gunboats, minesweepers, motorboats, auxiliary ships and other vessels; existing stocks of ammunition, explosives, torpedoes, naval mines, depth charges, and fuel, as well as expected future demand for these; and the requirements for maintaining, servicing, and improving naval bases.

This agenda was developed with an eye to the position of Spanish naval power at the time, comparing assets and proposed construction to the forces that it was anticipated France, Italy, and Great Britain would build. It was a novel plan that was realistic, comprehensive, and clearly in line with the Second Republic's political objectives. It could have given Spain, at an acceptable cost, a small but solid naval force, and in order to accomplish this it affected the entire organization.

As such, it proposed an investment of just over 908 million pesetas, 49% of which would go towards new ships, 25% towards ammunition, mines, torpedoes, charges, and explosives, 17% to renovating bases, and 8% to updating and improving units. Among the new ships, the budget included two 3,000-MT destroyers, eight 1,350-MT destroyers, twelve 575-MT submarines, three gunboats, six 600-MT minesweepers, twenty motor torpedo boats, and several auxiliary vessels for different kinds of missions.

This plan was not only balanced and comprehensive but also realistic; what is more, it was necessary if Spain did not want to find itself in an extremely

---

[22] AHN, Diversos, José Giral, leg. no. 8, Nl. P. 16.

[23] AGMAB, 'Writing presented to the Cortes by the ministry José Giral, justifying the included law project'. Leg. no. 8921.

vulnerable position in a potential conflict in the western Mediterranean; and it was urgent, given how quickly relations between Italy, France, and Great Britain were deteriorating. The plan was based on technical rather than ideological or industrial criteria, and there is no doubt that it would have given Spain its most effective navy in the first half of the twentieth century. It took into account the navy's deficiencies and needs from both a political and a strategic perspective. It can be judged one of the best naval plans of its time, both in its design and in its objectives and ambitions. Unfortunately, the assassination of the politician José Calvo Sotelo and the immediate outbreak of the Spanish Civil War prevented it from being implemented.

As we have been saying up to this point, it is right to underscore the outstanding merit of José Giral's plan and the acuity of his vision for the navy. The foundations of this vision reveal a clarity and realism that were uncommon among the ministers of the time. His plan, which took into consideration both political and strategic factors and economic resources, was possibly the only one that could have been undertaken successfully, to improve the conditions and the usefulness of the navy.

That said, Giral's policies also contained errors. Specifically, with respect to the application of the Republic's ideology, despite the fact that his policies resulted in an extraordinary tactical success, since they assured the Republic's control over almost the entire fleet and the most important ships at the beginning of the war, they also involved a profound strategic error, since they left the Republic's naval forces without commanders and beyond the control and discipline of the government for several months. This significantly diminished the navy's capacity to act, giving the rebel faction an overwhelming strategic advantage, even though this faction had started out at a clear disadvantage, given the fact that they had very few ships, submarines, or aeroplanes at their disposal.

The reorganization of the navy in 1931 by the minister of the navy who preceded Giral, Casares Quiroga, was based on several studies carried out before the regime changed and was intended to give the navy a more modern, efficient, and rational structure. In addition to this reorganization, several measures among the general reforms had already been adopted to ensure the loyalty of navy personnel.

In keeping with the Republican left political thinking, Giral also became involved in an issue that was very important for the survival of the new regime: the need to have the loyalty of the entire armed forces. To that end, he sought to apply Republican thinking, with the essential goal of promoting republicanism and commitment to the government among navy personnel. Possibly because of the need to achieve this objective in a short space of time, Casares and Giral directed their main efforts towards the subaltern ranks and the sailors, rather than towards the institution as a whole and, particularly, the general corps (i.e. the officers), who were entrusted with the main responsibilities.

Casares and Giral did this by pushing for the immediate implementation of organizational measures intended to improve the position of these lower ranks within the institution, decreeing reasonable and necessary social norms intended to improve the living conditions of the sailors.

Both men observed profound inequalities between the sailors and the officers on the ships, though this was typical of all navies at the time. Moreover, it was assumed that the officer class harboured anti-Republican sentiments, even though the change in regime had been received by the officers largely with indifference, and most of them in fact did not conform to this characterization. In any case, the disparities made it easier to radicalize navy personnel and this was exploited by revolutionary political organizations, which slowly and secretly insinuated themselves among the crews.[24]

Regarding the ultimate objective of many of the measures that were adopted, it is instructive to recall the words of lieutenant commander Ángel Rizo Bayona, the personal advisor of minister Casares, who explains the political reasons behind them:[25]

> I was well aware, through personal experience, of the anti-democratic atmosphere on the ships. My plan at the Ministry of the Navy was to break down the leaders' and officers' aristocratic pride, a pride based on caste. In order to do so, it was necessary to give a larger role to the Auxiliary Corps and the subaltern classes, among whom republicanism and, sometimes, freemasonry, were widespread. One of the ideas I suggested to Casares Quiroga, which he later formulated as a decree, was to make some Auxiliary Corps equal to certain ranks of officers in the General Corps. This triggered protests among the latter, but the Republic could thus count on having some loyal mainstays among the commanders of the ships.

Giral continued with this policy, for example granting different kinds of benefits to the auxiliary corps.[26] Regarding these and other Republican improvements, Giral would later criticize the way that some of the personnel in these corps joined the ranks of the Nationalists in July 1936 and fought against the Republic to which 'they owed so much' and which had 'reorganized and improved' the corps to their benefit.[27]

Giral's second term continued along the same lines as his first, with the publication of a series of regulations intended to satisfy the demands of certain political sectors and the subaltern classes, at a time when tensions

---

[24] Morales Trueba, *Marina de guerra*, pp. 276–278.
[25] Ayala Pérez, J.A., *La sombra del triángulo: biografía de Ángel Rizo, Gran Maestre del Grande Oriente Español* (San Cristóbal de La Laguna: Centro de la cultura popular canaria, 2002), p. 141.
[26] Decree 22 March 1932. GDM, n° 86/1932.
[27] AHN, Diversos, José Giral, leg. n°8, N1. P. 20.

were already running high. Again, in an effort to promote social equality, Giral extended permission to leave the ships and bases for the midday meal to all personnel who lived in the area, including corporals and the sailor ranks.[28] He also extended the forty-four-hour work week, established by the Ministry of Labour, to navy arsenals and bases.

While Giral focused on measures related to social equality during his first term, in his second he would introduce ideological measures that would make it easier for radical groups to grow and organize within the navy ranks, which in turn restricted the spread of opposing ideas. For example, he prohibited the reading of newspapers considered favourable to monarchy in naval bases.[29]

Beginning in February 1936, as the social and political situation in Spain was crumbling, Giral began to openly support small, secret extremist groups whose revolutionary objectives were inconsistent with consolidating the regime. Along these lines, Giral's most controversial decision – which would have disastrous consequences after the war broke out – was to authorize the reinstatement of all sailors, corporals, or volunteer infantry soldiers who had been discharged from service after 31 December 1930.[30] The decree clearly targeted those who had been expelled from the navy for their participation in an attempted coup by the revolutionaries in 1934. Many of them were implicated in subversive acts and other events that took place in October of that year. The implementation of this decree made it possible for many, who had been discharged for revolutionary activities or actions and punished by the military code, to return to their previous posts.

Likewise, starting many years earlier and as a result of the tensions arising from increasing subversion, indiscipline, and politicization of navy personnel, classified notes had been attached to the files of several people documenting activities along these lines. Many of these notes had been based on information provided by sources who, for reasons of personal safety, did not wish to be revealed. However, on 29 May 1936, with the acquiescence of Giral, the deputy secretary of the navy ordered the removal from all personnel files of all classified notes that had not been substantiated or produced according to regulation. This order, which might have been justifiable from a juridical or administrative standpoint, had the effect of boosting the type of clandestine activities that undermined stability and discipline within the navy.[31]

We should also note that in July 1936 Giral had put forward a new organizational plan, distilled in a proposed statutory law for the navy.[32] This proposal listed the main reasons for the reform as follows: the need to correct the

[28] Ibid.
[29] Order 27 February 1936. DOMM n° 48/1936.
[30] Decree 21 March 1936. GDM n° 84/1936.
[31] DOMM n°124/1936.
[32] AGMAB. Project of constitutive law of the navy. July 1936. Leg. no. 8921.

existing flaws in the organization, to simplify it, to encourage voluntary enlistment and to reduce mandatory military service to a minimum, to create a naval institute to train young men who would be selected to enter the naval academy; and given the disorganized and dispersed nature of existing regulations, to create a single, comprehensive code covering all of the organization's basic legislation.[33]

This proposal simplified the previous structure, with a sizeable reduction in the number of subdivisions and changes to the positions in the auxiliary corps, keeping only the lowest rank – the auxiliary – as non-commissioned officers, so that the essential links between officers, non-commissioned officers, and sailors were reduced to a minimum. It also created a new general corps, which included all the previous subdivisions – general, administrative, engineering – which would now be organized into three branches: administration, engineering, and general staff, for those belonging to the former general corps.

Another important innovation in this proposal had to do with entry to this corps. The traditional way had been selection of personnel by examination. The document stipulated that henceforward a minimum of 40% of positions would be reserved for personnel from the auxiliary corps and that the rest would come from a new naval institute. The latter was to be a civilian institution from which candidates for the general corps would be selected at twelve years of age. Admission to the naval institute would be based on a selection process in national schools with proportional representation from each province. This measure would have broken up the traditional pool of candidates, who were mostly the sons of officers and auxiliaries in the army and navy or from families in the liberal professions. It was a way to change the social and regional background of most naval officers.

As July approached, amid news and rumours about the possibility of a coup, Giral took several actions, including assigning an auxiliary radio operator by the name of Benjamín Balboa to the navy's central radio station in a way that failed to comply with regulation. Balboa was a freemason like Giral. He was also a member of the Anti-Fascist Republican Military Union (Unión Militar Republicana Antifascista) and was put on reserve between November 1934 and Abril 1935, for his involvement in revolutionary actions in October 1934.[34] At the beginning of the July rebellion, Balboa came to control the radio station and from there to coordinate the revolutionary committees who took over ships at sea and arrested and assassinated the officers before they could join the rebels, thus eliminating the leadership of the fleet's main units.

Although Giral cannot be called a radical or a revolutionary, it is true that at this point in time he understood that the Second Republic's survival

---

[33] AGMAB. Writing of the minister of the navy presented to the Cortes, included in the project of constitutive law of the navy. July 1936. Leg. no. 8921. P. 1.

[34] Cerezo Martínez, *Armada española*, II, p. 33.

depended on the actions of the radicals whose organized existence all ministers of the navy had been warned about. He was not willing to risk confiding in the officers and tragically lost the potential leaders of the Republic's fleet.

José Giral was the only minister of the navy during Spain's Second Republic who developed a true vision for the navy. Despite the fact that his credentials upon assuming the post suggested that he was far from understanding the technical details of his duties, he performed them successfully, adapting his plans for the navy to the political, strategic, and economic circumstances of Spain during the Second Republic, and always aligning them to overarching goals determined by the Republic's defence and security policy.

Unlike many of his predecessors, he championed a plan that was highly relevant, realistic, in line with the available resources, and most importantly based on detailed knowledge of the situation and the navy's requirements to be able to fulfil its mission effectively. Thus, in keeping with navy leaders in the previous regime, he believed that the best option for the Spanish navy – the one that would best contribute to the country's defence and neutrality – was to have a navy which, though modest, could tip the balance between France and Italy (whose navies at the time were roughly equal), both of which fearful about who would dominate the Mediterranean.[35]

All this aside, he made mistakes, the most important of which was not to target the navy as a whole in the efforts to ensure its loyalty to the regime, but rather to put his faith in the subaltern classes and the personnel that were most radicalized politically. Although this policy was initially successful in keeping the most important ships in the government's hands, it ultimately led to the tragic loss of their potential commanders and left the Republican fleet with an overwhelming material advantage but without effective leadership during the Spanish Civil War.

---

[35] AHN, Diversos, José Giral, leg. no. 8, Nl. P. 14.

9

The Quest to Understand Naval Leadership: Educating Admirals for High Command in the U.S. Navy from the Eighteenth Century into the Twenty-first Century

JOHN B. HATTENDORF

The U.S. Navy has only recently recognized that there is both an art and a science to leadership and that higher command at the flag and general officer level requires a unique approach in professional military education. As understanding slowly developed, the navy began by using history and biography, then they used applied social science theories and business management applications. In the early twenty-first century, the Naval War College began a new approach, a previously untried method of individual flag officer development.

In the late eighteenth century, the United States of America took form in the context of ideologies from the Enlightenment that informed not only the political context and debate over the purposes and functions of a navy but also how Americans initially viewed naval officers.[1] At the outset, Americans did not like the title of "admiral," which they thought inappropriate to their new republic. Primarily because of the Royal Navy's name, Americans viewed it as a product of the monarchical and aristocratic values they were trying to avoid. Many thought military and naval education a danger to the new republic,

---

[1] On the political issues, see "Debating the Purpose of a Navy in a New Republic: The United States of America, 1775–1815," in J.D. Davies, Alan James, and Gijs Rommelse, eds., *Ideologies of Western Naval Power, c. 1500–1815* (New York and London: Routledge, 2019), pp. 280–299; and Craig L. Symonds, *Navalists and Antinavalists: The Naval Policy Debate in the United States, 1785–1827* (Newark: University of Delaware Press, 1980).

believing in the militia and the innate abilities of Americans as militiamen and privateers.[2]

At the same time, they had no corresponding distaste for the rank of "general," which Congress gave to George Washington and others, associating it with Cromwell and the militia rather than the aristocracy.

The American Continental Navy of 1775–1785 and the United States Navy, established in 1794, used the rank of captain, not admiral, for its most senior officers. On 22 December 1775, Congress appointed Captain Esek Hopkins commander in chief of the Continental Navy with the courtesy title of commodore – the Dutch term that King William III had introduced into the Royal Navy in 1689. Congress overwhelmingly voted to deny Hopkins the perquisites of an admiral, such as table money for expenses.[3] Hopkins's career was short and unsuccessful. When Congress dismissed Hopkins from service, no one replaced him as commander in chief.

On 15 November 1776, the Continental Congress had created a table of equivalent ranks for the officers of the army and navy that included the naval ranks of admiral, vice admiral, rear admiral, and commodore. In the same legislation, Congress also established a pay table for naval officers and men, but it went no higher than a captain. Congress did not authorize the use of the flag ranks.[4]

Captain John Paul Jones of the Continental Navy coveted promotion to admiral, but with the disbandment of the Continental Navy in 1783, this became impossible. When Catherine the Great invited Jones to come to Russia in 1788 to command the Black Sea Fleet as a rear admiral, he wrote to Thomas Jefferson requesting that Congress backdate for him a rear admiral's commission to the 1779 battle off Flamborough Head. Angry and frustrated that the United States would not honour this request, Jones accepted Catherine's appointment in the vain hope that when the United States eventually decided to reestablish a naval force, the country would see the wisdom to call him to command it.[5]

---

[2] William P. Leeman, *The Long Road to Annapolis: The Founding of the Naval Academy and the Merging American Republic* (Chapel Hill: University of North Carolina Press, 2010), p. 5.

[3] William Bell Clark, William James Morgan et al, eds., *Naval Documents of the American Revolution* (Washington DC: Government Printing Office, 1964–), vol. 3, p. 207; "Journal of the Continental Congress," 22 December 1775, 20; "Diary of Richard Smith," vol. 2 , 1174 ff. "Rules for the Regulation of the Navy of the United Colonies".

[4] Clark, Morgan et al., eds., *Naval Documents of the American Revolution,* vol. 7, pp. 179–180; "Journal of the Continental Congress," 15 Nov. 1776.

[5] Samuel Eliot Morison, *John Paul Jones: A Sailor's Biography* (Boston: Little Brown, 1959), pp. 360–361; Evan Thomas, *John Paul Jones: Sailor, Hero, Father of the American Navy* (New York: Simon & Schuster, 2003), pp. 267–270.

After the establishment of the United States Navy in 1794, President George Washington issued the service's first naval officers' commission in 1797 to Captain John Barry. As the naval service's senior captain, he also used the courtesy title of commodore as a captain who had command over other warships.[6] The service followed this approach for the next fifty years, during which the navy firmly established its underlying service culture and understanding of naval command. American commanding officers typically had individual orders to operate their warships independently in achieving their objectives. They rarely operated in the context of a squadron or a fleet, but, when they did, they had neither a refined strategy nor tactics. Their efforts broke down in disputes over seniority and personal honor. In this context, the U.S. Navy built a command culture based on unquestioned authority over a ship's company, independence of action, quick and effective response without supervising guidance, or tactical direction from an admiral or any central authority. Operating on the intent of a commanding officer's broad orders, he adjusted his action in light of the situation he found on the distant scene of action.[7]

At the lower levels of the officer structure, it was relatively clear how an officer progressed from the grade of midshipman to that of captain in the navy. After initial entry-level practical training on the job at sea – or the U.S. Naval Academy, after it was established at Annapolis, Maryland, in 1845 – one rose to the command of a warship by mastering the practical, technical, and procedural skills necessary to operate a warship in peace and war. One learned these skills by serving at sea in positions of increasing responsibility while being promoted up through the pay grades to captain.

The prevailing culture of naval command continued, emphasizing individual ship command. However, in 1857, it became clear than there was a need to maintain discipline among individual captains. To meet this need, Congress created the temporary rank of flag officer for captains in command of squadrons.[8] Due to the practical necessities of the American Civil War, Congress established the permanent rank of flag officer in December 1861.

---

[6] Tim McGrath, *John Barry: An American Hero in the Age of Sail* (Yardley: Westholme, 2010), pp. 423–424.

[7] Gene R. Anderson, "Historical and Cultural Foundations of Navy Officer Development," in Kendall D. Gott, ed., *Cultivating Army Leaders: Historical Perspectives. The Proceedings of the Combat Studies Institute 2010 Military History Symposium* (Fort Leavenworth, KS: Combat Studies Institute Press, 2011), pp. 197–204. See also, Louis Arthur Norton, *Captains Contentious: The Dysfunctional Sons of the Brine* (Columbia: University of South Carolina Press, 2009).

[8] Donald Chisholm, *Waiting for Dean Men's Shoes: Origins and Development of the U.S. Navy's Officer Personnel System, 1793–1941* (Stanford: Stanford University Press, 2001), pp. 230, 232, 251, 259, 264.

Seven months later, on 16 July 1862, Congress modified its earlier action. The new Act replaced the rank of flag officer and established for the first time in the history of the U.S. Navy the ranks of rear admiral and commodore. At this point, Congress intended that the new ranks only for use during wartime, but soon the navy began also to use them to recognize exemplary wartime service.[9] In 1864, during the war, Congress authorized the president to promote Rear Admiral David Glasgow, the son of an immigrant to America from Minorca, for his victory at Mobile Bay. Again, in 1866, the navy honored Farragut for his victories by promoting him to full admiral and appointing in his place as vice admiral, David Dixon Porter. With Farragut's death in 1870, Porter moved up to admiral, and another Civil War hero, Stephen C. Rowan, became vice admiral. These appointments were limited to only three individuals, who were essentially retired but retained on active duty. With one exception, no other officers were promoted above the rank of rear admiral until 1915.[10]

The one exception was Commodore George Dewey, who had won the Battle of Manila Bay in 1898. Congress promoted him to rear admiral on hearing the news of that victory, and in 1899, authorized the president to promote him to admiral of the navy, a rank he held until his death. No successor has ever been appointed to succeed Dewey in his high rank. Aside from the particular cases of Farragut, Porter, Rowan, and Dewey, Congress retained its reticence about senior flag officers. After 1915, even with the revival of the appointment of vice admirals and admirals, these promotions were considered only temporary and dependent on filling particular positions that required such rank for a specific period. After serving in such a post, an officer reverted to rear admiral and could not rise above that rank permanently. This practice continued until 1944 when Congress created the five-star rank of fleet admiral. A step below the level of admiral of the navy that George Dewey had held, the position of fleet admiral was limited to officers who served in the Second World War. Only four naval officers obtained this rank, William D. Leahy, Ernest J. King, Chester W. Nimitz, and William F. Halsey, Jr. From that point onward, naval officers could retain the highest flag rank that they had held on active service.[11]

Americans were both hesitant about using the title of admiral and gave little thought to the higher aspects of command in the naval profession. In 1871, a group of officers established the U.S. Naval Institute to discuss such

---

[9] *Ibid.*, pp. 290–291, 295, 349.

[10] William B. Cogar, *Dictionary of Admirals of the U.S. Navy,* volume 1, *1862–1900* (Annapolis: Naval Institute Press, 1989), pp. xi–xvi, volume 2, *1901–1918* (Annapolis: Naval Institute Press, 1989), pp. ix–xiii.

[11] Public Law 333 – 79th Congress, Chapter 112 – 2d Session S. 1354. http://www.history.navy.mil/research/library/online-reading-room/title-list-alphabetically/p/public-law-333-79th-congress.html (accessed 2 January 2023).

issues. Before the U.S. Naval War College's first class convened in 1885, there was no formal training or preparation available for naval officers taking up positions of high command and senior leadership. Up until the 1880s, American warships continued to operate independently rather than in squadron of fleet formations. There was little practical need for admirals until the navy began to think of fleet operations and an administrative structure that could support and direct fleet operations. The founder of the Naval War College, Admiral Stephen B. Luce, was a crucial figure in developing a concept for the fleet in the U.S. Navy.[12]

In Admiral Luce's address to the first class at the College in 1886, he noted:

> Now, it must strike anyone who thinks about it as extraordinary that we, members of the profession of arms, should never have undertaken the study of our real business – war. For members of the naval and military profession, it should be not only the principal study, but it should be an attractive study.[13]

This subject soon occupied the curriculum of the new College and touched on a wide range of topics, from tactics and strategy to history and international law. As an institution devoted to preparing its students for occupying positions of high command and leadership, Luce was inspired in his approach by his personal friendships with Brigadier Emory Upton of the U.S. Army and his study of the German Army's general staff as well as with Professor Sir John Knox Laughton and his "Scientific Study of Naval History."[14] Developing these ideas further, Luce went on to suggest a comparative method for developing naval thinking. He pointed out that there was much to be learned from the biographies and letters of the great military commanders. He was strongly suggesting that naval officers could learn from the land campaigns of such great leaders as Marlborough, Frederick the Great, Napoleon, and Wellington.

Little existed in the way of focused studies on the topic of naval leadership. The traditional method has always been to look to biographical studies. In that regard, it is significant to note that one of the very first books that the Naval War College acquired in 1885 for its library was Clarke and M'Arthur's

---

[12] On the development of a fleet, see James C. Rentfrow, *Home Squadron: The U.S. Navy on the North Atlantic Station* (Annapolis: Naval Institute Press, 2014).

[13] Stephen B. Luce, "On the Study of Naval Warfare as a Science," in John D. Hayes and John B. Hattendorf, eds., *The Writings of Stephen B. Luce*. Historical Monograph no. 1 (Newport: Naval War College Press, 1975), p. 50.

[14] Andrew Lambert, *The Foundations of Naval History: Sir John Laughton, the Royal Navy, and the Historical Profession* (London: Chatham Publishing, 1998) and *Letters and Papers of Professor Sir John Knox Laughton, 1830–1915* (London: Navy Records Society, 2002).

Life of Nelson.[15] Luce specifically selected Captain Alfred Thayer Mahan to undertake for the Naval War College the two series of lectures that pioneered the link between naval operations and international politics. These lectures eventually became his famous books on *The Influence of Sea Power upon History, 1660–1783* (Boston: Little Brown, 1890), and *The Influence of Sea Power on the French Revolution and Empire* (Boston: Little Brown, 1892). Taken as a whole, Mahan presented two groups of arguments in his writings. On the one hand, he talked about grand strategy, and, on the other, about the naval profession. This second group focused on naval command and operational leadership.[16] Mahan was deeply sensitive to the increasing emphasis on technology in navies, but, in his mind, technology was not the key to success. "Historically, good men with poor ships are better than poor men with good ships," Mahan wrote.[17] "In following the story of Trafalgar, it must be remembered that the naval superiority of Great Britain lay not in the number of her ships, but in the wisdom, energy, and tenacity of her admirals and seamen."[18] Mahan saw that there must be a balance between the science and art of command. In educating leaders, Mahan believed that a critical study of history was the most important path for commanders to develop and to exercise intelligent judgment in war. While history did not provide direct answers, the study of it helped to mature a leader's discretion in ways that the memorization of maxims and doctrine could not. Doctrine, Mahan thought, created the formation of similar thoughts and helped build cooperation, an essential feature of successful operations, but it was no replacement for intelligent judgment.[19]

Less often noticed among Mahan's works is his short biography of Admiral Farragut, which he completed in 1892, just as he was returning to Newport, Rhode Island, to begin his second tour of duty as president of the Naval War College. The final chapter of that work is a study of Farragut's character, a

---

[15] The Rev. James Stanier Clarke and John M'Arthur, *The Life and Services of Admiral Lord Nelson, Duke of Bronte, Vice-Admiral of the White, K.B., etc., From his Lordship's Manuscripts*. London: Fisher, Son, & Co., 1840. See John B. Hattendorf, *Trafalgar and Nelson 200: Catalogue of an Exhibition of Rare Books, Maps, Charts, Prints, Models, and Signal Flags Relating to Events and Influences of the Battle of Trafalgar and Lord Nelson* (Newport: Naval War College Museum, 2005), p. 14. https://permanent.access.gpo.gov/gpo109166/trafalgarexhibit.pdf (accessed 5 December 2023).

[16] For a detailed analysis of Mahan's thinking, see Jon Tetsuro Sumida, *Inventing Grand Strategy and Teaching Command: The Classic Works of Alfred Thayer Mahan Reconsidered* (Baltimore: Johns Hopkins University Press, 1997), pp. 6–7.

[17] Alfred Thayer Mahan, *The Influence of Sea Power upon the French Revolution and Empire, 1793–1812* (Boston: Little Brown, 1892), vol. 1, p. 102.

[18] Mahan, *French Revolution, and Empire,* vol. 2, p. 141.

[19] Sumida, *Inventing Grand Strategy,* pp. 68–67.

pioneer professional analysis of an American naval leader, and a discussion of naval leadership.[20] As another author has written, "The history of Farragut's life is of importance less as a study of naval tactics, strategy, and history than a study of the character of one whom many believe as having been the ideal of what a naval commander should be. He proved that kindliness, honor, love of friends and family, and a tolerant disposition are not incompatible with inflexibility in discipline and greatness as a warrior. But the secret of this success in war was in straight thinking and determined action … ."[21] The closing chapter of Mahan's biography of Farragut included comparisons of the leadership of Nelson, St Vincent, and other commanders. He followed this book with the capstone volume to his four-volume sea power series, *The Life of Nelson: The Embodiment of the Sea Power of Great Britain* (Boston: Little Brown, 1897), and *Types of Naval Officers Drawn from the History of the British Navy* (Boston: Little Brown, 1901) that looked at the differing leadership styles of admirals Hawke, Rodney, Howe, Jervis, Saumarez, and Pellew. As Mahan put it, "Eminent all, though in varying manner and degree, each illustrated a distinct type in the same noble profession."[22] St. Vincent intuitively had broad and far-sighted views that he embodied in spontaneous and relentless action. Howe's actions were the result of conscientious and painstaking efforts that rose to greatness only in an emergency. Mahan thought that neither Saumarez nor Exmouth were great flag officers, but they were able and devoted. Saumarez was an accomplished master of his profession and an exemplar of the principal subordinate for a fleet commander, while Exmouth was the typical innate seaman and active warrior who does best with the freedom of detached service.[23]

Leadership studies at the Naval War College continued along such biographical lines for many years to come. In the first quarter-century of the college's existence, it had developed from a place of voluntary original research for the creation of the art and science of naval warfare, as Admiral Luce had established it. The approach to senior-level professional naval education had matured since 1884. The chief developments included the works of Captain Alfred Thayer Mahan on strategy, command, and leadership; Commander

---

[20] Alfred Thayer Mahan, *Admiral Farragut* (New York: D. Appleton & Co., 1892), pp. 308–326.

[21] U.S. Naval History and Heritage Command, website biography of Farragut. https://www.history.navy.mil/content/history/nhhc/research/library/research-guides/z-files/zb-files/zb-files-f/farragut-davidg.html (accessed 5 December 2023).

[22] Alfred Thayer Mahan, *Types of Naval Officers Drawn from the History of the British Navy with Some Account of the Conditions of Naval Warfare at the Beginning of the Eighteenth Century, and its Subsequent Development during the Sail Period* (London: Samson, Low, Marston, & Company Limited, 1902), p. 477.

[23] Mahan, *Types of Naval Officers*, pp. 477–478.

Charles Stockton's work in creating a basis for the law of naval warfare; and Captain Henry C. Taylor's adoption into the curriculum of Lieutenant William McCarty Little's adaptation of German ideas of *Kriegspiel* to create naval war gaming.[24]

The next phase in the development began in 1909, when Commander William L. Rodgers returned to Newport after serving as the liaison officer between the Naval War College and the newly established Army War College in Washington, D.C., under its first commandant, Brigadier-General Tasker Bliss. Bliss, having served as the first military faculty member at the Naval War College as a lieutenant in 1885–1887, was genuinely interested in developing a connection with Newport. Among other things, Bliss developed a system for the joint study of war problems by the two colleges. Bliss's successors continued his initiatives with the first naval officers attending the Army War College in 1906–1907. When Rodgers returned to Newport after his close observation of the Army War College, he brought with him the ideas that the U.S. Army had developed from its views of the German General Staff and the methods by which it trained its staff officers. Rodgers was particularly interested in what the Germans called "the applicatory system," which several American army officers had been working on to adapt for use in the United States. Major C.H. Barth's 1906 translation of Otto von Griepenkerl's *Letters on Applied Tactics* and Eban Swift's *Feld Orders, Messages and Reports*, along with army Captain Roger S. Fitch's 1909 *Estimating Tactical Situations and Composing Orders,* became the standard reference works for the U.S. Navy as it began to develop its adaptation of the applicatory system.[25]

Over the next half-century, the Naval War College developed and refined this approach in its curriculum that embodied a task-oriented approach to leadership. The approach focused on three major elements: the estimate of the situation, the philosophy of the order form, and the use of naval war gaming as a means to demonstrate the applicatory system in practice. The estimate of the situation created a logical mental process by which admirals and senior commanders reached and expressed a tactical or strategic decision. It involved four sequential steps: (1) the statement of the naval commander's mission, (2) an assessment of the strength, disposition, and likely intentions of an enemy force, (3) an evaluation of the disposition and strength of one's own forces, and (4) a determination of the courses open for action to achieve the mission. This system was not a prescription for action but a structured and logical method for analyzing particular operational naval problems. The next phase of the system was the philosophy of the order form and the drafting

---

[24] John B. Hattendorf, B.M. Simpson III, and John R. Wadleigh, *Sailors and Scholars: The Centennial History of the Naval War College* (Newport: Naval War College Press, 1984), Chapters 2–3.

[25] Hattendorf et al., *Sailors and Scholars,* pp. 69–71.

of orders. Future admirals learned to write their orders clearly and logically and in a consistent format.

Most importantly, they also learned in this phase of the curriculum that there were different types of orders for leaders, appropriate to their varying levels of command authority. The implications in the adoption of these new approaches were profound for the U.S. Navy. In the past, juniors blindly obeyed the directions of their seniors without question. Under the new approach, all could understand the full range of what was involved in any strategic or tactical situation. Juniors remained in their subordinate roles, but with an understanding of the situation and their seniors' reasoning and decisions, they could intelligently execute their orders. In place of blind obedience, they could now understand their seniors' objectives and the means at hand, allowing them to be able to adapt to the fluid and ever-changing conditions of war.[26]

In the early history of the U.S. Navy, both autocratic and paternalistic styles of leadership had predominated. Relationship-oriented leadership emerged in the early nineteenth century in association with an increasing focus on the abolition of flogging and the conditions under which seamen worked. Relationship-oriented leadership is focused on human relationships in a group and is more concerned with the overall well-being and satisfaction of group members than in meeting tasks. The new ideas surrounding the applicatory system that entered the U.S. Navy in 1909–1910 focused on task-oriented leadership. In this approach, a leader characteristically focuses on the tasks that need to be performed to meet defined goals. In the navy's case, the new system emphasized that the intelligent execution of orders was the product of mutual understanding between junior and senior officers about a commonly understood range of actions and procedures.

The concepts of the applicatory system soon became identified as doctrine, something that had not previously existed in the U.S. Navy before 1910 and now needed further development. This development was not an easy task, as the senior officers of the day had their initial naval training in the age of sail, although they also had some experience with steam engineering and electricity. Additionally, the intangible traditions of the naval service lay in the age of sail. Naval warfare in the early twentieth century, with its burgeoning technologies, increased mobility, and increasing firepower, required a more comprehensive approach to use these rapidly changing elements comprehensively. The mental processes involved in the estimate of the situation and the discipline in the philosophy of the order form filled the intellectual need and became the basis for the new American doctrinal approach to naval science.[27]

There was steady progress in developing this body of thought from 1910 up into the 1940s. Captain William S. Sims made one of the first notable

---

[26] Hattendorf et al., *Sailors and Scholars,* pp. 72–73
[27] Hattendorf et al., *Sailors and Scholars,* p. 74.

developments. A graduate of the Naval War College's first two-year "long course" in 1912, he went on to develop tactical doctrine as commander, Atlantic Fleet Destroyer Flotilla, in 1913. Sims's aide in that post, Lieutenant Commander Dudley W. Knox, made the next significant contribution. Knox had graduated from the next iteration of the college's long course in 1913. In 1915, he published the first public statement of the U.S. Navy's understanding of naval doctrine in a prize-winning essay on "The Role of Doctrine in Naval Warfare."[28] On Sims's return to the college presidency in 1919, after having commanded U.S. Naval Forces in European waters during the First World War as a four-star admiral, he reinvigorated the college's approach through his reflections on his own experiences in the war. As part of this effort, Sims reorganized the college into five departments, among them, the command department taught all the aspects of the applicatory system as well as leadership and doctrine.[29] Nominally headed by the college's chief of staff, a rear admiral, Captain Dudley W. Knox effectively led the department during Sims's presidency.[30]

During the interwar period, the Naval War College's focus lay increasingly at the tactical level of fleet operations. In these years, the repeated examination of the Battle of Jutland through war gaming also allowed students to examine the leadership of the key figures involved and to draw conclusions about their effectiveness.[31] Examining the battle from the standpoint of tactics and the performance of different types of ships, it was only in the area of individual leadership that War College students reached notably different views about the opposing commanders' leadership abilities.[32] Sims also began to widen out the curriculum with assistance from professional academics. In 1920, he brought in William Ernest Hocking, professor of philosophy at Harvard. Hocking regularly returned to the college lecturing on such topics as "Morale," "Psychology," and "Leadership."

---

[28] Dudley W. Knox, "The Role of Doctrine in Naval Warfare," *U.S. Naval Institute Proceedings*, vol. 41, no. 2 (March–April 1915).

[29] On Sims, see Benjamin J. Armstrong, *21st Century Sims: Innovation, Education, and Leadership for the Modern Era.* 21st Century Foundations (Annapolis: Naval Institute Press, 2015).

[30] On Knox, see David A. Kohnen, *21st Century Knox: Influence, Sea Power, and History for the Modern Era.* 21st Century Foundations (Annapolis: Naval Institute Press, 2016).

[31] David Kohnen, with Nicholas Jellicoe and Nathaniel S. Sims, "The U.S. Navy Won the Battle of Jutland", Naval War College Review, vol. 69, no. 4 (2016), 123–146. Available at: https://digital-commons.usnwc.edu/nwc-review/vol69/iss4/11 (accessed 5 December 2023).

[32] Hattendorf et al., *Sailors and Scholars,* p. 142.

Rear Admiral Edward C. Kalbfus[33] became president of the Naval War College in 1934 and began a significant effort to revise the course materials that were used to teach the estimate of the situation. Kalbfus wanted to turn what had been a short pamphlet into a book on the art of logical thinking that would be an appropriate guide to any military and naval situation. Kalbfus first turned to Professor Hocking and asked him to replace his usual topic with a lecture on "Logic and its Process." Kalbfus then used that lecture as the foundation for the faculty to begin to revise the pamphlet. Kalbfus made little progress during his first year. In the following year, army Major Edward S. Johnston reported to the college as a student in the senior class of 1936. A Phi Beta Kappa graduate of the University of Indiana, where his father was head of the Latin department, Johnston had already made a name for himself as a military thinker and critic of the *Army Field Service Regulations* for its failure to deal with the fundamental factors in warfare, rather than just focusing on the changing elements. In the year before coming to Newport, Johnston had been at the Army War College, where he had served on a committee that examined the fundamental factors involved in planning and executing joint operations.[34] Johnston played a critical role in the drafting of the Naval War College's new booklet that Kalbfus entitled *Sound Military Decision*. First printed in 1936, it was notable – and controversial – for rejecting the use of the army's nine principles of war. Such views were typical in the navy; Kalbfus was only the latest to object to them. There were many criticisms of the draft. Some thought it too long, some, too ponderous, and others said it was too complicated. Among them, three prominent faculty members at the college – Captain Raymond Spruance, head of the senior class tactics department; Captain Robert Theobald, head of the senior class strategy department; and Captain Richmond Kelly Turner, advisor on air operations – all had criticisms of the first draft, most of which were incorporated into the 1936 printed version.

The college continued to revise *Sound Military Decision* after Kalbfus left the college for the Battle Fleet in 1936. Three years later, in 1939, Kalbfus returned for a second term as president of the college. Disapproving what the college had done to *Sound Military Decision* in his absence, Kalbfus immediately began again to revise the work. He brought back to the college Edward S. Johnston, now an army lieutenant colonel. With Johnston's help and in light of Kalbfus's own recent experience as a four-star admiral and commander, Battle Force, they added an entirely new section that filled a notable omission on "The Supervision of the Planned Action," which became the fourth and final step of the Naval War College's process.

---

[33] Naval War College, *Sound Military Decision* (Newport, 1942), http://www.gutenberg.org/ebooks/28178' (accessed 2 January 2024).

[34] Hattendorf et al., *Sailors and Scholars*, p. 157; See also, https://www.findagrave.com/memorial/49239266/edward-s-johnston (accessed 5 December 2023).

"In war," Kalbfus wrote, "mistakes are normal; errors are usual; information is seldom complete, often inaccurate, and frequently misleading. Success is won, not by personnel and materiel in prime condition, but by the debris of an organization worn by the strain of campaign and shaken by the shock of battle."[35] Emphasizing issues below the strategic level, he explained that the nature of warfare requires that every plan needs constant supervision and revision in its execution. Through the collection, analysis, evaluation, and interpretation of new information, a commander will be able to maintain a grasp of both the progress of his forces and future possibilities. He can correct deficiencies and errors in the plan and its execution as he makes adjustments toward the attainment of the objective. Through this method, the commander can ensure that his forces conform their movements to the objectives and to each other, reapportioning strength to meet new conditions, comparing actual losses with those he had anticipated. Taking appropriate measures for freedom of action, the commander will evolve and adopt one. If the old plan requires changes to its broader aspects, he will make such changes. Otherwise, the commander will modify details of his plan as the situation may demand, always endeavoring to retain the integrity of its larger aspects and objectives.[36] The key to this final step in the process involved maintaining a running estimate of the situation that forced the commander to continually evaluate the situation and adjust his orders to the fleet in light of a continually changing situation. The chief of naval operations during the Second World War, Admiral Ernest J. King, summarized his idea of leadership that reflected both his Naval War College education in the 1930s and his own historical and biographical studies of commanders. "Leadership," King wrote, "requires the capacity to grasp the essentials of a particular job – plus the ability to impart knowledge and directions to subordinates in such manner that they can effectively do their several parts without close supervision."[37]

The approach that the Naval War College had begun in 1909–1910 reached its apogee with the 1942 publication of *Sound Military Decision*.[38] It was the most important expression of the college's teaching and influence in the interwar years. When the United States entered Second World War in 1941, nearly every flag officer eligible for command at sea understood in its concepts and procedures. Widely distributed throughout the navy and reprinted several

[35] Naval War College, *Sound Military Decision* (Newport, 1942), Chapter 9. http://www.gutenberg.org/ebooks/28178 (accessed 5 December 2023).

[36] Naval War College, *Sound Military Decision.*

[37] Naval War College, Naval Historical Collection, Buell-Whitehill-Fleet Admiral E.J. King collection, Ms. Coll. 37, Box 5, folder 10, 0134.

[38] For a scholarly edition in print, see Naval War College, *Sound Military Decision,* edited with an introduction by Frank M. Snyder. Classics of Seapower series. (Annapolis: Naval Institute Press, 1988).

times during the war, it was the U.S. Navy's only guide to operational planning and execution in that period. While the ideas found extensive use, some officers found the manual too ponderous and academic to use directly. However, the documentary evidence provided in the so-called "Nimitz Grey Book" – The Pacific Fleet Staff's running estimate of the situation – clearly shows that Admiral Nimitz followed the guidance contained in *Sound Military Decision* as he supervised, revised, and adjusted his orders throughout the entire war in the Pacific between 1941 and 1945.[39]

From the late 1930s to the 1950s, the leading student of military leadership in the United States was Douglas Southall Freeman. He was the editor in chief of the *News-Leader,* the major afternoon newspaper in Richmond, Virginia, which he edited for 34 years. As a sideline to his daily newspaper work, he became the most prominent military biographer in the United States. His four-volume biography on the Confederate States' leading general during the American Civil War, *R.E. Lee,* was published in 1934–1935 and was awarded the Pulitzer Prize in Biography in 1935. The award of the Pulitzer Prize led the Army War College in Washington, D.C., to invite Freeman to give the first of many regular lectures on military leadership. Freeman followed his first book with a three-volume study of *Lee's Lieutenants*, which appeared during the Second World War in 1942–1944, and widely read in wartime military circles. His final major work was his seven-volume study of *George Washington,* published between 1948 and 1957, which earned him a posthumous Pulitzer Prize in 1958, five years after his death. Freeman lectured at the Naval War College in 1948 and 1949. In his first presentation for a primarily naval audience, Freeman explained that the great American commanders have all been men of character. For Freeman, a senior officer's character was the most important quality in a leader. As he later defined it,

[Character] is that quality of man which is going to make a man, in an hour of strain, do the just and if possible the generous thing. Character is that quality of mind which makes truth-telling instinctive rather than strange. Character is the essence of all that a man has seen in life and regards as high and exalted. Character is like truth, the substance of the things that a man has forgotten but the substance of things that are worth remembering in life. Character is the starting point from which we go on.[40]

Freeman explained that the great American leaders of character had won their battles through three factors: superiority of numbers, the superiority of

---

[39] Hattendorf et al., *Sailors and Scholars,* pp. 157–161; Hattendorf, "Saving Nimitz's Gray Book," *Naval History Magazine,* vol. 28, no. 3 (June 2014). https://www.usni.org/magazines/naval-history-magazine/2014/june/saving-nimitzs-graybook (accessed 5 December 2023).

[40] Stuart W. Smith, ed., *Douglas Southall Freeman on Leadership* (Newport: Naval War College Press, 1990), p. v. [epigraph].

equipment, and superiority in morale. If one in this triumvirate of superiority were missing, the commander made up for it with overwhelming supremacy in one of the other factors. In 1949, Freeman spoke again at the Naval War College. This time he gave his standard postwar lecture on leadership that he had given at many other institutions. By this time, he had merged his historical studies abut leadership with his observations and discussions with many of the most prominent American military leaders who had fought in the Second World War. He distilled his definition of leadership into three concise points that emphasized the relationship between officers and ratings:

1 Know your stuff.
2 Be a man.
3 Look after your men.[41]

In the immediate postwar period, nearly every senior flag officer in the navy had extensive war experience and had little time or patience for the philosophical approach that had characterized the interwar years. Their view of successful command leadership was epitomized by Admiral Arleigh Burke, who served as chief of naval operations from 1955 to 1961. Burke pointed to decentralization as the critical facilitating element in American naval leadership.

> Decentralization means we offer officers the opportunity to rise to positions of responsibility, of decision, of identity and stature – if they want it, and as soon as they can take it.
> We believe in command, not staff. We believe we have "real" things to do. The Navy believes in putting a man in a position with a job to do, and let him do it – give him hell if he does not perform – but be a man in his own name. We decentralize and capitalize on the capabilities of our individual people rather than centralize and make automatons of them. This builds that essential pride of service and sense of accomplishment.[42]

The 1960s brought massive changes to all the military services with Secretary of Defense Robert McNamara's reforms that centered on procedural reforms and cost-management through the use of systems analysis and the insights of academics and industrial leaders, moving the Defense Department to emphasize civilian control over the armed forces. The colleges that focused on professional military education only slowly adapted to these changes as

---

[41] Smith, ed., *Freeman on Leadership,* pp. 205–214.
[42] Admiral Arleigh Burke to Rear Admiral Walter G. Schindler, 14 May 1958, quoted by David A. Rosenberg, "Admiral Arleigh Burke," in Robert William Love. Jr., ed., *The Chiefs of Naval Operations* (Annapolis: Naval Institute Press, 1980), p. 287.

they concentrated on the operational issues raised by current events such as the Cuban Missile Crisis and the Vietnam War. In 1965, McNamara's former deputy assistant secretary of defense for education and manpower, Edward J. Katzenbach, Jr., then the director of the American Council on Education, severely criticized all the country's senior professional military educational institutions in an article entitled "The Demotion of Professionalism at the War College."[43] Katzenbach argues that the colleges had become so civilianized in their outlook that they were no longer service-oriented, but, at the same time, did not reach the academic standard of civilian colleges and universities.

Between 1966 and 1974, the Naval War College underwent two periods of reform. The first period, under Vice Admirals John T. Hayward, Richard Colbert, and B.J. Semmes, began the process of raising the academic level and teaching the new ideas of defense management more effectively. The second reform period that Vice Admiral Stansfield Turner began in 1972 has, in many respects, continued to the present. The "Turner Revolution" began with a re-examination of what was essential in the education of a progressive, mid-career officer, focusing on first principles. At the same time, it returned the college to the basic idea of its founder, Rear Admiral Stephen B. Luce, that the Naval War College is a "place of original research on all questions relating to war and to statesmanship connected with war, or the prevention of war."[44] In Turner's approach, studies of leadership were part and parcel of the selected historical case studies that examined the elements of strategy and policy from the Peloponnesian Wars to the Second World War. Students read the book-length works of the best recent historians on the various subjects, leavened with the occasion novel, such as Stephen Crane's *Red Badge of Courage* on combat experience in the American Civil War and C.S. Forester's 1936 novel *The General*.[45]

While Turner's historical case study approach has continued within the study of strategy and policy, the teaching of leadership continued to develop three different methods: (a) adding ethical and moral dimensions, (b) introducing new management practices from industry, and (c) applying social science theories and applications.

In 1977, Vice Admiral James B. Stockdale became president of the Naval War College. As a naval aviator who had been shot down over North Vietnam in 1966, the North Vietnamese kept him a prisoner of war for nearly eight

---

[43] Edward L. Katzenbach, Jr, "The Demotion of Professionalism at the War College," U.S. Naval Institute *Proceedings* (April 1965), 34–41.

[44] Stephen B. Luce, "An Address ... ," in John D. Hayes and John B. Hattendorf, eds., *The Writings of Stephen B. Luce* (Newport: Naval War College Press, 1975), pp. 39–40.

[45] For Admiral Stansfield Turner's changes to the curriculum at the Naval War College, see Hattendorf et al., *Sailors and Scholars,* pp. 274–295.

years before they released him in 1973. Awarded the Medal of Honor for his valor and heroism as the senior American officer in the prisoner of war camp, Stockdale had an unusual basis for thinking about how to improve aspects of the Naval War College's curriculum. In particular, Stockdale wanted officers to appreciate more deeply the irrational and unpredictable elements of warfare that they might experience. His most important contribution was to expand the college's electives program and to include in the choices available for students a course that he taught on "The Fundamentals of Moral Obligation."

First taught in 1978, Stockdale enlisted the assistance of Professor Joseph G. Brennan, professor emeritus of philosophy from Columbia University's Barnard College, to team-teach the course with him. Stockdale began the course with his reflections on *The Enchiridion* by Epictetus, the Ancient Greek Stoic philosopher whom Stockdale had read while doing a master's degree at Stanford University in 1962.[46] The course included readings from the Book of Job, the Socratic dialogues of Plato, Aristotle's *Nichomachean Ethics,* Kant's *Foundations of the Principles of the Metaphysics of Words,* John Stuart Mill's *On Liberty* and *Utilitarianism.* Stockdale supplemented these with selections from Camus, Conrad, Dostoyevsky, Solzhenitsyn, and other writers before ending the course with a careful study of *The Enchiridion* and Wittgenstein's *The Ethic of Silence.* Professor Brennan elucidated the readings with lectures for the course, which he continued to teach for the next fourteen years.[47] To Stockdale, the point of the course was that individual character, freedom, and personal responsibility was more important than a rule book for a moral life.[48]

Stockdale's innovative and influential course at the Naval War College coincided with the aftermath of the Watergate scandal and the resignation of President Richard Nixon. An essential part of the reaction to these events in American politics was the action of Congress in passing the Ethics in Government Act of 1978. While this Act of Congress dealt with ethics at an entirely different level than Stockdale had discussed, the Act ushered in a series of subsequent laws and complex bureaucratic regulations that are in force today to promote ethical conduct in the armed forces and among civilian government employees.

In the 1950s and 1960s, the American engineer, statistician, and management consultant, W. Edwards Deming, became highly influential in Japan through

---

[46] James B. Stockdale, "The World of Epictetus," *Atlantic Monthly* (April 1978). Stockdale elaborated on this in later lectures. See, for example, his two lectures "Stockdale on Stoicism," https://www.usna.edu/Ethics/_files/documents/stoicism1.pdf and https://www.usna.edu/Ethics/_files/documents/Stoicism2.pdf (accessed 5 December 2023).

[47] Joseph Gerard Brennan, *Foundations of Moral Obligation: The Stockdale Course* (Newport: Naval War College Press, 1992).

[48] Hattendorf et al., *Sailors and Scholars,* pp. 309–311.

his advocacy among Japanese industrial leaders of what he called "Statistical Product Quality Control." Many credited him with being the inspiration behind Japan's economic recovery after the Second World War and the ideas of Total Quality Management (TQM) in the United States in the 1980s and 1990s. In 1984, the United States Navy began to work with this approach in its naval aviation supply system. In 1990, the chief of naval operations renamed the method "Total Quality Leadership (TQL)," adopting it for the entire service as the basis for its leadership approach.[49] It remained the navy's basic leadership approach into the early twenty-first century, when newer variants from industry, such as "Lean Leadership" and "Six Sigma," began to be used.

Based on Deming's management philosophy for improving quality, the approach was designed to improve mission effectiveness using (a) theory of variation; (b) application of systems theory to managing organizations; (c) psychology of work, and (d) use of the scientific method to pursue optimal mission performance.[50]

Under this system, leaders were the key elements to

- Teach their people how the work of the group supports the aims of the organization.
- Act as a coach and counselor, rather than simply as a judge.
- Not rely solely on formal authority, rather develop systems knowledge and interpersonal skills.
- Be an unceasing learner. Encourage everyone to study.
- Create an environment that encourages participation and innovation.[51]

At the Naval War College on 1 October 2007, college President Rear Admiral Jacob Shuford formally established a new section specifically designed to deal with leadership and named it the College of Operational and Strategic Leadership (COSL), initially headed by retired Rear Admiral Thomas E. Zelibor, who was followed as dean by Dr. Thomas Bayly and Rear Admiral James D. Kelly. This new organization joined five other colleges already established within the Naval War College. These are the College of Naval Warfare for senior-level U.S. students, the College of Naval Command and Staff for intermediate-level U.S. students; the Naval Command College for senior-level international officers; the Naval Staff College for intermediate-level international officers, and the College of Distance Education for off-campus, correspondence, and Internet-based courses.

---

[49] Archester Houston and Steven L. Dockstader, *Total Quality Leadership: A Primer* (Department of the Navy Total Quality Leadership Office, 1997), p. 11. https://www.balancedscorecard.org/portals/0/pdf/primer.pdf
[50] Houston and Dockstader, *Total Quality Leadership*, p. 13.
[51] Houston and Dockstader, *Total Quality Leadership*, p. 33.

Several developments led to the decision to create a college of operational and strategic leadership. In 2005, discussions surrounding the establishment of a proposed naval university to bring the Naval War College and its component colleges, the Naval Postgraduate School, and the Naval Academy under one organizational management led to the expansion of the Naval War College's responsibilities. Expanding from its traditional focus on intermediate- and senior-level officer professional military education, the college took up responsibility for professional military education above and beyond the entry level for all enlisted personnel and all officers within the U.S. Navy. Second, the Naval War College was assigned responsibility to develop and to deliver the Joint/Combined Force Maritime Component Commanders' (JFMCC/CFFCC) Course for selected groups of flag, general, and senior executive service officers, focusing on the operational level of war. The College of Operational and Strategic Leadership was the Naval War College's organizational response to these new assignments of responsibility to provide a wide range of team assistance, courses, panels, seminars, and discussion groups to develop leaders at the operational level of war further.

The group of selected students, named the Stockdale Group, was created within this new structure to examine the issues surrounding strategic and operational leadership. Over six years, they built cumulatively on the previous years' work to develop a set of recommendations

The idea of strategic and operational leadership as a specific type of leadership was a thought that had not been developed fully among naval scholars. In response to this challenge, the Naval War College's maritime history department undertook a pioneer attempt through a volume of comparative biography to try to identify the specific elements among twentieth-century American naval officers who were successful in the highest levels of operational leadership, developing over-arching strategic plans, and diplomatic work with allies and naval partners in implementing coalition strategies and operations.[52] Twenty-one scholars joined in the effort to produce a volume of nineteen biographical case studies. This work concluded that the case studies suggested that individuals who demonstrated an affinity for work in strategic, operational, or diplomatic leadership had not been taught, but had learned it on the job and by the example of their seniors.[53]

In January 2013, the chief of naval operations, Admiral Jonathan W. Greenert, issued The Navy Leader Development Strategy. Drafted by the College of Strategic and Operational Leadership, this document laid out a continuum for a comprehensive career-long development that integrated four

---

[52] John B. Hattendorf and Bruce A. Elleman, eds., *Nineteen-Gun Salute: Case Studies of Operational, Strategic, and Diplomatic Naval Leadership during the 20th and early 21st Centuries* (Newport: Naval War College Press, 2010).

[53] Hattendorf and Elleman, eds., *Nineteen-Gun Salute,* p. 257.

elements: experience, education, training, and personnel development. At the top level of the continuum were the flag officers, who were expected to be guardians of the Navy's core values of honor, courage, and commitment; exemplars for the navy of moral character; embracing forward strategic thinking in their judgment, and stewards of the naval profession of arms, who convey the highest standards of the service with strength, determination, and dignity.[54] Admiral Greenert's successor as the chief of naval operations, Admiral John M. Richardson, issued a new revision in January 2017 entitled *Navy Leader Development Framework* with a modified Version 2.0 in April 2018. The latest version emphasized two lanes to achieve its goals: operational and warfighting competence and character to behave by the Navy's core values. Richardson wrote:

> Effective Navy leaders demonstrate a deliberate commitment to grow personally and professionally throughout their careers. They work from a foundation of humility, embracing our core values of honor, courage, and commitment. They pursue excellence in accordance with our core attributes of integrity, accountability, initiative and toughness. They commit to improving competence and character in themselves and in their teams. They set ambitious goals, and then inspire their teams to learn so as to achieve their best possible performance to achieve those goals.[55]

For the highest levels, the *Framework* emphasized that "Senior leaders are almost exclusively judged by the performance of their teams. The standard for personal performance is extremely high; senior leaders are judged by their ability to consistently and sustainably produce winning teams."[56]

The Naval War College played an essential role in the implementation of this framework, providing original research, insights, and teaching. To implement this, the president of the Naval War College, Rear Admiral Jeffery A. Harley, moved the leadership and ethics components of the College of Strategic and Operational Leadership to a new deanery called Leadership and Ethics under the direction of retired Rear Admiral Margaret D. Klein. This new organization quickly implemented a graduate certificate of leadership and ethics that students at the Naval War College could earn through a ten-month series of focused electives, while also following the core course for one of the masters' degree programs. The elements of the certificate formed the basis for the shorter four-to-five-day courses for flag officers across the U.S.

---

[54] *Navy Leadership Development Strategy* (2013), pp. 7, 11. https://www.hsdl.org/?abstract&did=748304 (accessed 5 December 2023).

[55] *Navy Leadership Development Framework, Version 2.0* (2018), p. 2. https://www.navy.mil/cno/docs/NLDF_2.pdf.

[56] *Navy Leadership Development Framework*, p. 4.

Navy. The hallmark of this new program was the focus on the individual as a leader through psychological and personality assessments, self-examination of one's own character, values, and moral standards. This approach involved finding hidden biases and problem areas in which an individual needed further development. A key element was understanding oneself and to adjust one's leadership to the ethos of the profession of naval arms.[57] This approach capitalized on the still prevailing culture of American naval command that stretched back to the founding of the service in the eighteenth century. The new approach did not define a particular approach to leadership but built on individuals dealing with a multiplicity of different missions and tasks that they carried out independently within the navy.

The U.S. Navy has traveled a long way in its understanding of what has been called "admiralship."[58] For its first century, institutional thinking about the leadership of senior captains and admirals in the United States Navy was utterly ignored. The nascent historical studies began only in the mid-1880s with the founding of the Naval War College. By the first half of the twentieth century, the emphasis changed from the heroics of individual commanders with authoritarian and paternalistic styles of leadership to a focus on leadership of interrelated organizations and relationships within an organization to achieve specific goals. Defining leadership in ways that would be useful in the navy is an issue that has defeated academics. At the same time, the U.S. Navy's culture has, for most of its history, tended to define professional education as a cost rather than an investment. These trends have led to other approaches. The late twentieth century saw the widespread application of business and industrial management practices to senior naval leadership along with the rise of concern for the ethical and moral responsibilities of senior leaders. In the most recent developments, the focus has shifted. The new emphasis is on the development of an individual within the ethos of the naval profession of arms. At the same time, the current understanding of senior naval leadership often emphasizes the characteristics exemplified by the individual ship commander in the early years of the American Republic: taking charge at sea, carrying out an individual mission, and acting independently under general supervision.

---

[57] Hattendorf interview with Deputy Dean John Meyer, College of Leadership and Ethics, Naval War College, 24 September 2019.

[58] Edgar F. Puryear, Jr., *American Admiralship: The Moral Imperatives of Naval Command* (Annapolis: Naval Institute Press, 2005) and *American Admiralship: The Art of Naval Command* (Minneapolis, MN: MBI Pub. Co., 2008).

10

Reflections

RICHARD HARDING

This book has not been about strategy, but about the influence navies have exerted upon the strategy-making bodies in different societies. Navies cannot exist without the explicit support of political authorities, and those authorities rely upon their naval experts to help them make decisions to ensure naval power fits into national objectives. It is a symbiotic relationship that is common to almost all experts and their political masters in the modern world. In the twenty-first century the need for political authorities to understand naval power remains as important as ever, but, as the often repeated fears of 'sea-blindness' demonstrates, it is a difficult task. What these essays show is that the problems are not new. They have existed at least from the late sixteenth century when institutionalised navies imposed long-term fiscal, economic and political demands on societies' leaders. The complex demands placed upon those leaders by other actors influenced how they understood their navies and what they demanded of naval power was also highly variable.

Even in strongly maritime societies, navies are just one of many organisations and groupings that influence and inform political and defence policy decision-making. Defence demands have to be satisfied or negotiated among many other pressures facing modern industrialised societies. Today, when navies are an element within a broad 'defence' proposition, that is expanding from the other traditional domains of land and air to space and cyber, and the message is clearly that the effectiveness of defence will depend on the joint contribution of all these domains, navies have, as always, to compete to explain and demonstrate their place within this joint endeavour. The new digital media, in some ways, makes it easier, but in others it creates an even bigger wall of competing 'noise'.

On the other side of the equation, for societies to profit from sea power it requires an understanding and a willingness to accept the technical, social, and financial costs over a long period. Political leaders were not faced with the same defence problem, re-presented continually over space and time. What the problems are and how they are presented, varies according to the social, cultural, economic, and political circumstances. This has always demanded a constant dialogue between the political leadership of the state and seafaring, naval community. States found ways to accommodate their navies that reflected the balance of interests within the existing political authority. Today, as always, national maritime strategies reflect the way in which those interests are balanced. Information and understanding within that political authority will seldom be perfect or disinterested, so strategy will seldom represent a purely rational, objective assessment of 'national interest', costs and benefits.

These essays show different ways in which states have integrated naval expertise into the strategy-making process, with varying degrees of success. Although their conclusions can only hold as far they relate to the specific periods and places under investigation, they hint at a range of conditions which facilitate or hinder the influence of naval or maritime expertise on national strategy and decision-making which would repay further investigation.

Common to all the case studies we have seen is the physical and psychological distance of the naval experts from the centre of national decision-making. State navies are the conscious creations of the political leadership, but few of the policy decision-makers were experienced in the practicalities of naval warfare. How they learned depended upon to whom they were willing to listen. Our Spanish examples demonstrated a laudable willingness over nearly 200 years to hear the voices of the naval professionals at the highest level. Our French example shows how this expertise had to be moderated through the social expectations of the court. Other countries experienced, periodically, intense interest of the executive in the navy. In Britain the early institutionalisation of the navy, boosted by the personal interest of Charles II and James II between 1660 and 1688, established an understanding of the navy, its needs and its power that had a profound impact on a long-term investment in the navy. In Sweden the early Vasa monarchs (from the 1540s to the 1620s) took a close interest in their navies, and worked closely with seamen and shipbuilders. After 1680, and the removal of the main fleet base from Stockholm to Karlskrona, the close link between the monarch and the navy quickly withered and the Swedish navy never recovered its central role in Swedish defence policy.[1] In the United States, with attention divided between the great continental expansion, and a major maritime economic sector, clarifying the national role of the navy had to wait until the continental expansion had reached its natural conclusion by 1890. In the interim, the United States was also favoured by one of its leaders who understood the importance of naval power. President

---

[1] Glete, Jan. 'Bridge and Bulwark: The Swedish Navy and the Baltic 1500–1809'. In *In Quest of Trade and Security: The Baltic in Power Politics, 1500–1900*, edited by Goran Rystad, Klaus-R. Bohme, and Wilhelm N. Carlgren. Lund: Lund University Press, 1994, pp. 9–60.

Abraham Lincoln listened, learned, and took an active part in decisions about the navy during the Civil War.[2]

Perhaps the most significant example of personal impact of the political leader on naval power is that of Peter I of Russia (1672–1725). During his 'Great Embassy' to the United Provinces and England between 1697–1698, Peter immersed himself in the technicalities and possibilities of naval power. He moved his capital to St Petersburg, a new commercial and naval centre. The navy that he created in the Baltic demonstrated its power against the Swedes in the Great Northern War. In 1716 he was directly involved in naval operations, subordinating himself to Admiral Fydor Apraxin during the build-up to a proposed campaign with the Danes against the Swedes in Scania.

This is a subject that would repay much more detailed examination. While the enthusiasm of individual political leaders is often vital to connect the resources of the state to naval expertise, it seems equally true that unless this connection can be institutionalised, embedding the purpose and support of the navy deeply in the social and political fabric, achieving a sustained, long-term movement of naval expertise to inform the higher levels of national decision-making and ensure adequate resourcing, is extremely difficult. Navies have always been more complex to build and maintain than armies. The lead-times required to develop naval power usually exceeds the life span of any individual executive leader. Peter's death in 1725 deprived the new Russian navy of the drive and purpose it had possessed. Charles XII of Sweden and his successors, did not revive the navy as an instrument of Swedish power and for most of the eighteenth century its purpose was largely dictated by the domestic agendas of the nobility and bureaucracy. Few political leaders have had the freedom to concentrate resources on expanding naval power over long periods. In Spain, France, Portugal, and the Ottoman Empire, the navy had its moments of close engagement with the political decision-making process, but it was inconsistent and failed to embed itself in political assumptions of state institutions. As diplomatic circumstances shift the priority given to naval expertise rises or declines. Even in Britain, where diplomatic and military importance of the navy over 300 years, helped to create a valued institution, the conditions began to change in the mid-twentieth century so that it is now questionable how far British society still sees its defence as founded on a distinctive naval capability.

Given the long gestation period for state naval power and influence, the rapid changes in the military-diplomatic environment makes the influence of naval authority even more problematic. Since 1945 navies had been struggling to make the case for the role and relevance in a nuclear-armed stand-off between West and East. The end of the Cold War in 1990 continued to pose

---

[2] Symonds, Craig L. *Lincoln and His Admirals: Abraham Lincoln, the U.S. Navy, and the Civil War*. Oxford: Oxford University Press, 2008.

problems for political authorities trying to capitalise on an expected 'peace dividend' and adjust naval forces to the new conditions. In the thirty years after 1990, the shift from high level super-power geopolitical competition to geo-economic competition and back again to rising geopolitical inter-state confrontation has highlighted the confusion and expense of naval planning. The biggest defence spender, the United States, has highly developed legislative and executive mechanisms to manage the political and professional expectations of naval defence. Yet, even it cannot avoid confusions, delays, and wastage. For example, the end of the Cold War and the rising power of 'rogue states' redirected national missile defence research and expenditure towards countering ballistic missiles in the booster phase of their deployment. This was practicable and less confrontational to the old adversaries, so the planning and designs to defeat the missiles of the Soviet Union or China in the intermediate and terminal flight phases were dropped. The naval contribution had to be rethought and redeveloped with all the delay and cost that this involved.[3] The re-emergence of serious peer state rivalry since about 2014 has forced another rethink and changed planning assumptions. Since the Russian invasion of Ukraine in February 2022 everything from ammunition stocks to hyper-sonic missile defence development have had to be re-evaluated and priorities re-ordered. How navies are contributing to this re-evaluation in different states is an important element in understanding contemporary defence postures.

An examination of this contribution through the lens of institutionalisation seems promising.[4] It could build on a substantial body of previous writing. Mahan's famous six elements of seapower laid down a basis for this in 1890. Naval influence, like naval power, could depend on a state's geographical position, its physical conformity to a thriving maritime environment, the extent of its territory, the nature of its population, the national 'character' and the character of its government.[5] It opened the way for further explorations ranging from geographic or cultural determinism to more nuanced factors such as individual monarchical entrepreneurialism. This kind of detailed examination of the naval-political exchange of expertise, across many centuries and states may, in due course, have a significant contribution to make to the

---

[3] Binnendijk, H. and G. Stewart. 'Naval Contributions to National Missile Defence'. In *Globalization and Maritime Power*, edited by Sam J Tangredi. Honolulu: University of the Pacific, 2004, pp. 9–60. A number of the essays in this volume, illustrate the complexity of naval issues for contemporary governments.

[4] Hodgson, Geoffrey. 'What Are Institutions?' *Journal of Economic Issues* xl (2006): 1–25.

[5] Mahan, Alfred Thayer. *The Influence of Sea Power Upon History, 1660–1763*. Boston: Little Brown, 1890, pp. 26–75.

on-going debate between advocates of rationalist-materialism and culturalism in International Relations community.[6]

Whatever the factors were that hindered or facilitated the integration of naval expertise into the state's decision-making, one factor seems to stand out. Sailors have not been generally as effective as soldiers in influencing the decision-makers. It is interesting that Alfred Vagts' wide-ranging study *Defense and Diplomacy* (1956), is subtitled *The Soldier and the Conduct of Foreign Relations*. There is very little room for the influence of naval officers. Even in Great Britain, the social and professional distancing of the sailor from the key decision-makers gives them a very small direct role in informing or shaping policy. In Vagts' study, only Admiral Sir John Fisher, whose presence loomed large in the critical period between 1905 and 1914, features as a powerful influence.[7] Since the Second World War, the operational necessity of joint and combined command has led to stronger inter-service and inter-allied understanding and decisions, but this has not led to greater strategic influence of seamen in most nations.[8]

For most people, whatever the nation and whenever the time, wars are won by armies on land. Navies support this process. The wars in Afghanistan (Operation Enduring Freedom, 2001–2014) and Iraq (1990–1991 and 2003–2011) had important naval components, but these are seldom explored in popular histories. It remains to be seen how important the sinking of a single ship, the *Moskva,* was in April 2022 in the Western Black Sea. The loss of the *Moskva*'s air defence capability changed Russian operational possibilities in Western Ukraine and the Crimea that continue to play out. What impact this will have as the war progresses will not be known for many years, but set against the great battles on land the event has already faded out of the news cycles. This subordinate role navies play in the public imagination, their technical and operational obscurity to most landsmen, the complex mix of resources needed for constantly modernising navies, have all kept naval influence on the margins, or at least made it very difficult to articulate success fully. The essays in this volume have shown how, and to what degree, naval influence has imposed itself on state decision-making in specific situations in the past, but they demonstrate much more needs to be done to understand the phenomenon. If naval expertise is to be well understood, as it must be

---

[6] Sondhaus, L. (2006). *Strategic Culture and The Ways of War*. Abingdon: Routledge; Bloomfield, A. 'Time to Move On: Reconceptualizing the Strategic Culture Debate', *Contemporary Security Policy* 33(3) (2012): 437–461.

[7] Vagts, Alfred, *Defense and Diplomacy: The Soldier and the Conduct of Foreign Relations*. Defense and Diplomacy. New York: King's Crown Press, 1956, pp. 120–129.

[8] Freedman, Lawrence, *Command: The Politics of Military Operations from Korea to Ukraine,* London, Allen Lane, 2022. Apart from the Falklands War (1982), navies appear not to have made major contributions to policy decisions.

by political authority, it needs to be continually researched and reviewed. Strategy, operational capabilities and tactical competence are dependent on a mutual understanding between political leaders and military leaders regarding purposes and possibilities. Naval leaders probably face greater difficulties than their military and air force colleagues in achieving this mutual understanding, Exploring what has increased that comprehension and what has hindered it are important activities if 'sea-blindness' is not to remain a dangerous weakness in modern societies.

BIBLIOGRAPHY

Acerra, Martine, and Andre Zysberg. 1997. *L'Essor des marines de guerres Européennes (vers 1680–vers* 1790). Paris: SEDES.

Alcalá-Zamora, José N. and Quiepo de Llano. 1975. *Evolución del tonelaje de la flota de vela española durante los siglos modernos.* Zaragoza: Universidad de Zaragoza, Facultad de Filosofía y Letras.

Alzina Torrente, J. 2006. *Una guerra romántica, 1778–1783: España, Francia e Inglaterra en la mar.* Madrid: Ministerio de Defensa.

Anderson, Gene R. 2011. 'Historical and Cultural Foundations of Navy Officer Development'. In Cultivating Army Leaders: Historical Perspectives. *The Proceedings of the Combat Studies Institute 2010 Military History Symposium*, edited by Kendall D. Gott, 197–204. Fort Leavenworth, KS: Combat Studies Institute Press.

Anon. 1718. A Letter from a Merchant to a Member of Parliament relating to the Danger Great Britain is in of losing her trade by the great increase of the Naval Power of Spain London.

Anon. 1738. *The Ministerial Virtue: Or Long-Suffering Extolled in a Great Man.* London: J. Purser.

Anon. 1757. *The Present State of Europe Explaining the Interests, Connections, Political and Commercial Views of its Several Powers*, 4th ed. London: Longman.

Anon. 1778(?). *Journal de marine ou bibliothèque raisonnée de la science du navigateur, premier cahier.* Brest: Malassis.

Anon. 1881. 'Mémoire remis au Roi en 1765'. Journal des savants mars et and Avril, 171–184, 250–257.

Armstrong, Benjamin F., ed. 2015. *21st Century Sims: Innovation, Education, and Leadership for the Modern Era.* Annapolis: Naval Institute Press.

Antoine, M. 1970. *Le Conseil du Roi sous Louis XV.* Paris-Geneva: Droz.

Ash, Eric H., ed. 2010. *Expertise: Practical Knowledge and the Early Modern State.* Washington DC: Osiris.

Ayala Pérez, J.A. 2002. *La sombra del triángulo: biografía de Ángel Rizo, Gran Maestre del Grande Oriente Español.* San Cristóbal de la Laguna: Centro de la cultura popular canaria.

Barazzutti, Roberto 2010. 'Étude comparative des officiers généraux aux Provinces-Unies, en France et en Angleterre à l'époque de Louis XIV (1643–1715)'. *Revue d'Histoire Maritime* 12: 167–192.

Batista, J. 1992. *La estrategia española en América durante el Siglo de las Luces.* Madrid: MAPFRE.

Baudot Monroy, María, Manuel Díaz-Ordóñez, and Iván Valdez Bubnov. 2019. 'Política imperial y administración de industrias estratégicas: la Armada española en el largo siglo XVIII. Introducción'. *Espacio, Tiempo y Forma.* Serie IV, Historia Moderna 32: 13–18.

Baugh, D. 2004. 'Naval Power: What Gave the British Navy Superiority?' In *Exceptionalism and Industrialization: Britain and its European Rivals, 1688–1815*, edited by L. Prados de la Escoura, 235–257. Cambridge: Cambridge University Press.

Baugh, D. 2011. *The Global Seven Years War, 1754–1763.* Harlow: Longman.

Berbouche, Alain. 2011. *L'Histoire de La Royale: du moyen-âge au règne de Louis XIV.* St Malo: Pascal Galodé.

Bernal, A.M. 2005. *España, proyecto inacabado. Costes/beneficios del imperio.* Madrid: Marcial Pons.

Bernaola Martín, Íñigo. 2020. *Liderazgo naval y redes profesionales: el equipo de José de Mazarredo (1776–1814).* Madrid: Ed. Sílex.

Beunza, José María Imízcoz, ed. 2004. 'El entramado social y político'. Edited by A. Floristán, *Historia de España en la Edad Moderna.* Barcelona: Ariel.

Binnendijk, H., and G. Stewart, 2004. 'Naval Contributions to National Missile Defence'. In *Globalization and Maritime Power*, edited by Sam J. Tangredi, 455–469. Honolulu: University of the Pacific.

Black, Jeremy. 1992. 'Naval Power, Strategy and Foreign Policy, 1775–1791'. In *Parameters of British Naval Power, 1650–1850*, edited by Michael Duffy, 93–120. Exeter: University of Exeter Press.

Blanco Núñez, J.M. 1996. 'El marqués de la Victoria y la táctica naval'. *Cuadernos Monográficos del Instituto de Historia y Cultura* Naval 28: 35–50.

Blanco Núñez, J.M. 2001. *La armada española en la primera mitad del siglo XVIII.* Madrid: IZAR Construcciones Navales.

Blanco Núñez, J.M. 2004. *La armada española en la segunda mitad del siglo XVIII.* Madrid: IZAR Construcciones Navales.

Bloomfield, Alan. 2012. 'Time to Move On: Reconceptualizing the Strategic Culture Debate'. *Contemporary Security Policy* 33 (3): 437–461.

Bluche, François. 1990. *Louis XIV.* Translated by Mark Greengrass. New York: Franklin Watts.

Bonnel, U. 1959. *La France, Les États-Unis et la guerre de course.* París: NEL.

Bonnel, U. 1992. 'Fleurieu et les États-Unis. Guerre et diplomatie'. In *Fleurieu et la marine de son temps,* edited by U. Bonnel, 275–279. Paris: Economica.

Bonnichon, P. 2010. *Charles-Pierre Claret, Comte de Fleurieu (1738–1810).* Paris: Société des Cincinnati de France.

Bowen, Huw V., and A. González Enciso, eds. 2006. *Mobilising Resources for War: Britain and Spain at Work during the Early Modern Period.* Pamplona: EUNSA.

Bracker, Jeffrey. 1980. 'The Historical Development of the Strategic Management Concept'. *Academy of Management Review* 6 (2): 210–224.

Brennan, Joseph Gerard. 1992. *Foundations of Moral Obligation: The Stockdale Course.* Newport: Naval War College Press.

Burrage, Michael, and Rolf Torstendahl, eds. 1990. *Professions in Theory and History: Rethinking the Study of the Professions.* London: Sage.

Bustos Rodríguez, M. 2013. 'La Politique des Bourbons et la marine espagnole (1740–1805)'. In *Les Marines de la guerre d'Indépendance américaine (1763–1783). I. L'Instrument naval*, edited by O. Chaline, P. Bonnichon, and C. Vergennes, 107–128. Paris: PUPS.

Butel, Paul. 1990. 'France, the Antilles and Europe in the Seventeenth and Eighteenth Centuries: renewals of foreign trade'. In *The Rise of Merchant Empires: Long-Distance Trade in the Early Modern World, 1350–1750*, edited by James D. Tracy, 152–173. Cambridge: Cambridge University Press.

Calvo Maturana, A. 2008. 'Génesis del II Imperio Británico y el ocaso del universalismo español: la doble vertiente del conflicto de Nootka (1790)'. *Hispania* 228: 151–192.

Casado Rabanal, D. 2009. *La Marina ilustrada: sueño y ambición de la España del s. XVIII. Desarrollo y crisis (1702–1805)*. Madrid: Ministerio de Defensa.

Castellano, Juan Luis, Jean-Pierre Dedieu, and María Victoria López-Cordón. 2000. *La pluma, la mitra y la espada: estudios de historia institucional en la Edad Moderna*: Madrid: Marcial Pons Historia.

Castillo, A. 1930. *Spanish Mercantilism: Gerónimo de Uztáriz – Economist*. New York: Ad Press.

Cénat, Jean-Philippe. 2010. *Le Roi stratège: Louis XIV et la direction de la guerre, 1661–1715*. Rennes: Presses Universitaires de Rennes.

Cepeda Gómez, J. 2005. 'La Marina y el equilibrio de los océanos en el siglo XVIII'. In *El equilibrio de los imperios: de Utrecht a Trafalgar*, edited by A. Guimerá Ravina and V. Peralta Ruiz, 447–482. Madrid: Fundación Española de Historia Moderna.

Cerezo Martínez, R. 1983. *Armada española siglo XX*, 4 vols. Madrid: Poniente.

Chaline, O. 2017. 'Admiral Louis Guillouet, Comte d'Orvilliers (1710–1792): A Style of Command in the Age of the American War'. In *Naval Leadership in the Atlantic World: The Age of Reform and Revolution, 1700–1850*, edited by R. Harding and A Guimerá, 73–84. London: University of Westminster Press.

Chauca, J. 2005. 'La defensa de la América meridional durante la segunda mitad del siglo XVIII'. In *El equilibrio de los imperios: de Utrecht a Trafalgar*, edited by A. Guimerá Ravina and V. Peralta Ruiz, 631–645. Madrid: Fundación Española de Historia Moderna.

Chisholm, Donald. 2001. *Waiting for Dead Men's Shoes: Origins and Development of the U.S. Navy's Officer Personnel System, 1793–1941*. Stanford: Stanford University Press.

Clark, William Bell, ed. 1968. *Naval Documents of the American Revolution*, vol. 3 (1775–1776). Washington DC: Government Printing Office.

Clarke, James Stanier, and John M'Arthur, eds. 1840. *The Life and Services of Admiral Lord Nelson, Duke of Bronte, Vice-Admiral of the White, K.B., etc., From his Lordship's Manuscripts*. London: Fisher, Son, & Co.

Cobbett, William, ed. 1813. *Parliamentary History of England from the Earliest Period to year 1803*, vol. 15 (1753–1765). London: Hansard.

Cogar, William B. 1989. *Dictionary of Admirals of the U.S. Navy*. Annapolis: Naval Institute Press.

Collins, Harry, and Robert Evans. 2007. *Rethinking Expertise*. Chicago: University of Chicago Press.

Conrad, J. 2017. *Gambling and War: Risk, Reward, and Chance in International Conflict.* Annapolis: Naval Institute Press.
Corbett, J.S. 1907. *England in the Seven Years War,* 2 vols. London: Longman Green. Reprint, 1992.
Corbett, J.S., ed. 1908. *Signals and Instructions, 1776–1794.* London: Navy Records Society.
Corbett, J.S. 1911. *Some Principles of Maritime Strategy.* London: Longman Green.
Corbett, J.S. 1919. *The Campaign of Trafalgar,* 2 vols. London: Longman Green.
Corfield, Penelope J. 1995. *Power and the Professions in Britain, 1700–1850.* London: Routledge.
Cortezo, María Victoria López-Cordón. 2008. 'Tomar el timón, navegar por el mundo: Floridablanca, Ministro de Estado'. *Floridablanca: 1728–1808: la utopía reformadora.* Murcia: Fundación Cajamurcia.
Cremades, Gil. 1971. 'La Junta Suprema de Estado (1787–1792)'. Actas del II Symposium de Historia de la Administración, Madrid.
Crowhurst, Patrick. 1989. *The French War on Trade: Privateering, 1793–1815.* Aldershot: Scolar Press.
Cussik, J.G. 2007. *The Other War of 1812: The Patriot War and the American Invasion of Spanish Florida.* Athens: University of Georgia Press.
Darnell, B. 2016. 'Reconsidering the Guerre de Course under Louis XIV: Naval Policy and Strategic Downsizing in an Era of Fiscal Overextension.' In *Strategy and the Sea: Essays in Honour of John B. Hattendorf,* edited by N.A.M. Rodger, J. Ross Dancy, B. Darnell, and E. Wilson, 37–48. Woodbridge: Boydell Press.
Davies, J.D. 1991. *Gentlemen and Tarpaulins: The Officers and Men of the Restoration Navy.* Oxford: Oxford University Press.
Davies, J.D. 2017. *Kings of the Sea: Charles II, James II and the Royal Navy.* Barnsley: Seaforth.
Davison, Robert L. 2011. *The Challenges of Command: The Royal Navy's Executive Branch Officers, 1880–1919.* Aldershot: Ashgate.
De Conde, A. 1966. *The Quasi-War: The Politics and Diplomacy of the Undeclared War with France, 1797–1801.* New York: Scribner.
Delgado Ribas, Josep Maria. 1987. 'América en la teoría y praxis política de José Moñino y Redondo, conde de Floridablanca'. *Hacienda Pública Española* 108–109: 133–146.
Delgado Ribas, Josep Maria. 2007. *Dinámicas imperiales (1650–1796). España, América y Europa en el cambio institucional del sistema colonial español.* Barcelona: Ediciones Bellaterra.
Del Perugia, P. 1939. La Tentative d'invasion de l'Angleterre de 1779. Paris: Presses universitaires de France.
Denman, Timothy J. 1985. 'The Political Debate over Strategy, 1689–1712'. PhD thesis, University of Cambridge.
Desbrière, Édouard. 1909. *La Campagne maritime de 1805: Trafalgar.* Paris: Librairie militaire de R. Chapelot.
Dessert, Daniel. 1996. *La Royale: vaisseaux et marine du Roi-Soleil.* Paris: Fayard.
d'Ombrain, N.J. 1970. 'The Imperial General Staff and the Military Policy of a "Continental Strategy" during the 1911 International Crisis'. *Military Affairs* 34 (3): 88–93.

Domínguez Nafría, J. C. 2003. 'Perfiles institucionales del Almirantazgo en España'. *Cuadernos Monográficos del Instituto de Historia y Cultura Naval* 42: 13–56.
Duffy, M. 1998. 'World-Wide War and British Expansion, 1793–1815'. In *The Oxford History of the British Empire. Volume II. The Eighteenth Century*, edited by P Marshall, 184–207. Oxford: Oxford University Press.
Dull, Jonathan. 1975. *The French Navy and American Independence.* Princeton: Princeton University Press.
Dull, Jonathan. 2005. *The French Navy and the Seven Years War.* Lincoln: University of Nebraska Press.
Duro, C. Fernández. 1894–1902. *Armada española desde la unión de los reinos de Castilla y de León*, 9 vols. Madrid.
Elias, Norbert. 2007. *The Genesis of the Naval Profession.* Dublin: University of Dublin Press.
Erikson, A.S., L.J. Goldstein, and C. Lord, eds. 2009. *China Goes to Sea: Maritime Transformation in Comparative Historical Perspective.* Annapolis: Naval Institute Press.
Escudero, J.A. 1979. *Los orígenes del Consejo de Ministros en España. La Junta Suprema de Estado.* Madrid: Editora Nacional.
Escudero, J.A. 1999. *Administración y estado en la España moderna.* Valladolid: Junta de Castilla y León.
Estienne, R. 1979. 'La Marine royale sous le ministère du duc de Choiseul (1761–1766)'. PhD thesis, École des Chartes.
Farnham, Barbara, ed. 1994. *Avoiding Losses/Taking Risks: Prospect Theory and International Conflict.* Michigan: University of Michigan Press.
Fernández Durán, R. 1999. *Gerónimo de Uztáriz (1670–1732): una política económica para Felipe V.* Madrid: Minerva.
Fernández González, F. 2015. 'La construcción naval en la armada entre 1750 y 1820'. In *Vientos de guerra. Apogeo y crisis de la Real Armada, 1750–1823. Vol. I. Una armada en tiempos de la Ilustración. Política, ciencia, ingeniería y hacienda,* edited by J. Marchena and J. Caño, 520–660. Madrid: Ediciones Doce Calles.
Fernández, Juan Marchena, and Justo Cuño. 2018. *Vientos de guerra: apogeo y crisis de la Real Armada, 1750–1823.* Madrid: Ediciones Doce Calles.
Floridablanca, conde de. 1952. *Biblioteca de Autores Españoles… Obras originales del Conde de Floridablanca.* Madrid: Ediciones Atlas.
Franco Rubio, G.F. 2000. 'Reformismo institucional y élites administrativas en la España del siglo XVIII: nuevos oficios, nueva burocracia. La Secretaría de Estado y del Despacho de Marina (1721–1808)'. In *La pluma, la mitra y la espada. Estudios de historia institucional en la Edad Moderna,* edited by J.L. Castellano, J.P. Dedieu, and M.V. López-Cordón Cortezo, 94–130. Madrid.
Freedman, Lawrence. 2022. *Command: The Politics of Military Operations from Korea to Ukraine.* London: Allen Lane.
French, David, and Brian Holden Reid, eds. 2002. *The British General Staff: Reform and Innovation, 1890–1939.* London: Frank Cass.
Fuster Ruiz, F. 1997. *Final del descubrimiento de América. California, Canadá y*

Alaska (1765–1822). Aportación documental del Archivo General de Marina. Murcia: Universidad de Murcia.

Gámez Duarte, F. 2008. *Del uno al otro confín: España y la lucha contra el corso insurgente hispanoamericano, 1812–1828.* Cadiz: Diputación.

García Baquero, A. 1972. *Comercio colonial y guerras revolucionarias: la decadencia económica de Cádiz a raíz de la emancipación Americana.* Seville: EEHA.

García Hurtado, Manuel-Reyes, ed. 2012. *La armada española en el siglo XVIII: ciencia, hombres y barcos.* Madrid: Silex Editiones.

García Hurtado, Manuel-Reyes, ed. 2020. *Las innovaciones de la armada en la España del siglo de Jorge Juan.* Biblioteca de Historia. Madrid: Consejo Superior de Investigaciones Científicas.

García Martínez, José Ramón. 2000. *Méndez Núñez (1824–1869) y la campaña del Pacífico (1862–1869).* Santiago de Compostela: Xunta de Galicia.

García Martínez, José Ramón. 2000. 'Pagalugán'. *Revista Española de Historia Militar* 4: 202–209.

García Martínez, José Ramón. 2005. *Buques de la real armada de SMC Isabel II (1830–1868).* DVD editado por el Museo Naval de Madrid y Fluidmecánica Sur, SL.

Gibbs, Norman H. 1955. *The Origins of Imperial Defence.* Oxford: Clarendon Press.

Gildea, R. .1994. *The Past in French History.* London: Yale.

Giral González, F. 2004. *Vida y obra de José Giral Pereira.* Mexico: Universidad Autónoma Nacional de México.

Giral Pereira, J. 1932. 'La República y el Ministerio de Marina'. *Nuevo Mundo* 14 (April): 20–22.

Glasgow, Tom. 1968. 'The Navy in the Le Havre Expedition, 1562–64'. *Mariner's Mirror* 54: 281–96.

Glete, Jan. 1994. 'Bridge and Bulwark: The Swedish Navy and the Baltic 1500–1809'. In *Quest of Trade and Security: The Baltic in Power Politics, 1500–1900,* edited by Goran Rystad, Klaus-R. Bohme, and Wilhelm N. Carlgren, 9–60. Lund: Lund University Press.

Goerlitz, Walter. 1985. *History of the German General Staff.* Boulder: Westview Press. Original edition, 1951.

González Enciso, A., ed. 2012. *Un estado militar: España, 1650–1820.* San Sebastián de los Reyes: Actas.

González, J.A., 'Méndez Núñez y la revolución de 1868: tres cartas inéditas de Isabel II', *Revista de Historia Naval* 6 (1984): 89–97.

González-Aller Hierro, J.I. 1985. 'El navío de tres puentes en la armada española'. *Revista de Historia Naval* 9: 45–76.

Grafenstein Gareis, J. von. 2001. 'Insurgencia y contrainsurgencia en el golfo de México, 1812–1820'. In *La independencia de México y el proceso autonomista novohispano, 1808–1824,* edited by V. Guedea and et al., 185–228. Mexico: UNAM-Instituto Mora.

Graham, G.S. 1950. *Empire of the North Atlantic: The Maritime Struggle for North America.* Toronto: University of Toronto Press.

Griffin, C.C. 1937. *The United States and the Disruption of the Spanish Empire,*

1810–1822: A Study of the Relations of the United States with Spain and with the Rebel Spanish Colonies. New York: Octagon Books.
Grint, Keih. 1997. *Fuzzy Management: Contemporary Ideas and Practices at Work.* Oxford: Oxford University Press.
Guillamón Álvarez, F.J. 2009. 'Floridablanca y la crisis de guerra de Nootka (1789–1790)'. *Res publica* 22: 153–178.
Guimerá, A., ed. 1996. *El reformismo borbónico: una visión interdisciplinar.* Madrid: Alianza Editorial.
Guimerá, A. 2005. 'Trafalgar y la marineria española'. In *El equilibrio de los imperios: de Utrecht a Trafalgar,* edited by A. Guimerá and V. Peralta, 819–838. Madrid: Fundación Española de Historia Moderna.
Guimerá, A. 2011. 'Naval Leadership and Naval Expenditure in Spain, 1783–1795'. In *The Spending of the States. Military Expenditure During the Long Eighteenth Century: Patterns, Organization and Consequences, 1650–1815,* edited by S. Conway and R. Torres, 201–211. Saarbrücken: VDM Verlag Dr. Muller.
Guimerá, A. 2012. 'Estado, administración y liderazgo naval: Antonio Valdés y Lord Barham (1783–1808)'. In *Un estado militar: España, 1650–1820,* edited by A. González Enciso, 182–209. San Sebastián de los Reyes: Actas.
Guimerá, A. 2014. 'Defensa del liderazgo naval: el Secretario de Marina Antonio Valdés, según Alberto Sesma (1806)'. In *Herederas de Clío. Mujeres que han impulsado la historia,* edited by G. Franco Rubio and M.A. Pérez Samper, 263–275. Seville: Mergablum.
Guimerá, A. 2014. 'La marine espagnole contre la piraterie nord-africaine (1750–1785)'. In *La Piraterie au fil de l'histoire. Un défi pour l'état,* edited by Michele Battesti, 331–345. Paris: PUPS.
Guimerá, A. 2015. 'Teoría y práctica del imperio: el Secretario de Marina e Indias Antonio Valdés en la Junta de Estado (1787–1792)'. In *Andalucía, España, Indias. Pasión por la Historia. Homenaje al profesor Antonio-Miguel Bernal,* edited by C. Martínez Shaw, P. Tedde de Lorca, and S. Tinoco Rubiales, 513–543. Seville: Universidad de Sevilla-Marcial Pons.
Guimerá, A. 2018. 'La Stratégie navale et la navigation espagnole vers les Antilles et le Golfe de Mexique, 1759–1783'. In *Les Marines de la guerre d'Indépendance américaine, II. L'Opérationelle naval,* edited by O. Chaline, P. Bonnichon, and C. de Vergennes, 67–90. Paris: PUPS.
Guimerá, A., and Olivier Chaline, eds. 2018. *La real armada: La marine des Bourbons d'Espagne au xviiie siècle.* Paris: PUPS.
Guimerá, A., and N. García Fernández. 2008. 'Un consenso estratégico: las ordenanzas navales de 1793'. *Anuario de Estudios Atlánticos* 54–II: 43–48.
Guirao de Vierna, A. . 1984. 'Notas para un estudio del Almirantazgo'. *Revista de Historia Naval* 4: 83–100.
Hanlon, Gregory. 1998. *The Twilight of a Military Tradition: Italian Aristocrats and European Conflicts, 1560–1800.* London: UCL Press.
Harding, Richard 2007. 'British Maritime Strategy and Hanover, 1714–1763'. In *The Hanoverian Dimension in British History, 1714–1837,* edited by B. Sims and T. Riotte, 252–274. Cambridge: Cambridge University Press.
Harding, Richard. 2010. *The Emergence of Britain's Global Naval Supremacy: The War of 1739–1748.* Woodbridge: Boydell and Brewer.

Harding, Richard. 2020. 'Naval Ideology and its Operational Impact in Eighteenth Century Britain'. In *Ideologies of Western Naval Power, c. 1500–1815*, edited by J.D. Davies, Alan James, and Gijs Rommelse, 262–279. Abingdon: Routledge.

Harding, Richard, and Agustín Guimerá Ravina, eds. 2017. *Naval Leadership in the Atlantic World: The Age of Reform and Revolution, 1700–1850*. London: University of Westminster Press.

Harris, J.P. 1995. *Men, Ideas and Tanks: British Military Thought and Armoured Forces, 1903–1939*. Edited by I.F.W. Beckett, War, Armed Forces and Society. Manchester: Manchester University Press.

Harris, Robert. 1995. *A Patriot Press: National Politics and the London Press in the 1740s*. Oxford: Oxford University Press.

Hastings, Max, and Simon Jenkins. 1997. *The Battle for the Falklands*. London: Pan. Original edition, Michael Joseph 1983.

Hattendorf, J.B. 1987. *England in the War of the Spanish Succession: A Study of the English View and Conduct of Grand Strategy, 1702–1712*. New York: Garland Publishing.

Hattendorf, J.B. 2005. *Trafalgar and Nelson 200: Catalogue of an Exhibition of Rare Books, Maps, Charts, Prints, Models, and Signal Flags Relating to Events and Influences of the Battle of Trafalgar and Lord Nelson*. Newport: Naval War College Museum.

Hattendorf, J.B. 2021. 'Debating the Purpose of a Navy in a New Republic: The United States of America, 1775–1815'. In *Ideologies of Western Naval Power, c. 1500–1815*, edited by J.D. Davies, Alan James and Gijs Rommelse, 280–299. New York and Abingdon; Routledge.

Hattendorf, J.B., and Bruce A. Elleman, eds. 2010. *Nineteen-Gun Salute: Case Studies of Operational, Strategic, and Diplomatic Naval Leadership during the 20th and early 21st Centuries*. Newport: Naval War College Press.

Hattendorf, J.B., B.M. Simpson, and John R. Wadleigh. 1984. *Sailors and Scholars: The Centennial History of the Naval War College*. Newport: Naval War College Press.

Hennessy, Peter, and James Jinks. 2015. *The Silent Deep: The Royal Navy Submarine Service since 1945*. London: Allen Lane.

Hernández Franco, J. 1984. *La gestión política y el pensamiento reformista del conde de Floridablanca*. Murcia: Ediciones de la Universidad de Murcia.

Hernández Franco, J. 1992. *Aspectos de la política exterior de España en la época de Floridablanca*. Murcia: Ediciones de la Universidad de Murcia.

Hernández Franco, J. 2008. *Floridablanca, 1728–1808. La utopía reformadora*. Murcia: Fundación Cajamurcia.

Hernández Franco, J. 2008. *La gestión política y el pensamiento reformista del Conde de Floridablanca*. Murcia: Ediciones de la Universidad.

Hill, P.P. 2005. *Napoleon's Troublesome Americans. Franco-American Relations, 1804–1815*. Washington DC: Potomac Books.

Hodgson, Geoffrey. 2006. 'What Are Institutions?' *Journal of Economic Issues* XL: 1–25. doi: 10.1080/00213624.2006.11506879.

Hoefer. 1873. *Nouvelle biographie générale*. Vol. Didot. Paris.

Holmes, Geoffrey. 1982. *Augustan England : Professions, State and Society, 1680–1730*. London: Allen and Unwin.

Hoste, Paul, père. 1697. *L'Art des armées navales, ou traicté des évolutions navales.* Lyon: Anisson et Posuel.

Houston, Archester, and Steven L. Dockstader. 1997. *Total Quality Leadership: A Primer.* Washington DC: Department of the Navy Total Quality Leadership Office.

James, Alan. 2000. 'Les Amirautés à l'époque de Richelieu'. In *Pouvoirs et littoraux du XVe au XXe siècle,* edited by Gérard Le Bouëdec and François Chappé, 145–150. Rennes: Presses Universitaires de Rennes.

James, Alan. 2004. *The Navy and Government in Early Modern France, 1572–1661.* Studies in History. Woodbridge: Boydell and Brewer.

James, Alan. 2014. 'Une Époque sans amiral: les grands-maîtres de la navigation, 1626–1669', *Revue d'Histoire Maritime,* 19.

James, Alan. 2015. 'La Bataille du Cap Bévéziers (1690): une glorieuse victoire pour le roi stratège'. In *La Bataille: du fait d'armes au combat idéologique, XIe–XIXe siècle,* edited by Ariane Boltanski, Yann Lagadec, and Franck Mercier, 205–218. Rennes: Presses Universitaires de Rennes.

James, Alan. 2019. 'Colbert and "La Royale": Dynastic Ambitions and Imperial Ideals in France'. In *Ideologies of Western Naval Power, c.1500–1815,* edited by J.D. Davies, Alan James, and Gijs Rommelse, 122–136. Abingdon: Routledge.

Johnston, J.A. 1968. 'Parliament and the Navy, 1688–1714'. PhD thesis, University of Sheffield.

Kalbfus, Edward C. 1992 (1936). *Sound Military Decision.* Annapolis: Naval Institute Press.

Katzenbach, Jr, Edward L. 1965. 'The Demotion of Professionalism at the War College'. U.S. *Naval Institute Proceedings* (April): 34–41.

Kepner, Charles H., and Benjamin B. Tregoe. 1981. *The New Rational Manager.* London: John Martin.

Knox, Dudley W. 1915. 'The Role of Doctrine in Naval Warfare'. *U.S. Naval Institute Proceedings* 41 (2).

Kohnen, David, ed. 2016. *21st Century Knox: Innovation, Sea Power, and History for the Modern Era.* 21st Century Foundations . Annapolis: Naval Institute Press.

Kohnen, David, Nicholas Jellicoe, and Nathaniel S. Sims. 2016. 'The U.S. Navy Won the Battle of Jutland'. *Naval War College Review* 69 (4): 123–146.

Lambert, Andrew. 1998. *The Foundations of Naval History: John Knox Laughton, the Royal Navy and the Historical Profession.* London: Chatham Publishing.

Lambert, Andrew. 2012. *The Challenge: Britain Against America in the Naval War of 1812.* London: Faber.

Lambert, Andrew, ed. 2017. *21st Century Corbett: Maritime Strategy and Naval Policy for the Modern Era.* Annapolis: Naval Institute Press.

Lambert, Andrew. 2017. 'Writing the Battle: Jutland in Sir Julian Corbett's Naval Operations'. *The Mariner's Mirror* 103 (2): 175–195.

Lambert, Andrew. 2018. *Seapower States: Maritime Culture, Continental Empires and the Conflict that made the Modern World.* New Haven: Yale University Press.

Lambert, Andrew. 2021. *The British Way of War: Julian Corbett and the Battle for a National Strategy.* New Haven: Yale University Press.

Lambert, A.D., ed. 2002. *Letters and Papers of Professor Sir John Knox Laughton, 1830–1915.* (London: Navy Records Society.

Lambert, A.D. 2018. '"Doctrine, the Soul of Warfare": Sir Julian Corbett and the Teaching of Strategy in the Royal Navy before 1914'. In *Military Education and the British Empire, 1815–1949,* edited by D.E. Delaney, R.C. Engen, and M. Fitzpatrick, 48–68. Toronto: UBC Press.

Langford, Paul. 1973. 'William Pitt and Public Opinion, 1757'. *English Historical Review* 88 (January).

Langford, Paul. 1976. *The Eighteenth Century, 1688–1815.* Oxford: Oxford University Press.

Le Bot, P. 2018. 'La "nouvelle marine d'Espagne" vue par les Français, 1734–1735'. In *La real armada. La Marine des Bourbons d'Espagne au XVIIIe siècle,* edited by O. Chaline and A. Guimerá, 279–300. Paris: Sorbonne Université Presse.

Leeman, William P. 2010. *The Long Road to Annapolis: The Founding of the Naval Academy and the Merging American Republic.* Chapel Hill: University of North Carolina Press.

Legoherel, H. 1963. *Les Tresoriers generaux de la marine (1517–1788).* Paris.

Le Guisquet, B. 1992. 'Le Dépôt des cartes, plans et journaux de la marine sous l'ancien régime'. *Annales Hydrographiques,* 5th series, 18: 5–31.

Lemineur, J.C. 1997. 'La Marine de Louis XIV. Une marine nouvelle de conception française'. In *L'Invention du vaisseau de ligne, 1450–1700,* edited by M Acerra and José Merino. París: SPM.

López-Cordón, M.V. 2004. 'Entre Francia e Inglaterra. Intereses estratégicos y acuerdos políticos como antecedentes de Trafalgar'. In *Trafalgar y el mundo atlántico,* edited by A. Guimerá, A. Ramos and G. Butrón, 19–60. Madrid: Marcial Pons.

Love. Jr., Robert William, ed. 1980. *The Chiefs of Naval Operations.* Annapolis: Naval Institute Press.

Luce, Stephen B. 1975. 'On the Study of Naval Warfare as a Science'. In *The Writings of Stephen B. Luce,* edited by J.D. Hayes and J.B. Hattendorf, 45–68. Newport: Newport Naval War College Press.

Lynn, J.A. 2013. *The Wars of Louis XIV 1667–1714.* Abingdon: Routledge.

Mackay, R.F. 1973. *Fisher of Kilverstone.* Oxford: Clarendon Press.

Macleod, R., ed. 1988. *Government and Expertise: Specialists, Administrators and Professionals, 1860–1910.* Cambridge: Cambridge University Press.

Mahan, Alfred Thayer. 1890. *The Influence of Sea Power upon History, 1660–1763.* Boston: Little Brown.

Mahan, Alfred Thayer. 1892. *Admiral Farragut.* New York: D. Appleton & Co.

Mahan, Alfred Thayer. 1892. *The Influence of Sea Power upon the French Revolution and Empire, 1793–1812,* 2 vols. Boston: Little Brown.

Mahan, Alfred Thayer. 1902. *Types of Naval Officers Drawn from the History of the British Navy with Some Account of the Conditions of Naval Warfare at the Beginning of the Eighteenth Century, and its Subsequent Development during the Sail Period.* Boston: Marston. Reprint, Echo Library.

Maizeroy, Joly de. 1771. *Institutions militaires de l'empereur Léon le philosophe.* Paris: Claude-Antoine Jombert.

Malcolm, N., ed. 1906. *The Science of War: A Collection of Essays and Lectures by Col. G.F.R. Henderson CB, 1891–1903.* London: Longmans.

Maltby, William. 1990. 'Politics, Professionalism and the Evolution of Sailing Ship Tactics, 1650–1714'. In *The Tools of War: Instruments, Ideasa and Institutions of Warfare, 1445–1871,* edited by John A. Lynn, 56–73. Urbana: University of Illinois Press.

Maltby, William S. 1994. 'The Origins of a Global Strategy: England from 1558 to 1713'. In *The Making of Strategy: Rulers, States and War,* edited by Williamson Murray, Knox MacGregor, and Alvin Bernstein, 151–177. Cambridge: Cambridge University Press.

Marchena Fernández, J. 2018. *Vientos de guerra. Apogeo y crisis de la Real Armada, 1750–1823. Vol. II. Los buques de la Real Armada, 1700–1823.* Madrid: Ediciones Doce Calles.

Marchena, J., and J. Caño, eds. 2015. *Vientos de guerra. Apogeo y crisis de la Real Armada, 1750–1823,* 3 vols. Madrid: Ediciones Doce Calles.

Marder, Arthur J. 1940. *The Anatomy of British Sea Power: A History of British Naval Policy in the Pre-Dreadnought Era, 1880–1905.* New York: Alfred A. Knopf.

Martínez Martínez, M. 2011. *Los forzados de Marina en la España del siglo XVIII (1700–1775).* Almería: Universidad de Almería.

Martínez Ruiz, E. 1996. 'El Marqués de la Victoria y la política naval española'. *Cuadernos Monográficos del Instituto de Historia y Cultura Naval* 28: 7–20.

Martínez Shaw, C. 1985. 'Participación de la armada española en la Guerra de la Independencia de los Estados Unidos'. *Revista de Historia Naval* 3: 75–80.

Mauduit, Israel. 1760. *Considerations on the Present German War.* London: John Wilkie.

McGrath, Tim. 2010. *John Barry: An American Hero in the Age of Sail.* Yardley: Westholme.

Merino Navarro, J.P. 1987. 'La Hacienda de Carlos IV'. In *Historia de España fundada por Ramón Menéndez Pidal, vol. 31: La época de la Ilustración. Vol. I. El Estado y la cultura (1759–1808),* edited by María Jover Zamora José. Madrid: Espasa Calpe.

Merino Navarro, J.P. 2019. *La armada española en el siglo XVIII.* Madrid: Ediciones 19. Original edition, 1981.

Michel J. 1984. *Du Paris de Louis XV à la Marine de Louis XVI. L'Œuvre de Monsieur de Sartine. II, La reconquête de la liberté des mers.* Paris: Les Éditions de l'Érudit.

Molas i Ribalta, Pere, and Agustín Guimerá Ravina. 1991. *La España de Carlos IV.* Madrid: Asociación de Historia Moderna.

Monaque, R. 2000. *Les Aventures de Louis-René de Latouche-Tréville, compagnon de La Fayette et commandant de L'Hermione dans la guerre d'Indépendance américaine.* Paris: SPM.

Montferrand, Bernard de. 2016. *Vergennes. La gloire de Louis XVI.* Paris: Tallandier.

Morales Trueba, A. 2018. 'El marco del liderazgo naval español durante la Segunda República'. In *El liderazgo estratégico. Una aproximación interdisciplinar,* edited by A. Guimerá Ravina, 197–218. Madrid: Ministerio de Defensa.

Morales Trueba, A. 2018. *La marina de guerra de la Segunda República*. Madrid: Actas.

Morgan, William James. 1980. 'Naval Documents of the American Revolution'. In vol. 7 (1777). Washington DC: Government Printing Office.

Morgan-Owen, David G. 2017. *The Fear of Invasion: Strategy, Politics and British War Planning, 1880–1914*. Oxford: Oxford University Press.

Morison, Samuel Eliot. 1959. *John Paul Jones: A Sailor's Biography*. Boston: Little Brown.

Naval War College. 1942. *Sound Military Decision*. Newport. http://www.gutenberg.org/ebooks/28178

Naval War College. 2013. *Navy Leadership Development Strategy* https://www.hsdl.org/?abstract&did=748304

Naval War College. 2018. *Navy Leadership Development Framework, Version 2.0*. https://www.navy.mil/cno/docs/NLDF_2.pdf

Murphy, O.T. 1982. *Charles Gravier, Comte de Vergennes. French Diplomacy in the Age of Revolution 1719–1787*. Albany: State University of New York Press.

North, Douglas C. 1991. 'Institutions'. *Journal of Economic Perspectives* 5 (1): 97–112.

Norton, L.R. 2009. *Captains Contentious: The Dysfunctional Sons of the Brine*. Columbia: University of South Carolina Press.

O'Donnell, H. 2004. *El primer marqués de la Victoria, personaje silenciado en la reforma dieciochesca de la armada*. Madrid: Real Academia de La Historia.

O'Donnell, H. 2008. 'El marqués de la Victoria, una opinión discordante con la política naval de Ensenada'. *Anuario de Estudios Atlánticos* 13–41.

Olivares-Iribarren, I. 1992. 'L'Affaire de Nootka-Sound (1789–1790)'. *Mélanges de la Casa de Velázquez* 28 (2): 123–148.

Ortega del Cerro, P. 2016. 'La profesionalización de la oficialidad naval española, 1750–1800: aproximación a sus destellos desde las sombras'. *Vegueta* 16: 221–244.

O'Shaughnessy, A.J. 1997. 'The Formation of a Commercial Lobby: The West India Interest. British Colonial Policy and the American Revolution'. *Historical Journal* 40 (1).

Ostwald, Jamel. 2007. *Vauban under Siege: Engineering Efficiency and Martial Vigor in the War of the Spanish Succession*. Leiden: Brill.

Palmer, Michael A. 1987. *Stoddert's War: Naval Operations during the Quasi-War with France, 1798–1801*. Columbia: University of South Carolina Press.

Palmer, M.A.J. 1997. 'The Military Revolution Afloat: The Era of the Anglo-Dutch Wars'. *War in History* 4: 123–149.

Paret, P., Gordon A. Craig, and F. Gilbert. 1986. *Makers of Modern Strategy: From Machiavelli to the Nuclear Age*. Oxford: Oxford University Press.

Parker, Geoffrey. 2000. *The Grand Strategy of Philip II*. London: Yale University Press.

Payne, Kenneth. 2015. *The Psychology of Strategy: Exploring Rationality in the Vietnam War*. Oxford: Oxford University Press.

Perona Tomás, A. 1998. *Los orígenes del Ministerio de Marina. La Secretaría de Estado y del Despacho de Marina, 1714–1808*. Madrid: Ministerio de Defensa.

Peters, Marie. 1980. *Pitt and Popularity: The Patriot Minister and London Opinion during the Seven Years War.* Oxford: Clarendon Press.
Peters, Marie. 1993. 'The Myth of William Pitt, Earl of Chatham, Great Imperialist Part I: Pitt and Imperial Expansion 1738–1763'. *The Journal of Imperial and Commonwealth History* 21 (1): 31–74.
Pilgrim, D.G. 1975. 'The Colbert-Seignelay Naval Reforms and the Beginnings of the War of the League of Augsburg'. *French Historical Studies,* 235–262.
Podsoblyaev, Evgenii F., Francis King, and John Biggart. 2002. 'The Russian Naval General Staff and the Evolution of Naval Policy, 1904–1914'. *Journal of Military History* 66 (1): 37–69.
Pritchard, James. 1995. *Anatomy of a Naval Disaster: The 1746 French Expedition to North America.* Montreal: McGill-Queen's University Press.
Puerto Sarmiento, F. 2015. *Ciencia y política: José Giral Pereira (Santiago de Cuba, 1879–México D.F., 1962).* Madrid: Real Academia de la Historia-Boletín Oficial del Estado.
Puryear, Jr., Edgar F. 2005. *American Admiralship: The Moral Imperatives of Naval Command.* Annapolis: Naval Institute Press.
Puryear, Jr. Edgar F. 2008. *American Admiralship: The Art of Naval Command.* Minneapolis. Minnesota: MBI Pub. Co.
Rentfrow, James C. 2014. *Home Squadron: The U.S. Navy on the North Atlantic Station.* Annapolis: Naval Institute Press.
Renz, Bettina. 2018. *Russia's Military Revival.* Cambridge: Polity Press.
Richmond, H.W. 1946. *Statesmen and Sea Power.* Oxford: Clarendon Press.
Ritzer, George. 1975. 'Professionalization, Bureaucratization and Rationalization: The Views of Max Weber'. *Social Forces* 53 (4): 627–634.
Rodríguez González, Agustín Ramón. 1999. *La campaña del Pacífico: España frente a Chile y Perú (1862–1871).* Madrid: Agualarga.
Rodríguez González, A.R. 2013. 'Les objectifs de la marine espagnole'. In *Les marines de la guerre d'Independance américaine (1763–178). I. L'instrument naval,* edited by O. Chaline, P. Bonnichon, and C. Vergennes, 129–150. Paris: PUPS.
Rose, J.H. 1904. *Select Despatches from the British Foreign Office Archives: Relating to the Formation of the Third Coalition Against France, 1804–1805,* vol. 7. London: Royal Historical Society.
Rose, J.H., ed. 1904. *Select Dispatches Relating to the Third Coalition against France, 1804–5.* London: Camden Society.
Rose, J.H. and A.M. Broadley. 1908. *Dumouriez and the Defence of England against Napoleon.* London: John Lane Bodley Head.
Rowlands, Guy. 2002. *The Dynastic State and the Army under Louis XIV: Royal Service and Private Interest, 1661–1701.* Cambridge: Cambridge University Press.
Rowlands, Guy 2006. 'The King's Two Arms: French Amphibious Warfare in the Mediterranean under Louis XIV, 1664 to 1697'. In *Amphibious Warfare, 1000–1700: Commerce, State Formation and European Expansion,* edited by D.J.B. Trim and Mark Charles Fissel, 263–314. Leiden: Brill.
Ruigómez de Hernández, M.P. 1978. *El gobierno español del despotismo ilustrado*

ante la independencia de los Estados Unidos. Madrid: Ministerio de Asuntos Exteriores.
Ruiz Alemán, J., ed. 1983. *Floridablanca, conde de, escritos políticos. El memorial y la instrucción*. Murcia.
Rumeu de Armas, A. 1962. *El testamento político del conde de Floridablanca*. Madrid: CSIC.
Rumeu de Armas, A. 1966. *El testamento político del conde de Floridablanca*. Madrid: CSIC.
Sainsbury, John. 1987. *Disaffected Patriots: London Supporters of Revolutionary America, 1769–1782*. Kingston: McGill-Queen's University Press.
Sánchez Baena, J.J., C. Chaín Navarro, and L. Martínez-Solís, eds. 2011. *Actitudes y medios en la real armada del siglo XVIII*. Madrid-Murcia: Ministerio de Defensa-Universidad de Murcia.
Sánchez Montañéz, E. 2012. 'Vivir en el fin del mundo. El asentamiento español en Nootka a finales del siglo XVIII'. In *La constitución gaditana de 1812 y sus repercusiones en América*, edited by A.J. Gullón Abao and A. Gutiérrez Escudero, 17–38. Cadiz: Universidad de Cádiz.
Schivelbusch, Wolfgang. 2003. *The Culture of Defeat: On National Trauma, Mourning and Recovery*. London: Granta.
Schurman, Donald. 1981. *Julian S. Corbett, 1854–1922: Historian of British Maritime Policy from Drake to Jellicoe*. London: Royal Historical Society.
Scott, H.M. 1979. 'The Importance of Bourbon Naval Reconstruction to the Strategy of Choiseul after the Seven Years War'. *International History Review* 1: 17–35.
Seco Serrano, C. 1988. 'La política exterior de Carlos IV'. In H*istoria de España fundada por Ramón Menéndez Pidal y dirigida por José María Jover Zamora. Tomo XXXI. La época de la Ilustración*, edited by José María Jover Zamora, 449–732. Madrid: Espasa Calpe.
Semmel, Bernard. 1986. *Liberalism and Naval Strategy: Ideology, Interest, and Sea Power during the Pax Britannica*. London: Allen and Unwin.
Serrano Álvarez, J. M. 2015. 'La gestión económica de la armada española 1750–1820'. In *Vientos de guerra. Apogeo y crisis de la real Armada, 1750–1823.* Vol. I. *Una armada en tiempos de la Ilustración. Política, ciencia, ingeniería y hacienda*, edited by J. Marchena and J. Caño, 433–522. Madrid Ediciones Doce Calles.
Smelser, Ronald, and Edward J. Davies. 2008. *The Myth of the Eastern Front: The Nazi-Soviet War in American Popular Culture*. Cambridge: Cambridge University Press.
Smith, Stuart W., ed. 1990. *Douglas Southall Freeman on Leadership*. Newport: Naval War College Press.
Smith, Stuart W., ed. 1993. *Douglas Southall Freeman on Leadership*. Shippensburg, PA: White Mane Pub.
Soler Pascual, E. 1999. 'Floridablanca and the Nootka Crisis'. *International Journal of Canadian Studies* 19: 167–180.
Sondhaus, Lawrence 2006. *Strategic Culture and The Ways of War*. Abingdon: Routledge.
Sperling, John G. 1962. *The South Sea Company: An Historical Essay and*

Bibliographical Finding List. Boston: Harvard Graduate School of Business Administration.
Storrs, Christopher. 2006. *The Resilience of the Spanish Monarchy, 1665–1700.* Oxford: Oxford University Press.
Sumida, Jon T. 1997. *Inventing Grand Strategy and Teaching Command: The Classic Works of Alfred Thayer Mahan Reconsidered.* Baltimore: Johns Hopkins University Press.
Surreaux, S. 2017. 'The Reputation of the Vice-Admiral of France'. In *Naval Leadership in the Atlantic World: The Age of Reform and Revolution, 1700–1850,* edited by R. Harding and A Guimerá, 35–47. London: University of Westminster Press.
Symcox, G.W. 1974. *The Crisis of French Seapower, 1688–1697: From Guerre d'Escadre to the Guerre de Course.* The Hague: Nijhoff.
Symonds, C.L. 1980. *Navalists and Antinavalists: The Naval Policy Debate in the United States, 1785–1827.* Newark: University of Delaware Press.
Symonds, Craig L. 2008. *Lincoln and His Admirals: Abraham Lincoln, the U.S. Navy, and the Civil War.* Oxford: Oxford University Press.
Taillemite, Étienne. 2003. *L'Histoire ignorée de la marine française.* Paris: Perrin.
Tedde, P. 1998. 'Una economía en transformación: de la Ilustración al liberalismo'. In *Historia de España fundada por Ramón Menéndez Pidal, Vol. 30: Las bases políticas, económicas y sociales de un régimen en transformación (1759–1834),* edited by José María Jover Zamora, 327–425. Madrid: Espasa Calpe.
Thiers, A. 1840–1862. *Histoire du consulate et de l'empire,* 21 vols. Paris: Paulin
Thomas, Evan. 2003. *John Paul Jones: Sailor, Hero, Father of the American Navy.* New York: Simon & Schuster.
Thompson, Robert. 2018. 'Kenneth Payne, The Psychology of Strategy: Exploring Rationality in the Vietnam War'. *British Journal of Military History* 4 (2).
Torres Sanchez, Rafael, ed. 2007. *War, State and Development. Fiscal-Military States in the Eighteenth Century.* Pamplona: EUNSA.
Torres Sánchez, R. 2008. 'Las prioridades de un monarca ilustrado o las limitaciones del estado fiscal-militar de Carlos III'. *Hispania* 229: 375–406.
Torres Sánchez, R. 2013. *El precio de la guerra. El estado fiscal-militar de Carlos III (1779–1783).* Madrid: Marciel Pons.
Torres Sánchez, R. 2015. *Constructing a Fiscal Military State in Eighteenth Century Spain.* London: Palgrave Macmillan.
Torres Sánchez, R. 2015. 'El estado fiscal-naval de Carlos III. Los dineros de la armada en el contexto de las financias de la monarquía'. In *Vientos de guerra. Apogeo y crisis de la Real Armada, 1750–1823. Vol. I. Una armada en tiempos de la Ilustración. Política, ciencia, ingeniería y hacienda,* edited by J. Marchena and J Caño, 325–432. Madrid: Ediciones Doce Calles.
Torres Sánchez, R. . 2016. *Military Entrepreneurs and the Spanish Contractor State in the Eighteenth Century.* Oxford: Oxford University Press.
Tracy, N. 1992. 'Naval Tactics'. In *The Line of Battle. The Sailing Warship 1650–1840,* edited by R. Gardiner, 181–187. London: Conway Maritime Press.
Trim, D.J.B. 2019. 'Transnational Calvinist Co-operation and "Mastery of the Sea" in the Late Sixteenth Century'. In *Ideologies of Western Naval Power,*

c.1500–1815, edited by J.D. Davies, Alan James, and Gijs Rommelse, 153–187. Abingdon: Routledge.
Tunstall, Brian. 1990. *Naval Warfare in the Age of Sail: The Evolultion of Fighting Tactics, 1650–1815.* London: Conway Maritime Press.
Ulbert, Jörg, and Sylviane Llinares. 2017. *La Liasse et la plume: les bureaux du secrétariat d'état de la Marine (1669–1792).* Rennes: Presses universitaires de Rennes.
Uztáriz, G. 1724. *Theórica y práctica de comercio y de marina.* Madrid.
Vagts, Alfred. 1956. *Defense and Diplomacy: The Soldier and the Conduct of Foreign Relations, Defense and Diplomacy.* New York: King's Crown Press.
Valdés Ozores, M. 1989. 'El baylío don Antonio Valdés', PhD thesis, Universidad Complutense de Madrid.
Valdés Ozores, M. 2004. *El baylío don Antonio Valdés. Un gobierno eficaz del siglo XVIII.* Madrid: Libroslibres.
Valdez-Bubnov, I. 2015. 'De Monségur a Uztáriz. El origen de las reformas navales de Felipe V', in María del Pilar Martínez López-Cano, *Historia del pensamiento económico. Testimonios, proyectos y polémicas*, 68–90. Mexico: UNAM-Instituto Mora.
Valdez-Bubnov, I. 2009. 'War, Trade and Technology: The Politics of Spanish Shipbuilding Legislation, 1607–1728'. *International Journal of Maritime History* 21: 75–102.
Valdez-Bubnov, I. 2011. *Poder naval y modernización del estado: política de construcción naval española (siglos XVI–XVIII).* Mexico-Madrid: Bonilla Artigas/Iberoamericana Vervuert.
Valdez-Bubnov, I. 2015. 'Spanish Naval Strategy and the United States, 1763–1819'. *The Mariner's Mirror* 101: 4–20.
Valdez-Bubnov, I. 2015. 'Spanish Naval Strategy and the United States, 1763–1819'. *The Mariner's Mirror* 101: 9–19.
Valdez-Bubnov, I. 2018. 'Shipbuilding Administration under the Spanish Habsburg and Bourbon Regimes (1590–1834): A Comparative Perspective'. *Business History* 60: 105–125.
Valdez-Bubnov, I. 2019. 'Navios para un imperio global: la construcción naval y la matrícula de mar en España, América y Filipinas durante el largo siglo XVIII (1670–1834)'. *Espacio, Tiempo y Forma* 32: 123–160. doi: https://doi.org/10.5944/etfiv.32.2019.
Valdez-Bubnov, I. 2019. 'Pensamiento táctico y liderazgo estratégico: la evolución de la doctrina naval española entre los siglos XVII y XVIII'. In *Liderazgo estratégico en España, 1475–2018*, edited by A. Guimerá, 39–64. Madrid: Instituto Universitario General Gutiérrez Mellado.
Vargas Ponce, J. 1808. *Vida de D. Juan Josef Navarro.* Madrid: Imprenta Real.
Vázquez Lijó, José Manuel. 2006. *La matrícula de mar en la España del siglo XVIII: registro, inspección y evolución de las clases de marinería y maestranza.* Madrid: Ministerio de Defensa.
Vergé-Franceschi, Michel 1992. *Abraham Duquesne: Huguenot et marine du Roi-Soleil.* Paris France-Empire.
Vergé-Franceschi, Michel. 1993. 'Les Amiraux de France: 1492–1592 – treize

terriens'. In *La France et la mer au siècle des grandes découvertes,* edited by Philippe Masson and Michel Vergé-Franceschi, 171–191. Paris: Tallandier.
Vergé-Franceschi, M. 1987. 'Les Officiers generaux de la marine royale (1669–1774)'. *Revue Historique* 278 (564): 335–361.
Vergé-Franceschi, M. 1991. Marine et Education sous l'ancien regime. Paris: CNRS.
Villiers, P. 1998 (1985). 'La Stratégie de la marine française de l'arrivée de Sartine à la victoire de la Chesapeake'. In Les Marines de guerre européennes XVIIe–XVIIIe siècles, edited by M. Acerra, J. Merino, and J. Meyer, 211–247. Paris: Presses Universitaires de Paris-Sorbonne.
Virol, Michèle. 2003. *Vauban: de la gloire du roi au service de l'état.* Paris: Champ Vallon.
Walpole, Horace. 1734. *A Letter to the Craftsman, Upon the Change of Affairs in Europe by the War That is begun against the Emperour.* London: J. Roberts.
Williams, Basil. 1943. *Carteret and Newcastle: A Contrast in Contemporaries.* Cambridge: Cambridge University Press.
Woodfine, Philip. 1998. *Britannia's Glories: The Walpole Ministry and the 1739 War with Spain.* Woodbridge: Boydell Press.

INDEX

American Independence, War of (1775–1783), 54, 73, 77, 82, 94–95, 99–101, 111
Anglo-Dutch Wars (1652–1654; 1664–1668; 1672–1674), 32, 34, 37, 40
Anson, George (1697–1762), 52, 65–66, 121, 129
Aranda, Conde de (1719–1798), 13, 43–44, 47, 50–51, 66, 91

Beaufort, duc de (1616–1669), 21
Berryer, Nicolas (1703–1762), 94–95
Boscawen, Edward (1711–1761), 52, 82

Cadiz, 33–34, 36, 38, 40, 44, 47–49, 78, 85–88, 117, 124, 133–134, 148
Calder, Sir Robert (1745–1818), 121, 123, 129, 131–133, 136
Cape Sicié, Battle of (21st–22nd February 1744) (Battle of Toulon), 40–42
Cartagena (Spain), 38, 44, 47, 86, 148
Cartagena de Indias, 81, 114
Carlos III, King of Spain (1716–1788), 41, 70, 74–77, 79, 81, 100–101
Carlos IV, King of Spain (1748–1819), 77, 80, 84, 87–90
Casares Quiroga, Santiago (1884–1950), 144–145, 147–148, 152, 154–155
Catherine II, Empress of Russia (1729–1796), 160
Charles VI, Holy Roman Emperor (1685–1740), 56
Chernboyl, 2
Clausewitz, Karl von (1780–1831), 120, 128, 139
Colbert, Jean-Baptiste (1619–1683), 21, 23–24, 28–29, 34, 37, 39, 173
Corbett, Julian Stafford (1854–1922), 16, 52, 68, 120–140

Charles II, King of England and Scotland (1630–1685), 23
Choiseul, duc de (1719–1785), 42–43, 93–96, 98, 100
Churchill, Winston (1874–1965), 7, 10
Coligny, Gaspard de (1519–1572), 26
Condé, prince de (1552–1588), 27
Cromwell, Oliver (1599–1658), 59
Cuba, 35, 49, 70, 76–77, 173

Dewey, George (1837–1913), 162

Falklands War (1982), 6, 183
Ferdinand VI, King of Spain (1713–1759), 100
Ferdinand VII, King of Spain (1784–1833), 48–49
Ferrol, 38, 44, 47–48, 86, 145, 148
Fisher, Sir John, (1841–1920), 120, 122, 126, 131, 135–137, 183
Floridablanca, Conde de (1728–1808), 13, 44, 70–77, 79–80, 83–91, 97, 101–102
Freeman, Douglas Southall (1886–1953), 171–172
French Revolution, 91, 164

Gaztañeta, Antonio de (1656–1728), 13, 34–37, 40, 42–43
George II, King of Great Britain (1683–1760), 61, 63
George III, King of Great Britain (1738–1820), 67, 69
Giral Pereira, José (1879–1962), 15, 140–141, 144, 146, 149
Godoy, Manuel de (1767–1851), 45, 48
Guise, duc de (1550–1588), 27

Hawke, Edward (1705–1781), 52, 67
Hopkins, Esek (1718–1802), 160

Hoste, Père Paul (1652–1700), 20, 40, 42, 92

Isabel II, Queen of Spain (1830–1904), 13, 104, 109, 114–116

James II, King of England and Scotland (1633–1701), 23
Jones, John Paul (1747–1792), 160

Kalbfus, Edward C., (1877–1954), 169–170
King, Ernest, W. (1878–1956), 170
Knox, Dudley W. (1877–1960), 168

Laughton, Sir John Knox (1830–1915), 123, 125, 163
Llerena, Pedro González de, 80
Lloyd, Henry (1718–1783), 50
Louis, XIV, King of France (1638–1715), 9, 12, 19, 21–24, 28–30, 32–33, 95, 103
Louis XV, King of France (1710–1774), 93, 99–100
Louis XVI, King of France (1754–1793), 93, 95, 98–99, 101
Louisiana, 45, 48, 80
Luce, Stephen B. (1827–1917), 163–165, 173

Macdonnell, Enrique Reynaldo (1753–1823), 13, 46–51
Mahan, Alfred Thayer (1840–1914), 50–51, 122, 128, 132, 135, 138, 164–165, 182
Maurepas, comte de (1701–1781), 93–97, 99–101
Mazarredo, José de (1745–1812), 78, 83, 88, 91
Méndez Núñez, Castro (1824–1869), 14, 106–107, 109, 111, 117–118
Mexico, 45–49, 70, 74, 84, 110
Mexico, Gulf of, 45, 47, 49, 74, 84, 90, 102
Moreno Fernández, Francisco (1883–1945), 144–145

Napoleon, Emperor of France (1769–1821), 45, 48, 91, 95, 121, 123, 125–135, 138, 163
Navarro, Juan José, Marquess de Victoria, (1687–1772), 13, 38, 40–44, 51
Newcastle, Duke of, (1693–1768), 57, 59, 63
Norris, Sir John (1670/1–1749), 61, 64, 69

Nootka Sound, 83, 85–86, 88–91

Orvillers, comte d' (1710–1792), 99–100

Patiño, José (1666–1736), 13, 38
Peru, 14, 70, 83, 91, 110–113, 115
Philip V, King of Spain (1683–1746), 33–34, 39
Philippines, 86, 105, 109
Pitt, William (the Elder) (1708–1778), 52, 57–58, 67–68, 121, 129
Pitt, William (the Younger) (1759–1806), 126–129, 134–135, 138
Polish Succession, War of (1733–1738), 60
Pontchartrain, Jérôme, comte de, (1674–1747), 19
Pontchartrain, Louis, comte de (1643–1727), 21
Porter, David Dixon (1813–1891), 162
Professionalism, 4, 173
Puerto Cabello, 109

Quiberon, Bay, Battle of (20th November 1759), 67

Richelieu, Cardinal (1585–1642), 22, 25, 27–29
Russia, 1–2, 6, 9, 16, 75, 87, 113, 127–128, 132, 134, 160, 171, 181–183

Seignelay, Marquis de (1651–1690), 21
Seven Years War (1756–1763), 31, 41–43, 50–51, 58, 66, 96, 98
Santo Domingo, 47, 70, 74, 86–87, 97, 109
Sartine, comte d'Alby (1729–1801), 98–100
Sims, William S. (1858–1936), 167–168
Solano, José de, (1726–1806), 87
Spanish Succession, War of (1700–1713), 35, 37, 46
Stockdale, James B. (1923–2005), 173–174, 176
Sully, Maximilien, duc de (1560–1641), 21

Third Coalition, War of (1805–1806), 45, 48, 122
Toulon, 40, 44, 62, 100
Toulouse, comte de (1678–1737), 19, 23, 29–30
Trafalgar, Battle of (21st Oct. 1805), 6 48, 70, 78–79, 82, 84, 111, 120–127, 129, 134–140, 164

Turner, Stansfield (1923–2018), Admiral USN, 173

Uztáriz, Jerónimo de (1670–1732), 13, 34–39, 42–43, 50–51

Valdés, Antonio (1744–1816), 13, 70–73, 76–83, 86–89, 91
Vauban, Sébastien Le Prestre de, (1633–1707), 19–21
Vergennes, comte de (1719–1787), 94–95, 97, 101–102

Vernon, Edward (1684–1757), 52, 62, 65

Wager, Sir Charles (1666–1743), 59–61, 64, 69
Walpole, Sir Robert (1676–1745), 52, 57–60, 62–64
Washington, George (1732–1799), 102, 160–161, 171
West Indies, 56, 62, 67, 83, 100, 123, 127, 129
William III, King of England (1650–1702), 127, 160